KEEPERS
OF
THE
GOLDEN
SHORE

KEEPERS OF THE
GOLDEN SHORE

A History of the United Arab Emirates

MICHAEL QUENTIN MORTON

REAKTION BOOKS

Published by Reaktion Books Ltd
Unit 32, Waterside
44–48 Wharf Road
London N1 7UX, UK
www.reaktionbooks.co.uk

First published 2016, reprinted 2017
Copyright © Michael Quentin Morton 2016

Printed and bound in Great Britain by TJ International, Padstow, Cornwall

A catalogue record for this book is available from the British Library

ISBN 978 1 78023 580 6

Contents

Preface 7

1 Desert, Sea and Mountain: Southeast Arabia
in Prehistory 9

2 Emergence: Greater Oman, the Arabian Gulf and
the Bani Yas, AD 630–1909 28

3 A Maritime Kind: The Qawasim, the British and the
Trucial Coast, 1718–1906 54

4 Jewels of the Sea: The Rise and Fall of the
Pearling Industry, 1508–1949 75

5 Something in the Air: Dubai and the
Northern Sheikhdoms, 1901–39 95

6 The Hungry Years: The Trucial Coast in the
Second World War, 1939–45 116

7 Sweet Crude: Abu Dhabi and the Discovery
of Oil, 1909–71 130

8 Blueprint for a Nation: The Trucial States,
1945–68 151

9 Divided We Stand: Unification and Beyond,
1964–80 178

10 Only One Tribe: The United Arab Emirates,
1980–Present Day 200

Maps

Regional Map of the Arabian Gulf 218

The United Arab Emirates 219

Appendices

Al Nahyan – Selected Family Tree 220

Al Maktoum – Selected Family Tree 221

Timeline *222*

Glossary *224*

References *226*

Select Bibliography *232*

Acknowledgements *233*

Photo Acknowledgements *234*

Index *235*

Preface

WHO WERE THE people of this land and what happened to them? Since the discovery of oil, the United Arab Emirates (UAE) has experienced its own version of the Big Bang, being transformed from a traditional society to a modern state within the space of 50 years. If not for a keen interest in history among its people, many traces of the past might well have been obliterated in the process. But the past has not been forgotten, or destroyed, and each of the seven emirates of the UAE has a rich and diverse story to tell.

Keepers of the Golden Shore weaves these various strands together. It starts with a land that was a meeting place of many cultures, then traces the wanderers who emerged from the shadows of history and settled here, through their maritime encounters and tribal evolutions to the modern age – all bringing to life the tribes that became a nation. Many textures and nuances of their history still resonate today, and it is only by understanding the past that we can make sense of the politics and people of the present-day UAE.

It will be noticed that I have used the term 'Arabian' Gulf throughout the book rather than 'Persian' Gulf, unless the historical context requires otherwise. I realize that this is a contentious issue in the Gulf today but, since this book is about the Arab side of the Gulf, this description is used for practical reasons without intending to make any judgement in the matter.

The early sun on the scene seemed to clothe the morning with the quality of the age of Homer and the heroes – and it seemed an ageless and timeless morning, at once giving the impression of the dawn of man's history and of present vital reality.

Donald Hawley, Political Resident
On a journey between Dubai and Abu Dhabi in July 1960[1]

Dust storms blow over the Arabian Peninsula, covering parts of Saudi Arabia,
Yemen, Oman and the United Arab Emirates.

1

Desert, Sea and Mountain: Southeast Arabia in Prehistory

THEY KNEW ALL about the rock, where it was and what was written on it, even twenty years after it had been bulldozed for a new road. All their history was written on that rock and, in the space of a few seconds, it was gone. The old men only had their memories to fall back on, although that was not unusual in their world; the writing on the rock was the exception rather than the rule. There was no local tradition of the written word, and tribal memories were recounted through the centuries over the campfire or in the shade of palm trees. They told of great battles in which many proud warriors died, without any hint of disbelief or exaggeration; they called up events from hundreds of years ago as if they were within living memory; they told stories that were as fresh as the breaking dawn.[1]

But it is rocks that provide the earliest record of the land of the Emirates, though not exactly in the way the tribesmen remembered. One rock layer might inform the geologist that this part was once a river bed, or that part was a swamp or a desert. Fossils tell a story too, animal and plant remains trapped in time revealing the age of rocks, their original location and the prevailing climate when they were laid down. They can also tell us of a world turned inside out, where fossilized sea shells have been found in limestone rocks high up in the mountains, far from their ancient habitats on the seabed.

There are no eyewitnesses to these events, only the testimony of rocks. They tell us how the Arabian Plate started out in the southern hemisphere and drifted sedately northwards, travelling at only a few centimetres per year, or as fast as a fingernail grows. But the movement of the plate was enough to cause the tectonic equivalent of a car crash. Arabia collided with Asia, leaving mountain belts that are apparent today, such as the Zagros of Iran and the Al Hajar of Oman, of which the Ruus al-Jibal is a northerly extension. The Arabian Plate tilted, its eastern side pushed downwards and becoming part of a shallow, warm sea. This was the Tethys Sea, rich in the building blocks of petroleum, plankton and other organic material. Here, in the depths of the Earth, the great oilfields of the region were formed and the destiny of the United Arab Emirates (UAE) was made.

All the while, the climate was changing – at times, the land bore little resemblance to the arid deserts of the modern UAE. Between six and eight million years ago, we might find ourselves in a wilderness, teeming with elephants, giraffes, leopards, crocodiles and the like, where wide rivers ran through lush grassland and forest. Modern satellite images reveal the outlines of rivers twisting down from the Hajar Mountains to the Gulf coast, the only visible evidence of their existence today being the creeks that puncture the shoreline. The reason why mammals the size of double-decker buses are not strolling down Sheikh Zayed Road today is, of course, global climate change; the weather changed, the region became drier and the animals moved on.

In the same way that climate dictated the fate of species, so it affected patterns of human settlement and migration, bringing the first wave of humans from East Africa. Stone tools unearthed around Jebel Faya, a mountain in the emirate of Sharjah, suggest that they came out of Africa much earlier than previously thought, some 127,000 years ago. These early migrants might have crossed the Red Sea at the shallow Bab-el-Mandeb strait, which was then shallow enough to allow the passage of small boats, and then travelled through a relatively vegetated southern Arabia to arrive at Jebel Faya. Whether they went any further is open to speculation, and if they did, where might they have gone? It is likely that they travelled to Southeast Asia and beyond, even reaching Australia.

In this distant world, where nothing appears familiar to the modern eye, changes were gradual but profound. From our vantage point, it seems remarkable that about 75,000 years ago the sea retreated from the Arabian Gulf and left a ribbon of green in its wake. This 'Gulf Oasis' connected with the Fertile Crescent that runs from Iraq to the Levant, cutting a swathe through the heart of the region. There may also have been smaller oases dotted around the valley, fed by freshwater springs, but the truly impressive feature of this natural paradise was a river system, an extension of the Tigris and Euphrates, that flowed from the Taurus Mountains to the Strait of Hormuz, where it met the remaindered sea.

There was a price to pay for all this abundance. Much of the sea was locked up in ice and glaciers that covered large parts of Canada, northern Asia and Europe, and reached far into the United States. High atmospheric pressure formed above the ice caps, creating hostile climatic conditions on the Arabian Peninsula. Searing northerly winds blasted the land, carrying sand from the exposed Gulf basin and depositing it in the south, forming the great desert of the Rub al-Khali (the Empty Quarter). Like the scene in the film *Lawrence of Arabia* where the hero and his companions struggle through a raging sandstorm with their faces cloaked, early Arabians must have faced similar conditions in the winter months. The coast of today's UAE would have been virtually uninhabitable, situated on a bleak ridge above the Gulf Oasis, buffeted by the winter winds.

And in time, the Gulf Oasis yielded to climate change. Around 10,000 years ago, a slow and erratic process began whereby the ice caps melted and the sea level rose again, swallowing up the river valley and all its works. In the face of this onslaught, the dwellers of the valley were forced to retreat like flotsam on the crest of a wave, settling on the new shore, which roughly equates with the coastline of the modern Gulf.

This, at all events, is how the theory goes. But in an unguarded moment, perhaps at twilight when darkness is dimming the golden shore, we might imagine far-off days when a track led down to the ribbon of life that was once the Gulf Oasis. Here, in the dying light, one might imagine the ghosts of Adam and Eve walking in the Garden of Eden, Noah preparing his ark, or the flood in the *Epic of Gilgamesh* being played out.[2] Finally, when darkness falls and the lights of a passing supertanker twinkle in the night, we might be left with another thought, that the remains of a lost civilization could yet be found beneath the humdrum waters of today's Arabian Gulf.

For early 'Emiratis', life was short, brutal and hard. The men averaged 1.65 metres (5 ft 4 in) and the women 1.55 metres (5 ft 1 in) tall. They often squatted and were of muscular build, with a high level of inbreeding, and were accustomed to repetitive manual tasks. A small proportion showed signs of anaemia caused either by a lack of iron content in their diet or malaria. Only 39 per cent of the population lived beyond the age of 30. There was a relatively high incidence of head injuries, to both male and female skulls, signifying blows to the head with a blunt object; there was also evidence of 'trephination', the surgical opening of the skull. Such findings were made from a sample of human bones found at a Stone Age cemetery near the foot of Jebel Buhais in the emirate of Sharjah.

There are other clues to their lifestyle. A net sinker and shell beads found at the cemetery suggest a link between inland dwellers and those on the coast, either through occasional contact or seasonal migration. From the evidence of animal remains, it appears that the inhabitants kept sheep, goats and sometimes cattle, none of which were indigenous to the region. This begs the question of where they came from: wild goats may have lived in the Hajar Mountains to the east and wild cattle may have grazed along the eastern and western fringes of the peninsula, but wild sheep were unknown. DNA evidence from a cattle bone suggests a link with the southern Levant, today's Syria and Palestine, and local stone tools resembling arrowheads from that region support the theory that these early inhabitants came from the northwest and brought with them domesticated animals. Other early migrants may have arrived from southwest Arabia, from the land that is today known as Yemen.

An enduring theme of Emirati history is how the climate shaped people's lives. Periods when the climate was favourable widened the available life choices: in a time of ample rainfall and temperate weather, agriculture flourished and trade spread far and wide. Extreme conditions such as prolonged drought restricted opportunities: migration became a necessity as herders sought diminishing grasslands and followed meagre rains, *jebalis* left their mountain haunts to seek a living on the shore and the settled people clung to the oases of the dusty interior. These were not simply random events that could be shrugged off with the traditional stoicism of the Arab; they affected communities deeply, even within living memory. Add epidemics, invasions and famine to the mix and it is easy to see that life in this corner of Arabia was often a tentative affair.

And yet archaeological discoveries reveal a people who were resourceful and well connected: discoveries of stone tools and cairn burials on Marawah Island are signs of early settlement; and pottery fragments on Dalma Island betray links with the Ubaid culture of Mesopotamia. It is likely that the pottery was left by sailors from southern Iraq who came to trade rather than settle in the area. The latest evidence – such as that of fishing on Dalma – suggests that they were probably permanent settlements. As well as being connected to the maritime trade network, they interacted with other population groups inland, depending on their accessibility to and from the mainland.

One of the most intriguing finds came from the island of Akab in the emirate of Umm al-Qaiwain, from a site dating back to between 3500 and 3200 BC. Here, a mound of dugong bones and a surrounding settlement attracted the interest of archaeologists in the late 1990s. The dugong, or sea cow, is believed to have inspired the mermaid myth, for its shape in the water could easily be mistaken for a half-human, half-aquatic creature. It is a herbivorous sea mammal that grows up to 4 metres (13 ft) in length, weighs as much as 400 kilograms (882 lb), and used to congregate in herds of several hundred. Although this is rare in today's Gulf, the UAE has the second largest number of dugongs, after Australia, in the world. Feeding off sea grasses, the dugong was a valuable source of food, hides and oils for the early inhabitants of the shore. A pile of dugong bones might not, in itself, sound remarkable, but the fact that the mound was structured in a deliberate way convinced the archaeologists that this was more than just a site for slaughtering the animals and discarding their bones. The animals' skulls were aligned on a bed of jaw bones and ribs, with the upper jaw bones pointing to the east or northeast. Ornaments such as shells and beads were included in the structure, arranged around the skulls.

This is the only dugong mound of this type yet discovered on the Arabian Peninsula; its nearest equivalent is from thousands of years later (dating from the fourteenth century AD) and many miles away on the shores of Australia's Torres Strait. Here dugong mounds have a ceremonial significance. In Australia and Madagascar, the dugong is revered and special rites are observed in the various stages of capturing, killing and eating them. A similarity has also been noted with green turtle deposits discovered at Ras al-Hamra in the sultanate of Oman, some 300 miles away. These were dated to 3700 and 3300 BC, where the skulls were placed in a ritual fashion, with pebbles placed around the body in imitation of turtle eggs.

All this raises many questions. Who were the people who lived here, on the shores, in the deserts and mountains? What was their provenance and how do they relate to the people of today? Was there a civilization or lost cities waiting to be discovered? Such were the questions that faced archaeologists when they began their investigations in the late 1950s. In those days, little was known about the archaeology of the region – for the archaeologists, it was a blank on the map.

UNLIKE EUROPE, where archaeology has been practised for many centuries, even if sometimes at the level of a treasure hunt, much of the ancient history of the Gulf region remained a mystery until the twentieth century. In 1958 the British Petroleum (BP) representative in Abu Dhabi, Tim Hillyard, invited two archaeologists, Geoffrey Bibby and Peter Glob, to visit. They had been excavating sites on Bahrain Island and unravelling the story of Dilmun, an ancient civilization recorded by the Sumerians and believed to be centred on the island of Bahrain and the opposing shore of Arabia. From about 3000 BC there were trading links between Dilmun and lower Mesopotamia. But did this civilization stretch as far as the lower Arabian Gulf, or the Lower Sea as it was then known?

There was no UAE in those days, only a loose collection of territories ruled by sheikhs. The ruler of Abu Dhabi, Sheikh Shakhbut bin Sultan al-Nahyan, was an intelligent, if somewhat idiosyncratic ruler, who retained a keen interest in the archaeologists' activities. He had read a recent article in the *Illustrated London News* about the excavations in Bahrain, and had agreed for the archaeologists to come. He was naturally curious about the people from the 'Time of Ignorance', as the pre-Islamic period was called, of which little was known. There were no records, only stories and a few old ruins that were familiar to the bedouin and, of course, to the sheikh as well. He was keen for Hillyard to take the visitors to Umm al-Nar (Mother of Fire) Island where a number of tumuli were located. 'Who were the people who had lived in Abu Dhabi in the Time of Ignorance?' asked the sheikh at their first meeting. Bibby later wrote that their work had 'clearly captured the imagination of the enlightened Ruler of Abu Dhabi and he is very anxious that our investigations should continue'.[3]

The island of Umm al-Nar is a short distance from Al Maqta, where modern bridges connect Abu Dhabi Island with the mainland. In the late 1950s, there was no bridge, only a simple watchtower and causeway. Crossing the causeway and driving northeastwards along the coast, the archaeologists came upon a 'low dark hump' with a single palm tree at its northern end. A small boat waited to carry them across the narrow channel to the island. Within ten minutes of their arrival, they had found mounds and flint debitage, pieces of flint that had been chipped away while making arrowheads and axes, revealing a Stone Age past. Immediately the archaeologists' interest was fired. But at that time Abu Dhabi was a town of palm-frond huts and sandy tracks, with

Abu Dhabi during flooding in 1958–9. Houses built of palm fronds,
known as *'arish*, are visible in the background.

no modern facilities or infrastructure, and an archaeological expedition
would require considerable planning and backup. Thus it was not possible to commence excavations that season, and the archaeologists
returned to Bahrain, their appetites whetted, to prepare for an expedition
in the following year.

Amid the dirt and the ditches, gems of information can be retrieved
from the most trivial things: what narrative from the past might a small
bone, stone chipping or string of beads reveal? Such is the wonder of
archaeology, yet the first season at Umm al-Nar in 1959 uncovered no
evidence of links with other cultures. Then, during the next season, the
archaeological team unearthed a large quantity of broken pottery, known
as shards. These closely resembled items found in the Bampur Valley in
southeast Iran and in the Kulli culture in Baluchistan, but had no apparent connection with the Dilmun civilization. More important were the
50-plus large stone cairns, evidently man-made, and also different from
those they had been excavating in Bahrain. Bibby and his colleagues
were confronted with a startling prospect: that Umm al-Nar might have
been the outpost of an entirely different civilization, the legendary
copper-rich region of Magan, or Makan. Locating Magan was then
considered one of the great prizes of Middle Eastern archaeology.

Today, the region of Magan is generally regarded as being the
UAE and northern Oman. Sumerian tablets tell of copper being trans-
ported on ships from there up the Arabian Gulf to the city states of

Mesopotamia via Dilmun. And, more precisely, samples of copper excavated from sites in Iraq have traces of nickel that match deposits retrieved from ancient copper mines in the Wadi Jizzi, Oman. The wadi lies between the Batinah coast and the Al Ain/ Buraimi area, providing an important trading link between the Omani coast and the interior. Although the exact details are uncertain, it is possible that loads of copper were taken from along this route to Umm al-Nar and thence by sea to Dilmun. Thus the Umm al-Nar culture was part of a trading network that stretched from northern Oman through the Gulf to Mesopotamia. By the Bronze Age the lower Gulf was being described as the Sea of Magan.

On 7 March 1959 Sheikh Shakhbut's brother, Zayed, invited Bibby and Glob to visit him at his fort in Al Ain in the sheikhdom. Zayed, who went on to become ruler of Abu Dhabi and then president of the UAE, was then the ruler's representative in the eastern region. The area is dominated by Jebel Hafit, the 18-km/11-mile-long whaleback mountain that straddles the border between the UAE and Oman. In its shadow lies a collection of some 500 dome-shaped tombs dating back 5,000 years. More recent finds have included pottery that can be traced back to clay from Mesopotamia, more evidence of links between this area and the north. As well as visiting these tombs, Sheikh Zayed took the archaeologists to the northern part of the oasis, near the village of Hili, where a number of stone-built burials belonging to the Umm al-Nar culture were found. Most prominent among these was the so-called 'round structure', or the Hili tomb, decorated with low relief carvings depicting, among other things, two large cats, possibly leopards or cheetahs, attacking a gazelle; and two humans, holding hands and standing between a pair of Arabian oryx. The tomb was subsequently excavated in the 1964–5 season and contained many jumbled human bones, making analysis difficult. Similar, smaller tombs have been found at other Umm al-Nar sites in the Emirates, but the largest group by far is on the island of Umm al-Nar itself.

Since then, other scenarios have emerged. Tell Abraq, on the border of the Umm al-Qaiwain and Sharjah emirates, was first excavated between 1989 and 1998 by a team of archaeologists led by Professor Daniel Potts of the University of Sydney. The word 'tell' indicates a hill or mound that has been built up by human settlement, and here there is indeed a mound rising up about 10 metres (33 ft) from the surrounding plain. It was once a large settlement on the coast, but the sea has long since retreated, leaving traces of an ancient shore that are only visible when rainfall floods a hollow in the ground. Tell Abraq was a Bronze Age hub, a place where bronze goods were made from copper and tin, and traders met and did business. Pottery found at the site reveals the astounding scale of its links with the outside world: Mesopotamia, Iran, Bahrain, Afghanistan, Uzbekistan and the Indus Valley; and tin-bronze has been found at all levels of occupation. It also has the best-preserved tower from the period, a circular structure that once stood 8 metres (26 ft 3 in.) tall. This, and similar towers across the Emirates and Oman, were built around sweetwater wells. Their design brings to mind the Martello Towers of England, but any resemblance is purely coincidental. The Gulf towers were thousands of years older and probably designed as forts to house local rulers or notables and guard nearby settlements.

On the coast, we can imagine a landscape that was perhaps a little greener than today, with people living in palm frond huts along the shore, or mudbrick and stone houses inland, clustered around a tower that protected their settlement and guarded their land. These scenes are uncannily reminiscent of the Gulf towns and villages of the 1950s, when rulers' stone palaces rose above dusty settlements of *'arish* roofs. Nor do the comparisons stop there, for the folk who inhabited this landscape shared the same nomadic, pastoral, trading and fishing traditions with those who have emerged in more recent times. The Umm al-Nar people, for example, had widespread trading links, cultivated crops such as wheat, barley and date palms in the oases, managed sheep, goats and cattle, and fished in the sea.

Archaeologists have divided the Bronze Age into periods such as the Hafit (3200–2600 BC) and Umm al-Nar (2600–2000 BC), although the boundaries are somewhat blurred. The period known as Wadi Suq (2000–1300 BC) was named after tombs discovered in the early 1970s by the Danish archaeologist Karen Frifelt that were quite different to the discoveries from earlier periods. The tombs had been robbed and revealed few artefacts, but they still represented a break from the past, a time when Umm al-Nar culture gave way to a greater regional diversity. There are a variety of grave designs: some come in long shapes, others in T-shapes and horseshoes. Many are made of unworked stone, unlike the constructions of the earlier period. The presence of soft stone vessels, used for storing oily liquids such as perfumes and unguents, is carried forward but the decorations changed, as did the vessel types – and swords make an appearance for the first time.

Archaeological excavations of an Umm al-Nar structure at Hili in 1969.

At Shimal, a village of the Shihuh tribe in the shadow of the Hajar Mountains, several hundred tombs have been found, suggesting the largest settlement of the period. At Al Qattara near Al Ain, and Dhayah in Ras al-Khaimah, archaeologists have found beautiful gold pieces depicting animals, some resembling goats, with two necks and heads facing in opposite directions. At Tell Abraq, there is also evidence of a shift away from animal husbandry towards the consumption of fish and shellfish. Trading links with Dilmun continue, however, and copper shipments are still being made from Magan to Mesopotamia.

Many of these changes can be attributed to the collapse of neighbouring civilizations in Mesopotamia, Iran and the Indus Valley, a greater aridity in the climate, or a combination of both. No doubt these changes brought fresh waves of migration but the idea that they forced people into a nomadic existence can be discounted. Desert nomads would have struggled to survive without their beast of burden, the camel, which was not yet domesticated, being wild and hunted for its meat. These nomads of the future, the bedouins of the past, would have to wait a while longer for their trusty companions of the desert.

————

IN THE BRASH NEW WORLD of the UAE, life holds many surprises. The forces of change are so intense that the present is occasionally liable to crash into the past like a runaway truck. Indeed, the construction of a truck road brought matters to a head in 2013. The road was designed for the transport of rocks from the quarries and factories of the north, bypassing the city of Ras al-Khaimah in the process; but lying in the 'destruction corridor' was a group of fourteen megalithic tombs at Qarn al-Harf. Work was suspended while a three-month rescue excavation was undertaken.

The Qarn al-Harf tombs are among 60 on a fertile plain that is dotted with acacia trees and endowed with palm gardens that have been cultivated for some 4,000 years. The largest tomb is a 24-metre (79-ft) long, single-chambered structure, built of boulders that weigh up to a tonne that were carved from the mountains by men using bronze tools. Typical tombs of this period would hold 30 to 50 people, male and female, from stillborn babies to small children and the elderly; the full range of life captured in death.

Although the graves came from three periods, most were from the Wadi Suq culture. Each person was buried with at least one piece of pottery, some pieces being decorated with lines and dotted circles typical of the period; beads around a forearm and an earring by a skull indicate that they were wearing these ornaments when they were buried. The most impressive finds were of a silver lion, silver bull and a dog made from electron, all of which were probably used as pendants or brooches. But none of these discoveries made any real difference to the drive to progress: at the end of the project, three of the Qarn al-Harf tombs were bulldozed to make way for the new truck road, leaving the remainder intact.

Once known as the cultural 'dark age' of Emirati archaeology, the Wadi Suq period is now being unravelled piece by piece. From the number of graves uncovered so far, we can suppose that the coasts, wadis and oases of the Emirates, especially in the north, were well populated. But if the Wadi Suq still seems remote and strange to the present day, the Iron Age (1300–300 BC) brings the past a lot closer. This period saw the advent of the *falaj* (pl. *aflaj*) system, man-made water channels used for irrigation, and the domestication of the camel, which made the nomadic lifestyle possible. Legacies of these developments are clearly visible in the date gardens and camel markets of today's Al Ain.

But there is more to this than a few historical curiosities. As well as being found in the UAE, similar water channels exist in Oman and other places such as Iran, Baluchistan, Afghanistan, Spain and elsewhere in Europe. Until the last decade, however, few had seriously thought of the *falaj* of the UAE as a local innovation, assuming they had been introduced from abroad, perhaps from Iran. But in 2003 conventional wisdom was overturned when it was announced that the world's oldest known *falaj* system had been found in the Al Ain area. 'The *falaj* system existed in the Al Ain region at about 1000 BC, making it the oldest', said Dr Walid Yassin al-Tikriti, Adviser for Archaeology in the Department of Antiquities and Tourism in Al Ain.[4] On the basis that, in archaeology, a claim is as good as the latest discovery, this one still holds.

The Bronze Age people certainly knew a thing or two about digging wells and drawing water, but it was hard work carrying their waterskins over long distances. They could use donkeys and camels of course, but the *falaj* system enabled water to flow from wadis and wells in the foothills to the gardens and plantations of the plain. In this way, the *falaj* opened up fresh possibilities. Once a well (*umm al-falaj*, or mother of *falaj*) had been located, a gently sloping tunnel was then dug from the plantation or village back towards it, with vertical shafts at regular intervals to allow workers access to the tunnel and air for the workers to breathe. A number of smaller channels would branch out, feeding the date plantations and gardens of the district. Each farmer would be allocated a time when he could open a side channel in order to irrigate his crops.

The *falaj* brought a new dimension to the irrigation of gardens and plantations, increasing the arable land and probably triggering an upsurge in the population. If we were to see the Iron Age settlements as they were, we would be struck by their similarity to villages from the recent past, more like typical Middle Eastern settlements from the 1950s than anything from 2,000 years ago. The ancient settlements were walled, with the gardens lying outside the walls, reminiscent of modern gardens in Fujairah, or oases in the mountain wadis of Ras al-Khaimah. The houses were mudbricked or, if located near the mountains, built of stone, and the remains of a columned hall resembling a *majlis* are often present. The graves from this period have yielded a variety of weapons, ranging from arrowheads and short daggers to long swords and hand axes. The design of certain swords and metal bowls implies links with Iran, while there is a suggestion in texts that the area might have been part of a larger Assyrian state, or at least part of a confederation in which local leaders may have paid tribute to an Assyrian king in 640 BC.

Part of the *aflaj* water system that feeds the gardens and plantations of Al Ain.

One explanation for the region's expanding land-based trading links is the evolution of the camel from hunted beast to domesticated pack animal. Its latter use seems to have developed on the western coast of Arabia, where adverse winds hampered the progress of vessels sailing northwards. In a phenomenon noted by the fifteenth-century Arab navigator Ibn Majid, the wind in the Red Sea above Jeddah always seemed to blow from the north. While early sailors had to battle against it, a pack camel could make the same journey overland at a reliable plod, carrying goods such as incense from Hadhramaut to the cities of the Mediterranean. In fact the camel, with its immense powers of endurance and adaptability, largely replaced seaborne trade and made trade and travel across the length and breadth of Arabia a viable proposition.

It would be difficult to exaggerate the camel's place in the history and culture of the Arabs. Its domestication gave rise to the lifestyle known as 'bedouin', which generally denotes a nomad or wanderer of the desert. Some bedouins were traders, others herdsmen who took their flocks from one grazing ground to another as the rains came and went. They have a proud heritage, sustained by a folklore and tradition that underlies the culture of the modern UAE. There are everyday reminders of their roots in the tacky camel motifs and fluffy toys one sees in tourist shops at the airports, but there are also more discreet signs of an honourable past. The black double cords of the *agal* used to bind an Emirati's headdress in place is symbolic of the ropes used to hobble camels, an irrefutable sign that Emiratis are philosophically bound to their bedouin past.

It was a heritage forged in the unforgiving deserts of the Middle East. The UAE has its own deserts, such as Al Dhafrah, Ramlat al-Hamra and Al Kidan, which are extensions of the Texas-sized Rub al-Khali, the 'Empty Quarter', one of the most inhospitable places on Earth. The camel made these deserts accessible and, most of all, traversable. The animal is inimitably suited for desert travel, being remarkably well equipped for arid conditions. Contrary to popular belief, the camel's large hump is not for storing water, but fat. This enables the camel to maintain a thinner hide, which allows heat to be released more easily and the camel's internal organs to remain cooler. The camel can tolerate dry conditions much better than humans: it can withstand a dehydration rate of 40 per cent as compared with a human's 12 per cent.

Equipped with a reliable form of desert transport, new opportunities arose for the bedouin-cum-trader. The relationship between man and camel now developed from the camel as wild, hunted animal, a source of meat and milk, to a pack animal for transporting goods and supplies across the desert. When saddled and ridden, it became a vehicle for desert journeys and the object of sport in the camel racing that still persists in Arabia today. In times of war, particularly in the northern deserts, it gave the Arabs a distinct advantage not only as a tall, mounted steed for attacking the enemy but as a means of striking quickly by surprise out of the desert, and returning just as quickly, leaving pursuers behind in a cloud of dust.

A network of trading routes began sprouting up between southern Arabia and the Mediterranean. At Muweilah, for example, camel figurines imply that the beasts were domesticated and being used for transport in the southeast. Most of these camels were dromedaries, but there is evidence that the local inhabitants were also using a hybrid camel, the *bukht*, a cross between a single-humped dromedary and a two-humped Bactrian camel. This hybridization may have been introduced from

Iran and elsewhere in order to produce a stronger, faster animal capable of carrying heavier loads than their parents. These 'super' camels were the juggernauts of their world, and were probably used on long journeys to Hadhramaut, Dhofar, Hijaz and Mesopotamia.[5]

So, by the end of the Iron Age, the overland trade and the migration of tribes to southeastern Arabia had begun. In 331 BC Alexander the Great defeated the Persian king, Darius III, leading to the eventual disintegration of the Persian Empire that had once dominated the Gulf and its surrounds, including Magan.[6] This may well have created a power vacuum in the region, resulting in the growth of local political structures and fresh waves of refugees arriving in Magan. The discovery at Mleiha of monumental tower tombs similar to those found elsewhere in the Middle East support this theory.

Although much of this is guesswork – only about 1 per cent of Mleiha has been excavated so far – with ongoing archaeological work a clearer picture will emerge in time. The site certainly holds great promise: situated 20 kilometres (12.5 miles) from Al Dhaid, in the plain immediately to the west of the Hajar Mountains, Mleiha was continuously inhabited for 500 years, spanning the arrival of the Christian era. The remains of a fort, Al Husn, which was probably an administrative centre, have also been revealed. This hint of regional importance is reinforced by the discovery of a coin-minting mould, indicating that a local currency was minted here.

This is where we also meet our first 'Emirati', Abiel, whose name is written on ancient coins discovered at Mleiha. Imitations of Alexander the Great's coinage, they show a crude reproduction of the head of Heracles, with a picture of Zeus on the reverse, and 'Abiel' replacing 'Alexander'. The name of Abiel's father, with five different spellings, is also shown, and the fact that the Mleiha coin moulds were designed to produce these coins suggests that Abiel ruled these parts. Since these coins were produced over some four centuries, long past the lifetime of a single Abiel, there were probably many Abiels, a whole dynasty of unrelated examples spread around the region. The fact that Abiel was a female name also raises the intriguing prospect that the region was ruled by a queen, or a number of queens.

That Mleiha traded with the Greeks is undeniable: amphora jars and handles bearing their makers' stamps have been discovered, and traced back to the island of Rhodes. Therefore, while the first known trading routes linked southwestern Arabia with the Mediterranean, there was a wider movement of people and goods to and from the southeast, including trade with people as far away as the Greeks in the second century BC.

———

ON THE COAST of Umm al-Qaiwain, amid the sand dunes of the shore, ed-Dur is a site of numerous discoveries. It has revealed coins and artefacts from a wide range of places, glass jars from the Roman Empire, pottery from the Parthian Empire, Mesopotamia, Arabia, India, Iran and elsewhere, all signifying that ed-Dur was an important port and trading emporium. It is a candidate for the location of Omana, identified by the Roman author Pliny in his *Natural History* as a port of some importance; there were also links between ed-Dur and the inland agricultural centre of Mleiha, as indicated by the discovery of Abiel coinage at both sites. Pliny, incidentally, wrote that the islands of the Gulf were inhabited by a people known to the Greeks as the *Ichthyophagi*, or 'fish eaters'.

Other discoveries at ed-Dur include a bell-shaped diver's weight similar to those recently used by pearl divers, together with a stack of pearl-oyster shells at the entrance to one of the graves. Since there is ample evidence that the Romans were aware of pearl diving in the Erythraean Sea, the early name for the Arabian Gulf, it is likely that pearls were being exported from the region during this period. Among the graves and tumbled stones, however, there was a most curious find: a rectangular temple, the remains of an Umm al-Nar altar and three other sacrificial altars outside, with traces of ritual fires around the site. Inside the temple, written on a plinth, was an Aramaic inscription in which the word *shamash* stood out. This word, close to the Arabic word *shams* meaning 'sun', provided the first proof that the people of the area might have once worshipped the sun. Bronze wine sets found in some graves suggest that drinking rituals may have been part of funerary rites at the site.

Altogether these discoveries raise the question of early religions. Our knowledge is limited by the nature and extent of the material excavated from sites around the UAE, since there are no written records from that time. Iron Age vessels decorated with snakes found at various sites replicate snake imagery found in other Near Eastern religions and mythologies of the Iron Age; snake skeletons in ceramic bowls in a Dilmun palace on Bahrain suggest that snakes held a similar connotation there. We do not know exactly what happened to the temple at ed-Dur, only that the settlement was abandoned by AD 150, with parts being reoccupied in the fourth century.

The advent of Christianity in the region remains a puzzle. Most likely it spread to the Gulf from the north, via the Roman province of Arabia and along the trade routes to India between AD 50 and 350. The conversion of the Roman emperor Constantine to Christianity in 312 brought it widespread acceptance in the West but triggered a counter reaction in the East, where the Sasanian Empire of Persia suppressed it; this may have brought a flood of Christian refugees to the shores of the lower Gulf. But the first real evidence of Christians in the Gulf appears in a story about a monk, *Vitae Ionae*, dated to the fourth century AD, which describes a monastery 'on the borders of the black island'.[7] There is another account, the Nestorian *Chronicle of Seert*, which places a monastery on Ramat Island. Although the precise locations of these islands are unknown, a ruined monastery has been found on the UAE island of Sir Bani Yas, about 180 kilometres (112 miles), as the crow flies, to the west of Abu Dhabi city.

It appears that an eclectic community of 30 to 40 monks speaking Syriac, Persian or Arabic were on Sir Bani Yas, living in buildings that have been dated to about AD 600 – indeed, there may have been an earlier, simpler settlement. Until recently, no one had any inkling that there had been a Christian monastery in this part of the Gulf, particularly since Islam was beginning to spread across the Middle East shortly

Camels passing along the south Arabian shore.

afterwards. The excavated buildings include monks' cells, kitchens and animal pens around a courtyard, with a church at its centre. Pieces of plaster decorated with designs of grapes and crosses, similar to other Christian sites elsewhere in the Gulf, were uncovered. That it was an important stopover for pilgrims travelling to and from India is revealed by artefacts recovered from the site, such as bowls, jars, glass vessels and ceremonial vases linking it with Mesopotamia, Bahrain and India. A body in a single grave on the main entrance platform of the church might have been of the founder of the settlement, or a prominent figure such as an abbot. Although the monastery did not survive much beyond AD 750, there is no evidence that it was attacked or otherwise destroyed. In all probability, the monastery went into decline with the arrival of Islam, and the monks found it increasingly difficult to attract new recruits to a life of monastic frugality on an increasingly isolated island off the Arabian shore.

All this should be seen in the context of the region as a whole. Following a split with Rome in the fifth century AD, the Church of the East (often known as the Nestorian Church) expanded along the trade routes to India and the Far East. There were Christian communities in Kuwait, on the eastern shore of Saudi Arabia, in Bahrain and Qatar, all of which formed the ecclesiastical province of Bet Qatraye. Another province, named Bet Mazunaye, was probably named after Mazun, the old Persian name for the territories of Oman and the UAE, and there is a record of a bishop at Sohar, Oman, which suggests one or more churches in the area.

There certainly were Christians on the Arabian mainland, in eastern Saudi Arabia, for example, and bishoprics at least until the late seventh century AD. However, with the advance of Muslim armies into eastern Arabia and Persia, support for the Sir Bani Yas ministry may have waned. The monks may have had close links with the pearling industry of the lower Gulf, which would have been disrupted by warfare. Sir Bani Yas was cut off, the Christians were isolated and deprived, and their community died out; perhaps this is the most plausible explanation for their passing. There is also textual evidence that 'Nestorian' church leaders expressed their concern about people converting to Islam. Nonetheless, there were still a few Christians present on the mainland in the late nineteenth century. And in an interesting aside, a section of the Manasir tribe believes to this day that they were once Christians before their conversion to Islam.

If we now look back across the golden shore we might see three strands emerging: the desert *bedu*, the *bahari* seafarer and the *jebali* mountain man. There were nomadic tribes in the desert, herding their camels and following the rains to the next patch of grazing. Others divided their time between the different landscapes; some were settled farmers who used the *falaj* to bring sweet water down from the hills, cultivating terraces on the slopes or gardens on the alluvial plain, and others were fishermen and pearlers, traders and sailors along the coast. It was here, in a haphazard way, that the origins of the modern country appeared and developed over the centuries as people slowly drifted from a nomadic (*bedu*) life to a settled (*hadar*) one. Although this is only part of the story – the UAE is a rich tapestry of influences and people, including Persians, Indians, northern Arabs and others from Yemen, and the *Khaliji*, the Arabs of the Gulf – it was the tribes that held it all together.

2

Emergence: Greater Oman, the Arabian Gulf and the Bani Yas, AD 630–1909

THERE IS A BEDOUIN LEGEND of a 'great river' that once flowed from the Rub al-Khali to the Arabian Gulf, reaching the sea through Sabkhat Matti.[1] On 1 January 1990, when Sheikh Zayed bin Sultan al-Nahyan of Abu Dhabi told a group of palaeontologists at Jebel Dhanna about this legend, they were astounded. They had already discovered traces of an ancient river in the area which had existed long before modern humans evolved. In time, further investigations would confirm that there was such a river during the Pleistocene, part of a massive system of rivers and lakes that once existed in the region.

They are all gone now, of course. As the climate changed, fresh-water outflow from the centre of the Rub al-Khali ceased by the end of the Pleistocene – possibly recurring during times of higher rainfall between 10,000 BC and 4000 BC, which might account for the river being preserved in the bedouin memory. The *sabkha* (salt flats) along the coast began to form around 2000 BC, and would presumably have formed in the areas of Sabkhat Matti that were nearer to the coast at this time. Today, these developments have left behind a massive salt plain, which is as flat as a pancake, like quicksand when wet and inhospitable when dry.

Even those who might regard all deserts as much the same would admit that Sabkhat Matti is unmistakably different from the surrounding terrain. It was entirely appropriate that the early people of the region should have regarded it as a geographical boundary. Early Arab geographers knew today's UAE and Oman collectively as 'Greater Oman', and eastern Saudi Arabia and Bahrain as 'Greater Bahrayn'. This division roughly equates with the Magan and Dilmun of old, and the wide *sabkha* between them would have left travellers in no doubt that they were crossing a frontier to another land.

Although there is evidence of migration and travel to and from the two regions, the overland route was difficult and at times impassable, being covered with thick sand and frequented by warring tribes. This forced travellers to take the sea route from Bahrain to Julfar (near present-day Ras al-Khaimah), taking in islands on the way, before going inland to places such as Tuwwam (the area of Al Ain/Buraimi today) or Dibba on the Gulf of Oman. Trying to navigate around the Strait of Hormuz was a treacherous business, with terrors such as Al Dardur (the whirlpool) awaiting the hapless mariner, hence the overland route to and from Julfar was the preferred one, when it was available.

One of the first recorded tribal influxes came from a different direction, however – from the southwestern corner of the Arabian Peninsula that is known today as Yemen. In the sixth century AD the Marib dam burst, destroying fields and settlements and forcing sections of the Azd tribe to leave Yemen and seek their living elsewhere. In fact, although it is the drama of the inundation that is often recalled, these eastward migrations probably began and ended a few centuries either side of the event. People travelled along the southern edge of the Rub al-Khali or along its northern edge via eastern Arabia to arrive at the gateway to the region, Tuwwam.

There were other migrations too, such as those of the Nizar tribes from northwest Arabia, who counterbalanced the Azd and laid down the first fault lines of a rivalry that would stretch into modern times. Tribes were Hinawi (Azd) or Ghafiri (Nizari), and even those farther afield such as the Bani Yas of Abu Dhabi and the Qasimi tribes of Sharjah and Ras al-Khaimah – Hinawi and Ghafiri respectively – were defined in these terms. Although often blurred, the division was most apparent in the tribal alliances that formed from the seventeenth century AD onwards. Even in more recent times, many Omani towns were partitioned between the two factions, with a wadi and the ruler's fort to keep them apart.

It was in the seventh century AD that Islam made the greatest impact on the region. It is not entirely clear when the Arabic language arrived. Certainly, Aramaic was being used as a commercial language at ed-Dur, while an early pre-Arabic South Arabian language reached Mleiha and Muweilah. But the advance and migration of Arabic-speaking tribes, together with the advent of new religion, brought a common culture and language from the western coast of Arabia to the east.

In about 630 an emissary from Mecca, Amr ibn al-As, appeared in Oman with a letter from the Prophet Mohammed:

The name of God the Merciful and the Compassionate . . .
peace be on those who choose the right path. Embrace Islam,
and you shall be safe. I am God's messenger to all humanity,
here to alert all those alive that nonbelievers are condemned. If
you submit to Islam, you will remain kings, but if you abstain,
your rule will be removed and my horses will enter your arena
to prove my prophecy.[2]

Amr ibn al-As was duly received by the ruling Julanda brothers, Gaifar
and Amr, who at that time were vassals to the Sasanian kings of Persia
and collected taxes on their behalf. According to one account, the
brothers called a council of the Al Azd, whose members all converted
to Islam, and then expelled the non-believing Sasanians from the country when they refused to convert. The future of Oman (and what was
to become the UAE) as an Islamic country was assured, or so it seemed.

This was only the first round, however. After the death of the
Prophet in AD 632 there were widespread rebellions against Islam that
were suppressed in a series of campaigns known as the Ridda Wars. In
Oman, an Azdite by the name of Laqit bin Malik dhu at-Taj declared
himself a prophet and raised a revolt against the Julanda brothers
and by association against the Islamic state, the caliphate. In response its
leader, the caliph Abu Bakr, ordered three of his generals to invade Oman.
The caliphate armies faced a difficult overland journey across *sabkha* and
desert, but pressed on despite a large number of soldiers falling behind.
They met up with the Julanda brothers in the shadow of the fort at Sohar
and then marched on the rebels at Dibba, where a large battle took place.
In the midst of the excitement, as the caliphate army seemed to be
losing ground, the stragglers arrived. Laqit was killed, the rebels defeated
with the loss of 10,000 men; there is a large graveyard outside the town
that is believed to hold the dead from that battle. It is said that Dibba,
which had been a thriving port until then, never really recovered from
the sacking it received.

This victory, the so-called 'Day of Dibba' when Islam triumphed
over the forces of apostasy, set the seal on the caliphate domination of
Oman. Whether full conversion of the population to Islam was achieved
overnight is uncertain, but the might of the caliphate armies was overwhelming. After three years, the situation was deemed peaceful enough
to allow the general in charge of Oman, Hudaifah, to depart. He left
the territory in the hands of the Julanda brothers again, this time under

Al Utayba mosque, Abu Dhabi, built *c.* 1936. It has now been replaced by Sheikh Khalifa bin Zayed al-Nahyan Mosque.

the distant supervision of a caliphate governor based in Bahrain. The fact that the brothers were able to resume their leadership of the tribes at this juncture suggests that the underlying tribal structures had remained intact.

As it happened, Oman was not destined to stay within the Islamic mainstream. After Islam had cleaved between Shia and Sunni factions – a distinction that is familiar to most Western readers today – a third faction, Kharijites (later known as Ibadis), sprang up. From the eighth century AD, this breakaway sect spread through the high mountains and deep valleys of inner Oman. Mostly resembling Sunnism yet with important differences, Ibadis were led by an imam who was chosen for his moral rectitude, strong character and sound judgement. In this theocracy, succession was determined by elders and religious scholars, though at times it became more of a hereditary system – here, in fact, lay its main strength and weakness: while religious and secular leadership were fused in a single figurehead, thus presenting a powerful unified force against the caliphate, Oman also had a tendency to self-destruct with periodic bouts of in-fighting and upheaval.

In contrast, the tribes of the Gulf hinterland – the area roughly corresponding with today's UAE – had no centrifugal force to bind them together. Two broad confederations divided along Hinawi/Ghafiri lines emerged during the seventeenth century AD, but we know little about the tribes before then. It is apparent, however, that Tuwwam and Julfar were focal points of trade and communication from early times, giving the area a distinct identity. At various periods, Tuwwam and Julfar had paid tribute to foreign invaders such as the Carmathians from Al Hasa and the Buyids of Iran, signifying that they were important trading hubs in their own right. The Arab writer Al-Muqaddasi described them around 985:

> Hafit [Tuwwam] abounds in palm trees; it lies in the direction of Hajar [Al Hasa], and the mosque is in the markets . . . Dibba and Julfar, both in the direction of Hajar, are close to the sea . . . Tuwwam has been dominated by a branch of the Quraysh; they are men of fortitude and forcefulness . . . the people of these towns we have mentioned are heretical Arabs.[3]

Tuwwam straddled the trade routes between Sohar, the Arabian interior and the Gulf coast. Although Dibba had lost its former glory, it retained its trading links with India and China.

These are a few of the facts that can be extracted from the period between the end of the seventh and the beginning of the sixteenth centuries – otherwise, the history of the region remains scant, and its impact hard to discern. That the Kharijites (Ibadis) survived successive caliphate invasions is certain. The Umayyad dynasty (661–750) based in Damascus made a determined effort to conquer Oman, landing troops on the shore of today's UAE coast, at Baynuna or Julfar. But the collapse of the Umayyads saw a consolidation of Kharijite power in Oman and their subsequent evolution as the Ibadi sect. Although in the eighth and ninth centuries the Abbasid caliphate (750–1256) mounted successive invasions of Oman through Julfar, at one point seizing Tuwwam, their last invasion was conducted against an alliance of tribes in order to restore the Ibadi Imamate. Their interventions could be bloody affairs, as the exploits of one Abbasid general, Mohammed bin Nur, in the ninth century were described:

> He degraded the most honourable of the inhabitants, and reduced them to the most abject condition. He caused people to have their hands, feet and ears cut off, their eyes put out, and generally treated the inhabitants with the greatest severity

and contempt. He also filled up the channels [i.e. the *aflaj*], and Oman passed out of the hands of the people.[4]

Successive foreign invasions came and went like the seasons. The Safarid dynasty of Persia came to occupy parts of Oman, as evidenced by coins minted in the area. In about 925, the Carmathians of Al Hasa (today the Eastern Province of Saudi Arabia) arrived to conquer the territory and stayed for some 60 years, extracting tribute from local tribes. In 966 the Buyids invaded and ruled until about 1055, after which the Imamate was again restored. Again, coins from the Buyid period were minted in Oman, possibly in Tuwwam.

We now enter something of a dark age, as power struggles in Persia impacted and influenced events in southeastern Arabia. Julfar and the eastern coast eventually came under the control of the kingdom of Hormuz. Although not always a settled state of affairs, it was to Hormuz that a Portuguese fleet came at the beginning of the sixteenth century in order to seek the focal point of power in the lower Gulf.

But Julfar still remains something of a mystery. There are many references to it in the old texts but its exact location is unknown; indeed, the name 'Julfar' might have described both a port and an area in the same way that the modern capitals of the Gulf refer to a city as well as an emirate. The best that might be said is that the settlement of Julfar was probably in the vicinity of modern-day Ras al-Khaimah, though not in a fixed location – while the name of Julfar was in use until the eighteenth century AD, its population centre moved around the area. This was partly because of the silting up of creeks, some of which now lie well inland, which forced the people to seek new points of access to the sea. The tell at Kush in Ras al-Khaimah, for example, was abandoned because of this, and it appears that solid buildings began to appear on a sand spit north of the present-day town once Kush had been deserted.

Wherever its precise location, Julfar was renowned as a thriving port. The twelfth-century geographer Al Idrisi knew it as a centre of the pearling trade (although the pearling grounds are considerably to the west) where a sand bar prevented the docking of ships. It was in the fourteenth century that the area came under the control of the kings of Hormuz, who sought to protect the town and the agricultural land behind it, possibly from the interior tribes, by constructing a 7-kilometre (4-mile) long wall. Hormuz was known to the Venetians from the travels of Marco Polo, who twice visited Hormuz in the thirteenth century.

By 1490 when the first Portuguese arrived – probably Pero da Cavilha, who was investigating a maritime route to the East around the Cape of Good Hope – Julfar had established and maintained a long tradition as a centre of regional importance, renowned for pearling, trading and navigational expertise. From earliest times, the port was of great strategic importance, since control of Hormuz on the Persian side of the Gulf and Julfar on the other allowed a ruler to control shipping through the Strait of Hormuz. As has been seen, the port also gave foreign invaders easy access and a forward supply base for invasions of the interior.

By the fifteenth century, the lower Gulf was part of a trading network that stretched to the Far East, and Arab sailors had control of this network. There was trade between Dibba and China, probably Canton, before the coming of Islam, while Muslim merchants, not necessarily from the UAE area, had arrived in Canton much earlier. The renowned pilot Ibn Majid lived in Julfar, his bedouin family having migrated from the central Arabian desert, the Nejd. He was a prolific writer of books, among which *Kitab al-Fawaid fi Usul 'Ilm al-Bahr wa 'l-Qawa'id* (Book of Useful Information on the Principles and Rules of Navigation) is a remarkable navigational guide for the seas and coasts of the Arabian peninsula, the Indian Ocean and Southeast Asia.

In the late fifteenth century the Portuguese struggled to find a way to India, losing ships to reefs and treacherous currents along the way. The famous navigator Vasco da Gama arrived in the area in 1498 and, it was said, was shown the way to India by Ibn Majid – but this account has since been discounted since Ibn Majid would have been too old by then. It is likely that da Gama used an Indian pilot he met on the East African coast, who may well have used *Kitab al-Fawaid*. Da Gama certainly made it to India, and left his mark on the East: one of his voyages included burning a boat packed with Muslim pilgrims. The Portuguese aimed to monopolize the lucrative spice trade with Europe. Arab sailors, who had been accustomed to sailing to India without fear of being attacked, found themselves on the receiving end of a brutal campaign.

In 1507 a fleet of seven ships and 500 men under the command of Admiral Afonso de Albuquerque made its way up the Omani coast, taking ports such as Muscat and Khor Fakkan by force, while accepting submission from others. The seizure of Khor Fakkan served as a terrible warning to those wishing to resist. It was a large town, a fertile area and a major trading port with a significant number of Gujarati merchants. When Albuquerque's small fleet arrived, the inhabitants made a great show on the beach, marching up and down, beating drums, shouting and riding horses and camels along the shore. This fell short of a submission and, the following day, the unimpressed admiral sent his men ashore, where they proceeded to kill those who opposed them, taking any captured young men to work on their ships, hacking off the noses and ears of the old men, and keeping the women and children as prisoners. The town was razed, its fishing boats burnt and its crops destroyed.

Albuquerque sailed on to Hormuz. On his arrival he demanded that the twelve-year-old king become a Portuguese vassal and, when the king prevaricated, Albuquerque took the town of 30,000 people by force. But a mutiny forced the admiral to retreat and it was not until 1515 that he was able to return and retake Hormuz. The town and its (possible) vassal Julfar now found themselves under Portuguese tutelage, and its strategic position enabled the Portuguese to dominate the Gulf for many years to come, much as the kings of Hormuz had done before them.

An early Portuguese source described Julfar as a 'very large town' where

> There are many very respectable people, and many merchants and sailors. And there they fish up many large pearls and seed pearls, which the merchants of the city of Hormuz come there to buy, to carry them to India and other parts. This place is one of much trade and produces a great deal to the king of Hormuz.[5]

But there was another aspect to this: the capture of Hormuz was part of the Portuguese bid to control the Eastern spice trade. Driven by an acquisitive desire and religious zeal, they stamped their presence on the region by force of arms, occupying strategic points along the Omani coast. The Arabs, accustomed to a lucrative trade with the Far East, and with a long history of trade and seamanship, found themselves squeezed out. The Portuguese issued documents of safe passage known as *cartazes* for larger ships and free passes to local rulers, and imposed customs duties on cargoes and taxes on ports. As the ships of the Portuguese or their allies came to dominate the long-distance trades, smaller Arab boats concentrated on the coastal networks. This was the start of a European presence in the Gulf, and it did not bode well for the future.

In 1622 a joint Anglo-Persian force ousted the Portuguese from Hormuz. In 1633 Imam Nasir bin Murshid of the Yaruba dynasty of Oman expelled them from Julfar and Dibba. Ten years later he captured Sohar and in 1650 a new imam, Sultan bin Saif, took Muscat and expelled the Portuguese for good; they had been in the region for 150 years, but there was little to show for their presence. In addition to Julfar and a massive fort at Bahrain, their power base in the region had been in the forts of the eastern coast – at Fujairah, Dibba, Bidiya, Khor Fakkan and Kalba – and their interaction with the inland tribes had been minimal. All that remains today is a number of ruined forts and rusting cannons, some of which were taken over by local people after they had left. The Shihuh took over the Portuguese fort at Dibba Baiah, for example.

The tribes knew a great deal about building fortifications, no doubt, since the pre-Islamic era had seen many towers being erected. Now they were able to build new forts as well as utilizing the old ones. Forts were still being built long after the departure of the Portuguese: Qasr al-Hosn in Abu Dhabi was built in 1793; Al Fahidi Fort in Dubai around 1797; in Ras al-Khaimah, a line of forts and towers to Jazirah al-Hamra and Khatt from 1820, earlier forts having been destroyed by the British; Al Hisn Fort in Sharjah in 1820; and Al Jahili Fort in Al Ain in 1898. The larger forts, built by the ruling families, were known as *hosn* and provided safe refuges in turbulent times, or served as administrative bases during peaceful times. It is said that a watchman on the tower of a fort would fire one shot to warn of an approaching stranger, two shots for an attack, and three shots to signal an important event, such as sighting the new crescent moon which signalled the start of Ramadan, or the feast at its end, *Eid al-Fitr*.

The Europeans had no interest in the affairs of the Arabian interior, seeking to build up their respective trading positions in Persia and the Far East. By the mid-seventeenth century the clear winners were the Dutch, who traded through the Dutch East India Company (Vereenigde Oostindische Compagnie or VOC). They had established a base at Bandar Abbas, from where they sought to monopolize the trade in commodities such as sugar, spices, Indian cotton textiles, copper, iron and silk. The English, who had also had a factory in the town, traded through a rival company, the East India Company (EIC). Finding its efforts frustrated by the Dutch, the EIC set up a small factory at Basra in 1635 but the Dutch blockaded the port and the outbreak of war in Europe in 1653 pitted both nations against each other. A series of Dutch naval victories in the Arabian Gulf confirmed their supremacy in the region to the detriment of the English, who retained only a small share of Persian trade.

The Dutch era, as it is known, had little impact on the Arabian side of the Gulf but it was a time when history could have taken a different turn. In 1651 the imam Sultan bin Saif of Oman was so impressed by the Dutch that he visited their factory at Gombroon (Bandar Abbas) on the Persian coast and offered them a land route for their goods between Basra and the lower Gulf where the Bani Yas would provide camels for the journey. The Dutch had argued with the Persians over the silk trade and were looking for ways to avoid their customs dues, so the offer must have been tempting but, in the event, it was declined. Even so, the episode does raise some intriguing questions about how the region might have developed if the trade route had been adopted.

There were other European powers with an interest in the region, of course: the French, who lost one foothold in Persia and gained another through the arms trade in Muscat; and the Portuguese, who

An ancient cannon at the Qasr al-Hosn Centre, Abu Dhabi.

still maintained a trading presence despite their military defeats. Initially the Dutch were methodical, industrious and, above all, determined to monopolize the Persian trade. As with the Portuguese before them, their position in the Gulf was occasionally undermined by events in Europe; nevertheless they contrived to maintain a strong naval presence in the Gulf for 100 years. It was only in the mid-eighteenth century, in the face of strong British competition, that they decided to close their Persian factories and retreat to the island of Kharg, off the Persian coast, where they had a fort and trading station.

Here the Dutch took over many activities that had been run by Arabs, including the local pearl fisheries. This caused conflict among the inhabitants of Kharg and the nearby mainland, including a large Arab contingent who were opposed to their presence. In 1765 Mir Mahanna, a sheikh of the Zaab tribe and ruler of the nearby small town, Bandar Rig, took up arms against the Dutch. The Zaab were an Omani tribe that had settled on the northern shore of the lower Gulf on Jazirah al-Hamra in today's Ras al-Khaimah, and on the Persian shore where Mir Mahanna was ruler of Bandar Rig. His attacks on shipping were known far and wide, and any claim he might have had to being a simple freedom fighter against Dutch exploitation was contradicted by the fact that he had killed his mother and father and some fifteen members of his family in order to gain power. On any view, he was hardly a paragon of virtue.

Yet Mir Mahanna was an able commander. Having defeated a Dutch force on Kharg Island, he brought his 600-odd troops to bear on the island's fortress at Mosselsteyn where the remainder of the Dutch forces, 120 Arabs and 80 Europeans, were ensconced. Only a single Dutch ship at anchor in the harbour managed to escape capture. However, its captain decided to make sail in order to catch the seasonal winds for Indonesia rather than lend his support to the besieged garrison. The Dutch commander of the garrison, Van Houten, left the fort to parley with the sheikh only to find himself a prisoner of the Arabs; thus deprived of their commander, the garrison surrendered. Together with Van Houten they were allowed to go free, leaving Mir Mahanna to claim the spoils of victory. Now for the first time, the exploits of a Gulf Arab sheikh were reported in a newsletter sent from Basrah on 7 February 1766:

> The famous Mirmahana who exercises his piracy in the Persian [*sic*] Gulf has by surprise taken the island Karack [Kharg]

which was in possession of the Dutch since about 15 years. It is reported that the garrison of the fortress and the officers of the fort have been sent to Benderboucher and the booty taken by Mirmahana on this occasion amounts to several millions.[6]

The Dutch authorities had long been urging the VOC to withdraw from the region. In the event, the company's board of directors accepted the outcome as final, and so the fall of Kharg effectively brought the Dutch era in the Gulf to an inauspicious close. As for Mir Mahanna, despite his success he was overthrown by the people of Kharg in 1769. Fleeing to Basra, he was arrested by the Ottomans and strangled on the orders of the local governor.

The British, who had been building up their trading interests in Persia and India, now found themselves as the dominant European power in the region. In 1763 a Political Residency had been established in Bushire to administer British affairs; in time, EIC factories were replaced by a number of diplomatic outposts in the Gulf, known as agencies, which reported to the official in charge, the Political Resident based in Bushire. The needs of India dictated British policy, especially the need to protect communications and trade in the Arabian Gulf, the Euphrates Valley being the main channel for postal deliveries between London and Bombay, the seat of British government in India.

One consequence of the Mir Mahanna attacks on shipping was a system of British colours and passes that echoed the Portuguese *cartazes* of old. On payment of 100 rupees, a vessel would receive British protection. Although the system was soon suspended, it was later re-introduced and would have a major impact on the ensuing history of the region. Alongside the British rise to prominence was an ongoing struggle between indigenous groups over trade routes in the Gulf: the Omanis of Muscat, the Qawasim (singular Qasimi) of Ras al-Khaimah and the Utub of Bahrain. As we shall see in the next chapter, the British remained largely uninterested in the region until attacks on shipping brought a decisive struggle with the Qasimi tribes.

———

THE BEDOUIN did not write things down, relying instead on an oral tradition of songs and stories in which the great deeds of their forefathers were repeated over unfathomable periods of time. The picture is vague and uncertain until the seventeenth century, when tribal groupings start to emerge in southeast Arabia. The Bani Yas was a confederation of tribes believed to have originated in the Nejd and to have migrated towards the Liwa Oasis. According to one account, a leader called Yas dug the first well in the oasis and the tribes congregated around it, taking his name; such is the simplicity of legends. More confident genealogies assert that the Bani Yas name derived from Yas Bin Amer, a tribal leader whose lineage can be traced farther back into the mists of time.

Liwa became an important tribal centre for a community of date farmers and camel herders who relied on occasional rains and dew collected in dune basins to provide sweet water for their plantations and animals. The Bani Yas sported a variety of lifestyles: nomadic, sedentary or a mixture of both. It was the habit of many tribesmen to spend the winter tending their herds and date plantations in the Liwa Oasis and then migrate in the summer to the fishing and pearling grounds off the coast, using the shore and islands as a base for their activities. In 1580 the Venetian jeweller Gasparo Balbi travelled to the Gulf in order to investigate the pearl trade and noted an island called Sirbeniast – Sir Bani Yas – which suggests a Bani Yas presence there at that time.

The next references can be found in Sirhan ibn Said's *Annals of Oman* and Razik's *The Imams and Seyyids of Oman*. The Yaruba dynasty of Oman, which had been established in 1624, faced internal challenges from forces such as those led by Nasser bin Qahtan al-Hilali. Around 1633 Nasser was forced to retreat to Ezh-Zhafrah ('Al Dhafrah') fort, which was probably located at Mantakha As'sirra in western Abu Dhabi, where he was welcomed by the Bani Yas. A reference in *Annals* has a battle fought at Al Shaib near Al Dhafrah with the imam's forces, during which the Bani Yas leader Saqr bin Isa and his brother Muhammad were killed.[7]

At the heart of the Bani Yas confederation was the Al Bu Falah tribe, which had been among those who had migrated from Greater Bahrayn to Greater Oman, settled in the borderlands of Baynuna and gained control of the Liwa Oasis, which is about 120 kilometres (75 miles) from the Gulf coast. The Al Bu Falah, as their name suggests, took their name from Falah, a respected leader of the early eighteenth century. The name of the ruling family, Nahyan, is derived from Falah's son and successor, who was named after the Wadi Nahyan in Yemen. The Arab naming system reflects this interest in genealogy, giving someone a family name that links them to a patriarch or tribe:

A bedouin family on the move: as well as the traditional tribal range (*dirah*), there were seasonal migrations between the interior and the coast for the pearling season.

thus Dhiyab bin Isa al-Nahyan denotes Dhiyab, son of Isa of the Nahyan dynasty.

The emergence of the Bani Yas brings a tribal network into view. At the head of each tribe was a sheikh, and the paramount sheikh among them ruled over all the tribes of a particular tribal grouping. In the case of the Bani Yas, the leading family was the Al Nahyan and so the head of that family was the ruler of the Bani Yas. Ruling sheikhs were appointed by a council of tribal elders and family members and their removal was – occasionally – by assassination.

Sheikh Dhiyab bin Isa al-Nahyan was the ruler of the Bani Yas. It was during his time that the settlement of Abu Dhabi was founded. Today, Abu Dhabi describes a city as well as an emirate, but originally it was a meagre settlement on a coastal island in the Gulf, separated from the mainland by a narrow creek at Al Maqta. As the story goes, in 1761 a group of tribesmen were hunting gazelle on the island when they discovered a supply of fresh water. A number of Bani Yas, including some Al Bu Falah, decided to make it their home. Hence the modern city of Abu Dhabi was born, but then only as a scant collection of huts and coral-stone dwellings along the shore with a small watchtower to guard a precious well.[8] It is believed that the name Abu Dhabi, meaning 'Father of the Gazelle', takes its name from the event that started it all; but perhaps all this is too convenient, since there is a different story about the city's origins, which has a lone fisherman scooping up the sand to discover the first well on the island, thus choosing to start a settlement there.

Whatever the explanation, the island was worth defending. Three watchtowers were built: one by a well, another at Al Maqta to protect the crossing onto the island, and a third recently discovered at Al Bateen, on the east side of the island. According to Reverend Zwemer's account in 1902, crossing by Al Maqta was a treacherous business, with a tidal channel to be negotiated under the full gaze of watching guards and only a slip or stumble separating the camels from certain death. Although the leader of the Al Bu Falah, Sheikh Dhiyab bin Isa, spent only a few months each year on the island, within two years there were 400 'arish houses built just inland from the shore, with pearling and fishing the main occupations of the inhabitants.

The tranquillity of this little island world was briefly shattered in 1793 when news arrived that Dhiyab had been assassinated by his cousin, Hazza, at the Liwa Oasis. Dhiyab had visited Abu Dhabi to tell a branch of the Al Bu Falah to stop stirring up trouble with a neighbouring tribe. Hazza, their leader, who was in Bahrain at the time, hurried back and killed Dhiyab during the course of an argument between the two. The effect of this convulsion was short-lived, however, as the Bani Yas elders swung behind Dhiyab's son, Shakhbut. Hazza went into exile, and his supporters were slaughtered.

In 1795 Sheikh Shakhbut moved his place of residence from Liwa to Abu Dhabi, effectively making the latter the capital of the Bani Yas. The first watchtower became part of a fort that was modified and extended over the years, and still stands today. Known as Qasr al-Hosn, it was once an important landmark for sailors, an administrative base and home to the ruling family. Today, the restored fort is a museum resting in the shade of skyscrapers at the centre of a modern, thriving city.

The nomadic Bani Yas spread to the west and east of the western desert, movements that would have repercussions when it came to settling the boundaries of the Emirates in later years. The limits of their expansion roughly coincided with the territorial limits of the modern state of Abu Dhabi. Arabian boundaries could be changeable, however, depending on the allegiances of a particular tribe, and the extent of their *dar*. While bedouins had a keen eye for the terrain, they were little concerned about lines on maps; confederations like the Bani Yas were dynamic affairs, and tribes would come and go.

The history of Abu Dhabi was never a simple affair. In a pattern that would become depressingly familiar, there were coups and counter coups as sections of the family struggled for control. In 1816 Sheikh Shakhbut was deposed by his son Mohammed, who in turn was forced to step down in favour of his younger brother, Tahnoun. In 1818 Mohammed went into exile in Doha but remained a thorn in Tahnoun's side, returning in 1824 to attack Abu Dhabi in alliance with the Manasir, only to be repelled by Tahnoun. Described as a 'fine-looking man, possessing much of that open and hospitable frankness generally attributed to

A scene from the Liwa Oasis, 1962.

the Arab', Tahnoun was a firm ally of the sultan of Muscat.[9] Shakhbut stayed on as his son's right hand, signing agreements on his son's behalf and remaining active until the 1840s. Indeed, many Bani Yas still regarded him as their overlord.

From these years, we find enmities and alliances that endured into modern times: the Wahhabis and the Qawasim were enemies of the Bani Yas, while Omanis and the Awamir were friends. The Wahhabis, a radical religious sect under the Al Saud family from the Nejd, took their name from the movement's founder, Sheikh Muhammad ibn Abdul al-Wahhab. This was the so-called 'Arabian Reformation' when Wahhabis were to Arabia as Calvinists were to Europe, aiming to sweep away what they claimed were the baubles, idolatry and false saints of the old religion and return to worshipping the one true God. They were expansionist and highly ruthless, ready to put opponents to the sword as they fought their *jihad* across the Arabian peninsula; those who refused to submit were killed, the rest were converted. They appeared in Buraimi in 1802 and sought to dominate Oman for the next sixteen years. Yet even they could not resist the might of Egypt and, when the Nejd was invaded by Ibrahim Pasha in 1818, the Wahhabi threat to southeastern Arabia fell away.

In one sense, the Wahhabi attacks were the making of the Bani Yas, since they caused them to strengthen their ties with the Al Bu Said sultans of Muscat, and spread their influence in the Buraimi area. Sheikh Shakhbut built up his authority among the local tribes to such an extent that 30 years later his son was telling the Political Resident that the country of the Dhawahir (to the south of Buraimi) belonged to his father. However, Tahnoun's alliance with the sultan of Muscat incensed their traditional foe, the Qawasim, and their ruler, Sheikh Sultan bin Saqr al-Qasimi of Sharjah. In an attempt to strike at the Bani Yas homeland, Sheikh Sultan supported the deposed sheikh of Abu Dhabi, Mohammed, in an attack on Abu Dhabi town; but Mohammed's forces were repelled by Tahnoun, forcing his retreat to Sharjah.

One writer has likened the worst days of the Al Bu Falah in the nineteenth century to those of the Borgias or the Medicis.[10] Certainly, underlying themes of mistrust, betrayal and murder run like a dark river through the narrative. About the Bani Yas it was noted: 'So soon as they were deprived of a ruler they quickly supplied themselves with another, and as quickly became reconciled to the sway he held over them.'[11]

Abu Dhabi from the air, 1949.

And so the carousel turned once more. In 1833 Tahnoun was murdered by two of his brothers, Khalifa and Sultan, with the first shooting and the other stabbing him. Khalifa was ambitious but impetuous; upon becoming ruler and finding himself in a precarious position, he bought the protection of the Al Saud by paying tribute to them. Outrage over this agreement destabilized his weakened sheikhdom, and even the ex-ruler Sheikh Mohammed popped up again, hoping to regain his former status. But the patriarch of the tribe, Shakhbut, decided to throw in his lot with Khalifa and Sultan, thus ensuring their survival. In August and September a plot emerged to replace Khalifa with his cousin, leading the new ruler to exact a terrible revenge on three conspirators, although he relented against another two of them. So alarmed were some members of the Bani Yas, about 3,600 people in all, that they decamped and set up in Bur Dubai under the leadership of Sheikh Maktoum bin Buti of the Al Bu Falasah section.

Dubai had been the scene of many Qasimi–Bani Yas skirmishes over the years. The town's creek, which marked the vague boundary between their two territories, was controlled by a fort at Deira until it was burnt down as part of an Omani-brokered peace in 1827. Now another fight broke out as Khalifa tried to oust the Al Maktoum, but without success. After two years, a truce was struck whereby Khalifa was forced to recognize Dubai as an independent sheikhdom. It was a fragile peace: Sheikh Khalifa made two more attempts to take the town, in 1838 and 1841, before finally accepting defeat.

The Al Maktoum were not the only ones to suffer; the almost constant state of warfare cost the Bani Yas dearly. In addition to the cost of prosecuting the war, there was the effect of attrition and the disruption of the economic cycles: the date harvest lost, the pearling season interrupted. Bani Yas sailors attacked a number of native boats in order to catch debtors or seize their vessels in lieu of unpaid debts. The British took a dim view, however, deeming their actions as 'piracy'. At this juncture, the mollifying influence of Sheikh Shakhbut came to the fore. Khalifa was persuaded to accept terms, which included forfeiting his finest ships, the *Mombasa*, *Ghanomee* and *Bellaly*, giving full redress and paying an indemnity.

This settlement had an unexpected outcome. In 1835 a number of the Qubaisat clan, also part of the Bani Yas confederation, left Abu Dhabi in order to avoid paying their share of the costs that the British had imposed on Sheikh Khalifa. They settled in Khor al-Udaid, the inlet on the eastern coast of the Qatar peninsula, and set about raiding the ruler's fishing boats there. In May 1837 Sheikh Khalifa sent a force that killed 50 of their number, threw their bodies down a well and destroyed their homes. The remaining Qubaisat then returned to Abu Dhabi, having been offered generous peace terms.

Towards the end of his reign, this conciliatory streak prevailed as Sheikh Khalifa negotiated a truce with the Al Maktoum over the Al Ain/Buraimi Oasis and expelled the Naim from some of its villages. By late 1844 the British agent in Sharjah was writing, 'It appears to me at the present time that there is not throughout the interior one bedouin tribe that is opposed to him.'[12] The fact that Khalifa was able to unite the tribes without fear of Qasimi reprisals said much about the latter's loss of influence. The result was a prosperous and reasonably secure Abu Dhabi stretching from Dubai to the foot of the Qatar peninsula, with a strategic foothold in the Al Ain/Buraimi Oasis and a thriving pearling industry on the coast. All appeared set fair for the future but, as the past had shown, the greatest danger was from within.

In 1845 Sheikh Khalifa and his brother, Sultan, were assassinated at a feast. It was July, a time when the date harvest and pearling season coincided, and many tribesmen were away. Over the next few months Abu Dhabi went through a troubled period during which the assassin Isa bin Khalid and his sons were slaughtered. The Bani Yas sought to restore Tahnoun's bloodline by appointing his second son, Said, as ruler. This approach had the desired effect, uniting the Bani Yas under a popular leader who had the necessary family pedigree.

Sheikh Said's energies were immediately taken up by a renewed Wahhabi threat to Buraimi and its western approaches. Joining forces with the Naim and other tribes of the oasis, Said's tribesmen were able to block Wahhabi supply columns making their way across Al Dhafrah, winning a famous victory at Ankah in November 1848 in which it is said that 700 warriors died. The Wahhabi commander Saad ibn Mutlaq retreated to the coast and, although a peace treaty allowed him to occupy Buraimi, his authority there was effectively broken. After Sheikh Sultan bin Saqr of Sharjah had become disenchanted with the Wahhabi cause, conditions were right for Said to expel them from the oasis in November 1850. But the Wahhabis returned in the spring of 1853 with a large force of 300–500 horsemen and ten times as many camel riders under Emir Abdullah bin Faisal, leading to a Wahhabi occupation of Buraimi that would last for another sixteen years.

Back in Abu Dhabi, there were murmurings of discontent. In 1849 Sheikh Said entered into an alliance with the Muhariba tribe, rivals of the Qubaisat, both of whom were sub-tribes of the Bani Yas. As a result, a number of Qubaisat failed to return to Abu Dhabi at the end of the pearling season and took their boats to Khor al-Udaid. Said took the remaining Qubaisat as hostages and used them to persuade the seceders to return. When they did come back, Said appeared conciliatory at first, but that night his retainers attacked the Qubaisat boats, removing their masts, rudders and sails, making escape impossible. Then, for good measure, they received fines that they could only pay by selling their boats. Finally, Said sent a boatload of dead and dying donkeys to Khor al-Udaid to poison the wells there.

Of course a sheikh had to be a strong leader, but some things went beyond the pale. In 1854 an elderly tribesman killed his brother. In accordance with the tribal law of retribution, Sheikh Said demanded the murderer's life, but the Bani Yas, believing that the man had just cause for killing his brother, would only agree to pay blood money. In

A bedouin guide, Ali bin Thamer, pictured here in 1961.

1855, on Said's promise not to harm him and forgo blood money, the tribe agreed to produce the murderer. He was brought before Said, who drew his dagger and stabbed him to death, whereupon the Bani Yas 'rose to a man' and would have killed Said there and then had he not fled immediately, leaving his brother Saqr in charge of the fort.[13] He was duly expelled when news reached the Bani Yas that Said had contacted the Political Resident with a view to regaining the sheikhdom.

The tribe appointed 24-year-old Zayed, son of the long-deceased ruler Khalifa, to rule jointly with his brother Dhiyab. But in July 1856 Said and his elder brother Hamdan returned with a vengeance, captured the Maqta watchtower, plundered parts of the town and caused the people to flee to the safety of the fort commanded by Dhiyab. Sheikh Zayed, who was away in the desert at the time, gathered his forces and engaged his cousins, who were killed in the battle. The British administration, taking the view that the hand of Sultan bin Saqr was apparent in the affair, fined the Qasimi sheikh 25,000 Maria Theresa dollars, which was paid in full by the end of May 1860.[14]

One of the first issues that came before Sheikh Zayed was the case of Abdul Karim, a Bahraini whose *shu'ai* had been attacked at Khor al-Udaid by two *baghalas* from Abu Dhabi; Karim himself was wounded and one of his men killed. The incident occurred during Sheikh Said's reign and he, having been unable to identify the offenders, later used the incident in an attempt to enlist British help. Zayed declined to settle the case on the grounds that it had occurred during his predecessor's reign, but eventually he paid full compensation for the robbery and blood money of $600 on account of the murdered man.

Khor al-Udaid remained a trouble spot for the new ruler. In 1869 there was another migration: the Qubaisat again left Abu Dhabi and settled there. At first, they sought British protection but, when this was not forthcoming, they turned to the Ottoman Turks, who were looking to expand their influence down the Gulf coast. As a result of the Qubaisat's wish to ingratiate themselves with the Turks, the Ottoman flag was occasionally seen flying over Abu Dhabi territory. In 1877 HMS *Teazer* was sent to subdue Murrah raiders operating out of Khor al-Udaid. The inhabitants were forewarned and fled before the British ship appeared, with many seeking the protection of the sheikh of Qatar. Meanwhile, Sheikh Zayed bided his time and, when the time was right, offered an amnesty to the Qubaisat, many of whom returned to Abu Dhabi for good.

There is an interesting aside to this episode. As part of his policy of appeasement, Zayed arranged for the leader of the Qubaisat, Buti bin Khadim, to marry his uncle's daughter. Among their children was Salama bint Buti, who in turn would marry Sultan bin Zayed and give birth to another Zayed, the twentieth-century 'Father of the Nation'. As we shall see, Sheikha Salama had an important role to play in the ongoing saga of the Al Bu Falah in the twentieth century.

Meanwhile, the dispute over Khor al-Udaid rumbled on. When the Turks protested about HMS *Teazer*'s intervention, the Foreign Office ignored their complaint. The area was in disarray as it was raided by various tribes. The year 1883 saw Zayed campaigning against the tribes with the support of the Sheikh of Dubai:

> The Chief of Abu Dhabi had several affrays during the year with marauders of the tribes, Al Murrah, Manasir and Beni Hajir. In August he asked the assistance of the Chief of Dubai, who allowed his bedouin dependants to join the Bani Yas. In October the combined forces defeated the Al Murrah, killing about 30 and capturing some cattle. In October the Al Murrah and Manasir made reprisals and in November Sheikh Zayed despatched a force of 750 men of various tribes as far as the vicinity of Al Udaid, where they came upon the Al Murrah and killed 17 of that tribe, and captured over 1,000 camels. Other encounters occurred, but in December the Bani Yas Chief came to terms of peace with the Al Murrah and other hostile tribes.[15]

The news from Abu Dhabi that year included a report of heavy gales on the coast in February and March during which several boats were wrecked, a bad outbreak of malaria from which there were many deaths, and a new pearl bank discovered off Halul Island.

Both Qatar and Abu Dhabi claimed ownership of Halul Island as part of an ongoing territorial dispute between the two sheikhdoms. Sheikh Qasim of Qatar desired to build a fort at Khor al-Udaid, but was warned off by the British, who held a frigate in reserve should he go ahead with his plan; the Turks mooted the prospect of building a military post at Udaid, but were again discouraged from doing so. In 1888 skirmishes between Abu Dhabi and Qatar resulted in the death of Sheikh Qasim's son. In 1906, in an attempt to settle the matter once and for all, the British confirmed in writing to Sheikh Zayed that Udaid belonged to Abu Dhabi.

Wahhabi rule in Buraimi ended in 1869 when Azzan bin Qais of Oman defeated them in battle and retook the oasis. In February 1870 Azzan entrusted Sheikh Zayed to keep the peace on his behalf before withdrawing to Oman. As a result of these struggles the Bani Yas had drawn closer to the Al Bu Said dynasty of Oman, both being on the Hinawi side of the tribal divide. The Qawasim were Ghafiri supporters

A guard looks through an opening in the gate of the ruler's palace,
Qasr al-Hosn, Abu Dhabi, 1961.

and staunch allies of the Wahhabis. Between the opposing factions were
other tribes such as the Naim and Beni Kaab, which played both sides
to their advantage. As the Bani Yas had strengthened their position in
the Al Ain/Buraimi area, the Naim lost ground. In 1891 Sheikh Zayed in
alliance with the Sheikh of Dubai captured Al Ain and in 1897 took over
the settlement of Jahili, bringing the number of the oasis villages under
his control to six.

Sheikh Zayed was a calming influence among the tribes. When the
Awamir tribe threatened to take up arms against the Naim, the latter
wrote to Zayed's *wali* in the oasis asking for his decision in the dispute
rather than risk Zayed's armed intervention in the event of war. His
influence spread as far as inner Oman, where the sheikhs appealed for
his help to prevent the Manasir from attacking them. The Political
Resident Percy Cox, travelling through the area in 1902, found that
Zayed's influence in the Dhahira Plain (south of Jebel Hafit) was in fact
stronger than the sultan's, despite the fact that the latter was its nominal
ruler. The sheikh was, according to Reverend Zwemer

> A well-preserved old man; although his years are over three
> score, he has twelve sons and the full number of wives that
> Moslem law allows. We found him genial, hospitable . . . and
> very intelligent.[16]

Not all Zayed's forays were successful. For a decade, he tried to establish a foothold in Zora, a strip of land situated between Ajman and Hamriyah, but the intervention of Cox put paid to that idea. Another long-running dispute, with the ruler of Umm al-Qaiwain, was eventually resolved peacefully, but only after Zayed had clapped his rival in chains. Again, Cox intervened, securing his release.

While Zayed extended his influence in the Al Ain/Buraimi area in alliance with the sultan of Oman, Wahhabi interest in the area revived under the emir of the Nejd, Abdul Aziz bin Rahman (Ibn Saud). Intending to travel to the Trucial Coast in the summer of 1905, Ibn Saud found the weather too hot and postponed his visit to the spring of 1906, writing to the rulers accordingly. Although masked in platitudes, the gesture was a dangerous one, threatening to excite the Ghafiri tribes. In September 1905 Sheikh Zayed met the rulers of Dubai, Ajman, Sharjah and Umm al-Qaiwain in a vain attempt to prevent the latter from enlisting the Bani Kitab in his dispute with Abu Dhabi. In the event, a stiff warning from Percy Cox put the dampers on the northern sheikhs' enthusiasm to receive Ibn Saud, whose visit never materialized, and the respective spheres of influence of Abu Dhabi and Umm al-Qaiwain were settled in 1906.

As the nineteenth century unfolds, we see an increasingly prosperous Abu Dhabi, certainly when compared with its neighbouring sheikhdoms, and much larger in terms of territory, too. The days of Dubai's commercial prosperity were yet to come, and Sharjah and Ras al-Khaimah did not have the resources to compare with the Bani Yas. With their move to Abu Dhabi, the Bani Yas had diversified their economic base and strengthened the reach of their marine activities, especially pearling. The traditional base of the Liwa Oasis, where palm plantations produced dates and firewood, was still prosperous, and Sheikh Zayed had six villages of the Al Ain/Buraimi Oasis under his sway. The Al Bu Falah sheikhs grew rich on the proceeds of pearling, agricultural dues and payments from the sultan of Muscat for looking after northern Oman.

Sheikh Zayed died in 1909, leaving a flourishing legacy; it is not difficult to see why he is remembered as Zayed 'the Great'. His rival, Sheikh Sultan bin Saqr al-Qasimi, had died in 1866 of 'paralysis of the loins', having married a fifteen-year-old girl the year before, a demise that was somewhat overdue since he was reputed to have been 115 years old.[17] Two years later, as the armies of Abu Dhabi and Sharjah squared up to each other, Zayed stepped in front of his men and challenged the new ruler of Sharjah, Khalid bin Sultan, to single combat. His challenge accepted, Zayed won and killed his opponent. After that, Sharjah separated from Ras al-Khaimah and the Qawasim were never able to replicate the power of Sheikh Sultan and challenge the Bani Yas as they had done in the past, and Zayed was generally recognized as the most powerful ruler in the area.

He was certainly a charismatic and popular leader, but he was also an astute ruler who furthered his tribe's expansion through the clever use of arms and alliances. He made a series of tactical marriages during his reign for himself and other members of his family in order to keep fractious elements within the family fold. Finally, he was generous, relying on his revenues and making few financial demands of his people; in any event, such demands were amply compensated by his largesse.

And yet, while Abu Dhabi had a significant fleet, it was mainly a desert sheikhdom, in contrast to Ras al-Khaimah, Sharjah and Dubai, which were maritime ones. The Bani Yas had consolidated their position in Abu Dhabi and fallen into conflict with the Qasimi tribes, but it was the latter's struggles with Great Britain that would determine all their destinies. It is now time to consider that other part of the Emirati equation, the so-called 'piracy' of the Arabian Gulf.

3

A Maritime Kind: The Qawasim, the British and the Trucial Coast, 1718–1906

THE SETTLEMENT OF Ras al-Khaimah – literally the 'head of the tent' – was said to take its name from the golden tent top of the Persian commander who landed there in the eighteenth century on his way to fight the Yaruba dynasty of Oman; or from the Qasimi sheikh's custom of setting up his tents on a spit of land overlooking the sea, where they could be seen by passing ships; or from the simple fact that a dune at the end of Ras al-Khaimah spit resembled a tent. Whatever the explanation, the port had a proud and ancient history, being the successor to the ancient port of Julfar. It was a centre of the pearl trade, with vessels setting out for the pearling banks during the season and returning with their haul, which was then exported. A variety of goods were imported, such as horses from Basrah, carpets from Persia, dates from Oman, cotton from India and slaves from Zanzibar.

Although the British used the name Qawasim to denote a group of tribes in the northeastern sheikhdoms, it derived from the leading dynasty of the area, the Al Qasimi. Their origins are vague but the old writers were of a mind that they were members of the Huwala tribe of Siraf in Persia, which settled in Ras al-Khaimah. The Dutch first recorded a Qasimi sheikh, Rahma bin Matar, as the emir of Julfar around 1718. At the end of the eighteenth century, after a roller-coaster ride of alliances and conflicts, the Qawasim found themselves in a commanding position. The Qasimi tribes were a naval force to be reckoned with and, having established a presence on the Persian coast at Qishim and Lingah, and on the Arabian coast in and around Ras al-Khaimah, they had much of the lower Gulf in their sights. They were, above all, a maritime kind.

The Strait of Hormuz, separating the Arabian Gulf at its narrowest point, was vital to regional trade, much as it is today. While the Qawasim might have sought to control it, there were other interested parties.

The Al Bu Said dynasty of Oman had ambitions in the Gulf, Great Britain's EIC plied its trade and postal communications through the Gulf, and the Wahhabis of the Nejd, driven by a religious zeal to convert the tribes of Arabia to their brand of radical Islam, were poised to break out of their desert fastness. The decline of Persian influence, and the vulnerability of Bahrain, were also factors in the struggle for the Gulf.

Oman presented the most obvious threat to the Qawasim. In the mid-eighteenth century the Al Bu Saids had emerged as the power in the land, expanding their maritime interests through the port city of Muscat. Under the leadership of Seyyid Sultan bin Ahmed, the ruler of Muscat between 1792 and 1804, the Omanis sought to dominate the Arabian Gulf. They challenged the Utub tribes of Bahrain and carried their naval campaign as far as Basrah at the head of the Gulf. Their ambition towards Al Sir, the strip of coastline adjoining Ras al-Khaimah, brought an intermittent naval campaign against the Qawasim, in which they harassed their ships and blockaded their ports. But when Seyyid Sultan entered treaty relations with the British in 1800, a local contest became a matter of regional concern; the British were now allied to Oman and ranged against the Qawasim.

Until this point, clashes between Qasimi and British vessels had been few and far between, and the EIC, facing a series of expensive military commitments in India, remained reluctant to undertake a major naval campaign in the Gulf. In December 1778, after a three-day battle, six Qasimi ships captured an EIC brig and held it for a ransom of 4,000 rupees. When challenged by the British Resident in Bushire, Sheikh Rashid of the Qawasim claimed that the brig had been flying Omani colours, and its seizure was justified as an act of war (the Qawasim were then at war with Oman). In 1779 raiders engaged separately with the EIC ships *Success* and *Assistance* and were beaten off, but neither incident can be definitely attributed to the Qawasim. In 1790 Qasimi raiders seized the *Beglerbeg* off the Musandam Peninsula. In 1797 a Qasimi fleet captured the *Bassin* and released it after 24 hours. When confronted with the latter incident, the ruler of Ras al-Khaimah, Sheikh Saqr bin Rashid al-Qasimi, explained that it was a simple misunderstanding and the Qawasim remained 'honourable friends' of the British.[1]

In the same year, the British ship *Viper* was attacked while at anchor in the Bushire Roads. It was a bizarre incident, bearing in mind that Britain and Oman were on friendly terms at the time. The captain of a

Qasimi squadron anchored in the harbour obtained a small supply of shot from the captain of the *Viper* on the pretext of using it to attack Omani ships due to pass by. However, the Qawasim then attacked and attempted to board the *Viper*, but were repelled. Although the Qasimi captain was Salih bin Muhammed, a nephew of Sheikh Saqr, the latter disowned his actions, claiming that Salih had left Ras al-Khaimah some time before in order to reside on the Persian shore. It was hardly a convincing argument, since Saqr and Salih were clearly at one in their opposition to Oman. Indeed, Saqr may have recognized the true facts of the case when he summoned Salih, possibly to rebuke him.

On Sheikh Saqr's death in 1803 his son, Sultan, became ruler of Ras al-Khaimah and of the Qasimi tribes. We have already seen how Sheikh Sultan battled the Bani Yas for control of the Al Ain/Buraimi Oasis, and his influence in the area would extend over succeeding decades. The fact that he managed to retain power over the Qasimi tribes in one form or another for nearly 60 years says much for his abilities. He was an ally of the Wahhabis but not driven exclusively by their demands, and a friend of the British when it suited him. 'He is "wily and politic"', wrote Lieutenant James Wellsted, who visited Ras al-Khaimah in 1835.[2] Although Wellsted never met him, his observation best summarizes the British view of the redoubtable sheikh at that time.

Sheikh Sultan's early years were not so assured. Three years before his accession, the Wahhabi general Salim al-Hariq had reached Buraimi and, using the oasis as his base, launched a campaign against Oman. It is not entirely clear exactly when the Wahhabis arrived in Ras al-Khaimah, but the Qasimi tribes seem to have been more receptive to their radical message than others, with the result that they accepted their emissaries and a requirement to pay them tribute, namely *zakat* and one-fifth of their booty. However, Sheikh Sultan was pragmatic in his dealings with the Wahhabis, remitting *zakat* as required but ignoring the one-fifth rule – a fact that did not go down well in the Wahhabi capital of Diriyah.

In the British mind, the arrival of the Wahhabis marked a new intensity in maritime affairs: in 1804, after a hiatus of seven years, attacks on shipping resumed. The crew of the East India cruiser *Fly* were particularly unfortunate. First, they were attacked and taken prisoner by a French privateer, then, while returning home, their *baghala* was set upon by two Qasimi dhows and they were taken prisoner again, eventually being allowed to buy their freedom. The British believed the

Qawasim were to blame but, seeing a Wahhabi hand in these events, they held back. With the Napoleonic Wars raging in Europe, they were anxious to safeguard the Euphrates Valley mail route to India from Wahhabi disruption, and even considered the Wahhabis as prospective allies against their rivals in the Middle East, the Ottoman Turks.

In November 1804 Sayyid Sultan, the ruler of Muscat, was killed at sea. This set the Gulf alight as the Qawasim sought to exploit the Al Bu Said's weakened situation. Having joined forces with the Bani Muin tribe of Qishm Island and their own kinsmen at Lingah, Qasimi forces occupied Bandar Abbas, besieged Minab and captured Kharg Island. As a result, the Qawasim, who had once been confined to their ports by the Omani navy, now found themselves free to roam the lower Gulf, controlling considerable stretches of the Persian coast, as well as their own territory on the Arabian side.

In December two British brigs, *Shannon* and *Trimmer*, were attacked. After little resistance from the *Shannon*, both ships were captured and a number of their crew members killed. Since Captain Babcock of the *Shannon* had been seen firing a musket during the skirmish, the Qawasim severed his left hand, but he survived to tell the tale. The crew were taken prisoner and brought ashore, with most of them eventually escaping. The Qawasim retained the vessels for their own use, fitting them out

An ancient tower on the shore in Ras al-Khaimah.

with additional armaments and Arab crews in order to support their activities in the Gulf.

These events could not be ignored. Both ships belonged to Samuel Manesty, an English merchant of Baghdad and EIC representative in the Gulf. Manesty is an example of how, in the early days, the British spread their influence in the Gulf through trade. Based in Basra, he acted as the company's agent while building up his own interests through private trading – at one time he owned six vessels that were used for trading in the Gulf. Much of his business involved transporting company mail and exporting horses, and trading in luxury items, such as tobacco, wheat and barley. Although Manesty was well connected, he was also a difficult man, and fell out with many of the people he had dealings with, including those of the company and the Ottoman authorities. Remarkably, he had remained on good terms with Sheikh Sultan bin Saqr of Ras al-Khaimah and Sharjah until the *Shannon* and *Trimmer* incidents, which he blamed on the Qawasim. In 1805, at his prompting, Qasimi vessels were banned from entering Indian ports under British control.

Whether Manesty's conclusion was correct is highly debatable; in any event, the Muscat Resident, Seton, decided to reach an agreement with Sheikh Sultan rather than take up arms against him. A treaty, signed by the sheikh's representative at Bandar Abbas on 6 February 1806, was drawn up without prior consultation with the Wahhabis. The Qawasim agreed to respect the flag and property of the EIC and its subjects, failing which they might be fined 30,000 Maria Theresa dollarrs. If the *jihad* compelled the Qawasim to break the maritime peace, they were to give three months' notice. Seton dropped the claim to the cargo of the *Trimmer* and the ban on Qasimi ships visiting certain Indian ports was lifted.

Although the Wahhabis rejected the treaty, the Arabian Gulf remained peaceful. This was largely due to the presence of a British fleet – HMS *Fox* and eight company ships – that was detailed to keep a watching brief while events in Persia played out: a renewed French interest in the country and a war with Russia were potential threats to British interests. The fleet stayed in the Gulf for the next two years, and its departure brought a fresh wave of maritime disturbances.

In April 1808 an attack on a company ship, *Lively*, was beaten off. Qasimi activities intensified, bringing some twenty ships into the Arabian Sea in the coming months; soon there were wild reports of a 50-strong Qasimi fleet setting sail for the Indian coast. On 2 May 1808 two dhows attacked a company ship, *Fury*, and were driven off. In the autumn, the company ship *Neptune* was attacked but managed to escape. An incident involving another ship, *Sylph*, illustrated the problem of British standing orders, which required ships only to fire in self-defence. The *Sylph*'s captain allowed a large ship and two boats to draw close before opening fire, resulting in the loss of life on both sides, which might have been avoided if the captain had been permitted to fire from a distance. The Qawasim boarded and killed a number of the crew before another ship, the *Nereide*, came to the *Sylph*'s rescue with its 36 cannons and sank one of the attacking dhows.

Sheikh Sultan's response may have been a sign of his weakening influence over the Qasimi tribes, rather than mere bluff: he admitted that the attackers of the *Sylph* were Qawasim, but were not under his control. Indeed, more evidence emerged that Sheikh Sultan's power base was being eroded. Soon afterwards, the Wahhabis recognized Sheikh Hasan bin Ali of Rams as the nominal chief of many northern tribes, covering places such as Shinas, Khor Fakkan, Dibba and Fujairah, thus curtailing Sheikh Sultan's authority over the area. The new arrangements included a resident Wahhabi *qadi* and an Al Saud official designated to collect *zakat* and their share of plunder. And it was probably this – a desire to maximize tax and the collection of plunder – that led the Wahhabis to tighten their grip on the area.

In March 1809, Sheikh Sultan appears to have set out with *qadis* to argue his case with the Wahhabi emir at Diriyah. Whether he went voluntarily or was carried off is not entirely clear, and details of his movements after appearing in the Saudi capital are sketchy. In his absence, his cousin Hasan bin Rahma took over the chieftainship of Ras al-Khaimah.

An English traveller, James Buckingham, met Hasan bin Rahma and described him as a 'small man, apparently some 40 years of age, with an expression of cunning in his looks, and something particularly sarcastic in his eyes'. In the absence of any other description of this Qasimi sheikh, we are left with a suspicious Englishman eyeing an equally suspicious Arab, where words such as 'cunning' and 'sarcastic' reflected the extent of the mistrust between them. Possibly, if he had recorded his impressions of their meeting, Hasan would have described Buckingham in similar terms. There was no doubt that Hasan was a committed Wahhabi, since he considered himself the 'emir of the true believers'.[3]

Hasan's brother Ibrahim was reputed to be the 'commodore' of the Qasimi fleet and also loyal to the Wahhabi cause. Under their direction, the naval campaign against foreign vessels endured. Sheikh Sultan was now in Diriyah arguing his case with the Saudi emir, but explanations and exculpations were of little interest to the British authorities. Despite their desire not to aggravate the Wahhabis, they were discussing plans for an expedition against the Qawasim, planning to attack Qasimi ports and destroy their fleets.

While this went on, the attacks continued. On 23 May Qasimi boats fell upon the *Minerva*, another of Manesty's ships. After a running fight lasting two days, the vessel was captured and taken back to Ras al-Khaimah. The exact details of what happened are not entirely clear: initial British versions suggested a large number of mortalities, while a later report said that no lives had been lost, except those captives who tried to defend themselves. Some of the crew were probably circumcised before all the survivors were released. Mrs Robert Taylor, the wife of a British official at the Bushire Residency, was detained and eventually ransomed for 1,000 thalers. In the British mind, it was a situation that cried out for retribution.

In fact, the Supreme Government of Calcutta had already approved a military expedition to Ras al-Khaimah, with Captain John Wainwright as its leader. Qasimi towns and coastal bolt holes were to be targeted, and any direct contact with Wahhabi forces was to be avoided:

> We consider it of some importance to manifest as much as possible both by declaration and by action, that the expedition is directed, not generally against the tribe of Wahhabis but exclusively against the piratical branch of that tribe which has so long infested the commerce of India and the Gulf.[4]

On 14 September, a fleet of sixteen ships and more than 1,300 troops set sail from Bombay, arriving off Muscat some five weeks later, having been delayed by adverse winds. Here they spent ten days taking on water before proceeding to Ras al-Khaimah. On 11 November, the town hove into view but the sea was too shallow to bring the larger ships within firing range. A number of Qasimi men were aboard Manesty's captured vessel *Minerva*, which British ships intercepted, recaptured and burnt. The following day, the town was bombarded by the small cruisers and gunboats. In the evening, the tribal leaders held a *majlis* to discuss their predicament and decided not to surrender. Women and children were evacuated during the night, leaving the men to stay behind for the battle.

British troops landing at Ras al-Khaimah, 1809, from Richard Temple's
Sixteen Views of Places in the Persian Gulph (1813).

Early in the morning of the 13 November, troops boarded boats
and headed for the shore. The Qawasim, who were in the mosque at
prayer, rushed out to engage the gunboats that were bombarding the
town. But this attack was a distraction while the main force landed
to the south. Realizing their mistake, the Qawasim turned on the dis-
embarking troops but many were cut down by grapeshot from the
British boats. By 10 am the battle was over as British troops roamed the
streets, setting light to houses and vessels. By 4 pm the town and about
50 dhows had been destroyed. The force retreated to their ships without
attempting to impose peace terms on the defeated tribes.

Instead, the squadron turned its attention to the Qawasim and
their allies on the other side of the Gulf. They found Lingah abandoned,
destroyed twenty ships there and sailed for Qishim. Wainwright discussed
the surrender of the town of Luft with the sheikh of the Bani Muin,
Mullah Hussein, but when these talks failed, he ordered the troops
ashore. The Bani Muin retreated to a large fort on the top of a steep cliff
to witness the destruction of their fleet: eleven ships were burnt in the
harbour while both town and fort were bombarded. Mullah Hussein
agreed to surrender the following day, after about 80 tribesmen had
been killed and wounded in the battle.

The squadron spent the next few weeks searching the Arabian
Gulf for Qasimi ships and destroying any they found – the final tally ex-
ceeded 100. The British had already banned the export of Indian teak to
Qasimi ports in order to stop them rebuilding their fleet. Although no

financial demands for compensation had been made and no company property recovered, the operation was regarded among military circles as a success: many of the Qasimi ships had been destroyed and their bases severely damaged.

For the Qawasim, the outlook was bleak. Their livelihoods had been destroyed – not just their 'pirate' ships but those that were used for fishing and pearling – their homes razed, their prospects of renewal dashed. However, they were a determined and resourceful people; by 1812 they were rebuilding their ships with wood imported from Africa. In 1814 the new Wahhabi emir Abdulla ibn Saud renewed his support, and Qasimi ships began appearing again off the coasts of India and the Arabian Gulf.

Sheikh Sultan bin Saqr was back on the scene as ruler of Sharjah, then reckoned to have a population of around 500. The ruler of Muscat, Seyyid Said, saw the sheikh's return as an opportunity to join forces, restore him as paramount ruler of all the Qawasim and thus put an end to the attacks on Omani shipping. Certainly, Sheikh Sultan must have nurtured the hope of regaining his power over the Qasimi tribes. However, although plans were drawn up for a fresh naval assault on Ras al-Khaimah and a limited degree of British support was obtained in the form of a cruiser, the expedition came to nothing. In all, Seyyid Sultan conducted three expeditions against Ras al-Khaimah between 1812 and 1814, but failed to disable what was left of the Qasimi fleet.

As new attacks were reported, the British remained convinced that the Qawasim were to blame. They duly laid their allegations at Hasan bin Rahma's door. Both Hasan and the new Saudi emir, Abdullah, presented a united front in reply. Abdullah denied that the Qawasim had taken any ships bearing British passes, and Hasan instructed his representative to make a full investigation into their claims. But while the Qawasim admitted sending their ships to Sind[5] – not then under British control – there was another incident that involved a British-flagged ship; and this time the British were not in such a forgiving mood.

The ship in question, the *Ahmad Shah*, was a native vessel under British colours that ran aground near Qais Island and was then plundered by the sheikh of Charak, with part of the booty comprising a number of horses being taken to Ras al-Khaimah by what was believed to be a Qasimi vessel. The *Ahmad Shah* was then set alight. The incident posed a dilemma for Bruce, the British Resident in Bushire, since the sheikh of Charak was a Persian subject and the British government was in treaty relations with Persia. Hasan bin Rahma denied any involvement in the affair, but admitted that his ships had been raiding Sind and agreed to pay compensation for any acts against British-flagged ships that could be *proved* against his people.

On 6 October 1814 Hasan bin Rahma's agent, Hassan bin Muhammed bin Ghayth, signed an agreement with Bruce which included an undertaking that Qasimi ships would not attack vessels flying the British flag; that the ports of India and those of Ras al-Khaimah would be open to Qasimi and British vessels respectively; that Qasimi ships would fly a distinctive flag; that any property shown to have been taken by the Qawasim from the *Ahmad Shah* would be forwarded to the EIC representative in Muscat; and that Hasan would send a representative to Bombay to discuss a more permanent agreement. Bin Ghayth professed the hope that Qasimi ships would still be allowed to attack their enemies, otherwise their standing in the Arab world would diminish.

The provisional treaty was ratified in Bombay but then put on hold by the new governor. It had little effect apart from recognizing that the Qawasim were a power to be reckoned with. More reports arrived of Qasimi 'piracy', including an attack on a Muscat ship, which the Qawasim justified as an act of war. Bruce sent his *baghala* with friendly messages to Ras al-Khaimah, calling in on Sheikh Sultan bin Saqr at Tunb Island on the way. The ruler received the envoy and then confiscated part of the vessel's cargo of dates, claiming that the small amount of dates taken was a measure of the high esteem in which he held Bruce. Upon reaching Ras al-Khaimah, the *baghala* was attacked by twenty armed raiders, causing most of its crew to flee in terror. Hasan bin Rahma would later claim that this was the work of the Naim from Ajman, a separate tribe but nominally part of the Qasimi grouping.

At times, the British authorities struggled to make sense of it all. A lack of reliable intelligence, informants and spies on the Trucial Coast meant that assumptions were made that were not always supported by facts. The appearance of Qasimi vessels that would track a ship for days before attacking, the dread sight of their red flags fluttering in the breeze and their men armed to the teeth as they came aboard: these were tales that would make the most hardened traveller's hair stand on end. But there were shades of activity that lay between warfare and piracy just as there were different tribes and sub-tribes engaged in it. Even those cases that appeared clear-cut were never quite so. In 1815 men of the Sudan (Suweidi) tribe, a coastal section of the Bani Yas, seized a British-flagged *baghala* and took it back to Sheikh Sultan's port of Sharjah, but the sheikh seized their prize. The tribesmen, thus offended, migrated en masse to Ras al-Khaimah. Muddying the waters some more, Sheikh Sultan refused to offer restitution to the vessel's owners, claiming that the vessel had simply melted away.

In 1816 reports reached Bombay that Qasimi ships had captured three British-flagged vessels bound from Surat to Mocha on the Red Sea, sparing only a few of the crew. When Bruce complained to Ras al-Khaimah about this apparent breach of the 1806 treaty, there was a flat denial of the capture of any vessels in the Red Sea at the time in question. Hasan bin Rahma reaffirmed that the property of the English, those of the 'sect of Jesus', would be respected but the Qawasim retained their right 'to destroy all idolatrous Indians, and to extirpate from the face of the earth all the worshippers of false gods'.[6] Otherwise, he declined to cooperate. The year ended with a British naval demonstration off Ras al-Khaimah that was meant to signal their government's displeasure. As it happened, it was a public relations disaster. The British could not bring their ships in close to the Qasimi dhows and their shots fell short, while the Qawasim returned fire and hit part of a cruiser's foremast, leaving locals shouting and jeering from the shore.

But here lay the cause of Bin Rahma's undoing for, as more incidents of Qasimi 'piracy' were reported, so the case for Britain's military intervention gathered pace. In September 1818 the governor of Bombay, Sir Evan Nepean, submitted a report to the governor-general of India, the Marquis of Hastings, recommending military action against the Qawasim and setting up a base in the Gulf. Hastings's view was that India did not have the 5,000 men required, therefore the expedition would have to be postponed for a year. The Qawasim would be weaker by then, having lost Wahhabi support when the Egyptians expelled the Al Saud from Diriyah and executed Emir Abdullah. A British attempt to enlist Egyptian support did not materialize but the sultan of Muscat promised to equip some 70 ships for carrying men and equipment, as well as attacking Ras al-Khaimah with an army of 4,000 tribesmen by land, and three ships and some 600 men by sea.

In October 1819 the British fleet was assembled. Under the command of General William Grant Keir, this was the largest expedition ever sent to the Arabian Gulf. It comprised three Royal Navy warships, nine EIC cruisers, twenty transport vessels and an armed force of approximately 3,000 men, about half of which were British artillerymen and the remainder Indian infantrymen. On 30 November, the lead ships, *Liverpool* and *Eden*, were off Ras al-Khaimah to assess a suitable landing point. That night, three Qasimi vessels tried to sneak past the British fleet and reach the harbour, but they were intercepted. The sultan of Muscat arrived on 2 December with two frigates and 600 men. At 5 am on 3 December, the assault began, with British soldiers landing unopposed 3 kilometres (2 miles) southwest of the town. Muscati crews assisted with the landings, although the Omani land army did not arrive until after the battle had ended.

The men marching along the shore would have had an idea of what lay ahead, having glimpsed the town's defences from the sea, but their full extent was revealed on a closer view. There was a castellated wall with towers that ran along the cliffs down to the creek, with a fortified gate at its centre and a massive fort behind, all defended by men armed with cannons and muskets. There were estimated to be some 7,000 inhabitants in the town, of which a number of elderly, women and children had again retreated to the date groves, leaving about 4,000 men to take up the defence under the leadership of Hasan bin Rahma and his brother Ibrahim. The Qasimi tribes might have been hopelessly weakened and divided, having lost support of the Wahhabis and allies such as Sultan Saqr bin Sultan of Sharjah and Rashid bin Humaid of Ajman, but the two brothers were determined to repel the invaders. In the morning, a body of men appeared from inland and made their way towards the town, being greeted by a *feu de joie* from the battlements; for these

The EIC ship *Aurora* engaged in battle, 1812,
from an oil painting by Thomas Buttersworth.

were reinforcements from other towns and villages in the area. The scene was completed by a man riding a camel and carrying a large red flag, galloping furiously towards the gates, which he reached despite a fusillade from the British forward troops.

For the next two days, the British shelled the walls and fort with a massive bombardment from their eighteen- and six-pounder guns, mortars and howitzers, arranged before the defences, and from the expedition ships which came in close to the shore; but they failed to make a serious impression on the sturdy fortifications. On the third day, however, the main tower was breached. All the while, the Qawasim resisted as best they could, and when they were running out of ammunition, they piled stones into their cannons and, during lulls in the fighting, scrambled to retrieve unexploded shells from the British guns. At night, as the British were unloading extra guns from the ships, Ibrahim led a party to capture a British battery, which included mortars, but he was killed when the position was retaken by the 65th Regiment. In the morning, the Qawasim launched another attack on the British positions, but this again failed.

On 8 December the British, having unloaded two of *Liverpool*'s heavy guns onto the beach, began to damage the fort while the Qawasim fought back with small-arms fire. During the day, the walls were breached and, throughout the night, Hasan and Keir parleyed, but without success. When the bombardment was renewed in the morning, the fort was infiltrated and a British force went in, seizing the main tower and raising the British flag over the deserted town, the people having fled by crossing the creek at low tide. It was a distressing scene: old men, women and children struggled to wade across the creek before the tide came in, while the last of the warriors followed behind, all making for the safety of the mountains. The British, having seized some 60 ships and many cannons, proceeded to destroy the fortifications, keeping one of the buildings as accommodation for the officers and troops. By 10 December, with the town a smouldering ruin, Hasan arrived at the British camp to sue for peace.

Naval operations ensued up and down the Gulf, the objective being to destroy all remaining Qasimi strongholds. The town of Dhayah, home of Sheikh Hussan bin Ali of Rams, fell after heavy bombardment, its small fort and the sheikh's house destroyed. Upon returning to Ras al-Khaimah, having received no further instructions for the peace, Keir decided to release Hasan bin Rahma. Slowly but surely, the remaining sheikhs signified their surrender: the ruler of Jazirat al-Hamra was first to arrive in Ras al-Khaimah on a guarantee of safe passage, followed by Sheikh Sultan bin Saqr of Sharjah. The rulers of Dubai, Ajman and Umm al-Qaiwain sought peace. Although the Bani Yas had not been involved in attacks on shipping, as a matter of prudence (and security) their tribal patriarch Sheikh Shakhbut put in an appearance. The sheikh of Bahrain, wishing to avoid maritime tolls, also asked to be included.

In January 1820, over a period of ten days, a number of sheikhs signed preliminary treaties requiring them to surrender their strongholds, guns and vessels apart from pearling and fishing boats – the corollary was that their towns were to be spared. In an interesting aside, Sheikh Sultan's claim to suzerainty over Umm al-Qaiwain and Ajman was rejected, thus preserving them as independent sheikhdoms. Leaving aside the sheikhs of Jazirah al-Hamra and Rams, who were subsequently deposed, there were six signatories from the lower Gulf. This configuration of six, fashioned by the exigencies of the time, was the basis of the sheikhdoms (with the addition of Fujairah in 1952) that would form the Trucial States and, ultimately, the United Arab Emirates.

Finally, the sheikhs were presented with, and agreed, a final treaty known as the 'General Treaty of Peace'. Acts of piracy were prohibited and the Arabs were required to fly a red flag with a white border, although several variants developed along the coast. For example, Abu Dhabi used a one-third vertical white stripe (later a canton) against the red while Fujairah, not being officially recognized by the British at that time, retained the traditional all-red flag. There were also provisions about Britain's role in the Gulf, discipline and peace on the seas, and a prohibition on slave trading. This last provision, added at the insistence of ardent abolitionist Captain Thomas Perronet Thompson, proved to be unenforceable; the trade continued well into the twentieth century. A plan to establish a naval base on Qishm Island was abandoned in favour of a base at Qais. Hasan bin Rahma was replaced in Ras al-Khaimah by Sheikh Sultan bin Saqr and consigned to two minor sheikhdoms. After a series of small operations designed to destroy any outstanding ships, peace returned to the Gulf once more. The last members of the expeditionary force departed in July 1820, leaving behind a small garrison to enforce the terms of the treaty.

Ras al-Khaimah and Rams had fallen, and Qasimi boats had been destroyed. Elphinstone, the new governor of Bombay, regarded Keir's treaty as too lenient towards the Qawasim, but was unable to change it for fear of being accused of treachery; so matters stayed as they were. We have seen how, in 1835, attacks on shipping by the Bani Yas and others led to a Maritime Truce banning maritime warfare during the pearling season, which was renewed annually.

In 1853 there was a permanent ban on maritime warfare in the Gulf in return for British protection. The Perpetual Treaty of Maritime Truce signed by the rulers of the territory that today forms the UAE gave the area a new name – the Trucial Coast or the Trucial States.[7] From now on, so Lorimer's *Gazetteer* noted, the word 'piracy' was replaced in official correspondence with the term 'maritime irregularities', a change attributed to the 'great and peaceful revolution' effected by British political officers – but rather overlooking the fact that the Qasimi challenge to British supremacy in the Gulf had been crushed in 1819.[8] The distinction between warfare on land and at sea had some bizarre outcomes, too: the British authorities would not have opposed Sheikh Said bin Tahnoun's attack on Abu Dhabi in July 1856 if it had taken place by land rather than by sea, for example.

By other agreements with the Trucial sheikhs, anti-slavery measures and an arbitration council for cases of runaway debtors, who were disrupting the pearling industry, were introduced. The appearance of French agents on the coast in 1891 with offers of assistance to the Trucial sheikhs triggered alarm bells that prompted the Political Resident to ask the sheikhs to make new agreements. The result was the so-called 'Exclusive Agreements' of 1892, by which the sheikhs agreed not to enter into relations with any power other than the British government, or allow representatives of foreign governments to reside in their territory without British approval, or dispose of any territory except to Great Britain. In return, the British accepted responsibility for the defence and foreign relations of the Trucial States.

For many years, Westerners knew the land of the Emirates as the 'Pirate Coast' – indeed the name lived on until the 1950s. It derived from the nineteenth-century EIC officials and ship owners who stigmatized the Qawasim as pirates. But modern Arab writers such as Sheikh Sultan III bin Muhammed al-Qasimi (the ruler of Sharjah since 1972) have rejected this view, pointing out that it was the British, not the Qawasim, who were the intruders. From a forensic view, some attacks cannot be nailed to the Qasimi mast while others can be explained as acts of war against third parties or legitimate activities. These include incidents where the Qawasim demanded tariffs from vessels

معاهدات فيما بين دولت البهية البرطانية و مشايخ المتصالحين في عمان -

للملاحظة

اذا بعد هذا حصل الاشتباه في معنى بعينه في جزء من نص الشرائط المعاهدات كان انكليسيا او عربياً فالنص الانكليسي مرثوق به للترضيح ذلك تطعياً

معاهدة العمومية مع الا قوام العرب فى خليج فارس فى سنه ١٨٢٠ ع

— بسم الله الرحمن الرحيم —

الحمد لله الذى جعل الصلح خيراً للانام وبعد قد صار الصلح لدوثيم بين دولة سركار الانكريز و بين الطوائف العربية المشروطين على هكذا الشروط —

الشرط الاول — ان يزال النصب والغارات فى البر والبحر من طرف العرب المشروطين فى كل الا زمان —

الشرط الثانى — ان نعرف احد من قوم العرب المشر وطين على المترددين فى البر والبحر من كافة الناس بالنصب و الغارات لاب حرب معروف فهو عدو لكافة الناس فليس له زمان على حالة ولا مالة و الحرب المعروف هو الذى مناداً به مبيّن مامور به من دولة الى دولة وقتل الناس و اخذ المال بغير منادية و تبيين و امر دولة فهو النصب و الغارات —

الشرط الثالث — ان العرب المصالحين لهم فى البر والبحر علمٌ احمر فيه حرف اوبلا حرف على مطلويهم وهو فى كفّه ابيض عرض الا بيض اللذي فى الكفة يعادل عوض لاعمركا هو مصوّر فى الحاشية وان هذا هو علّم العرب المصالحين فيستعملون به ولا يستعملون بغيره —

الشرط الرابع — ان الطوائف المصالحين كلهم على حالة الاول لا انهم صار الصلح بينهم و بين دولة سركار الانكريز و ان لا يحرب بعضهم بعضا و العلم هو والشاهد هو ذلك فقط و ليس هو شاهد على غيره —

A page from the Perpetual Treaty of Maritime Truce, 1853, with a depiction of the red flag with white border imposed by the British in 1820.

for using the shipping lanes and only seized them when the dues were not paid. Today, the debate is more about cultural perceptions and the battle between two seagoing powers over control of the Gulf trade routes, with the traditional assertions of piracy replaced by more nuanced points of view. Perhaps now we can see the era for what it truly was, a struggle for mastery of the sea that determined the future of the region for the next 150 years.

THESE MARITIME TREATIES laid the foundation for future relations between Great Britain and the Gulf states, and ensured Britain's predominance in the region well into the next century. They also gave the sheikhs legitimacy, recognizing them as the rulers of particular areas and tribes and, although the boundaries remained vague in parts and allegiances could still change, a degree of security. The British adopted a light-touch approach, hoping to stay out of the sheikhs' internal affairs and keep order at the least cost with the minimum degree of force. But there was a price to pay: the treaties ossified the region, preserving its territorial and ruling patterns for generations to come.

In the early days, Britain's administration of the Gulf was simply an extension of their system in India. The Indian Civil Service oversaw the arrangements through the Political Resident, who was the senior British diplomatic officer in the Gulf, based in Bushire until 1946 and then in Bahrain until 1971. The post was considered so important that Lord Curzon deemed the holder 'the uncrowned king of the Gulf'.[9] The Resident was entitled to receive a seven-gun salute in his honour, the ruler of Abu Dhabi five guns and the remaining sheikhdoms three. In time, to reflect his town's growing importance, the ruler of Dubai would also receive a five-gun salute.

The Resident relied on a system of Residency (or Native) Agents, usually Arab, Indian or Persian, to represent his interests. They tended to be merchants or traders in their own right, often lining their pockets but always acting as a conduit between rulers and the Resident, delivering advice to one and intelligence to the other. It was said that the pay was so poor that only those with other sources of income could afford to take the job. An agency was established at Sharjah in 1823, but the ruler did not warm to the first two agents and it was not until the 1850s that the Native Agent became an accepted channel of communication.

In the rulers' eyes, Great Britain was *al-daulah* (the power) and the Political Resident was *hakkam* (the ultimate arbitrator) and *mujjawir* (protector). There was the semblance of an informal tribal structure that the sheikhs could easily recognize, relate to and accept as a basis of government. The agreements of 1892, which settled these arrangements, gave Britain control over the sheikhs' foreign policy while leaving them to deal with internal affairs – political officers and agents might proffer advice across the full range of issues that came before a ruler but decisions over his own people were his alone.

Overseeing the naval arrangements was the Senior Naval Officer Persian Gulf (SNOPG), who reported to the Resident and was responsible for the operational activities of a naval squadron with a brief to 'watch and cruise'. Patrolling naval ships became a regular feature of the maritime scene as they criss-crossed the Gulf to intercept ships and check their credentials, and to search for guns and slaves. They visited ports up and down the Gulf, bringing the Resident to meet and discuss matters of mutual interest with local sheikhs. Occasionally, more intractable issues of diplomacy might require a gunboat to be sent as a show of force to persuade a sheikh to the British point of view; in the event of the sheikh turning a blind eye, fines imposed and warnings issued, a gunboat would appear over the horizon and fire a few shells at one of the sheikh's watchtowers, dislodging a stone or two, until his agreement was reached. It was, from the British point of view, a cost-effective method of policing and negotiation, and it was used for many years to bring sheikhs into line. As late as 1921, the fort at Ajman was bombarded, and that of Fujairah in 1925, both resulting from disputes over slavery.

The main advantage for the British in these arrangements was that they tied the region into a defensive framework, all aimed at protecting imperial interests in India. For the remainder of the nineteenth century, British policy was determined by these interests. The Gulf was one of several buffer zones that the British constructed around their jewel in the imperial crown. Thus Russian ambitions to secure a warm water port were to be thwarted, German expansion towards the upper Gulf resisted and Ottoman designs on the lower Gulf watched.

The Qawasim had lost their struggle for supremacy in the Gulf but would, in time, rebuild and focus its fleets on pearling and the deep-sea trade with East Africa. And yet, as the days of the 'Pirate' Coast slipped into history, the theme of foreign encroachment in the Gulf reappeared under a different guise, a strange new contraption called the steamship.

The first example in the Gulf was the paddle wheel INS *Hugh Lindsay*, which 'caused no small sensation by her novel appearance and evolutions' in 1838.[10] The real impact of steamships was rather more invasive, however. As they became involved in trade, so steamships disturbed the equilibrium of local shipping. The mercantile families of the main trading centres of the Gulf could not match the resources of the steamship companies. They lacked the type of ocean-going vessels that might carry cargo and passengers in the manner of a modern ship, and the capital to invest in them. Apart from rare voyages – such as that of the *Sultanah*, an Omani vessel that visited New York in 1840 – there was no history of sailing to Western ports, and no financial resources and organization to underpin a profitable steamship service.

The Arabian Gulf had a long tradition of coastal trading, with a network reaching as far as the ports of India and East Africa. Sailors relied on their own knowledge rather than modern navigational aids. It was a proud tradition:

> Every man in the ship knew those waters: there was none among them who had not been sailing for at least ten years. Nejdi [the captain] knew every bank, every overflow, every low sanded point.[11]

The Arab captains knew the coastal routes and were saddened by the decline in Arab navigation, which they blamed on 'cut-throat' competition from Western shipping.

There is no doubt that steamships affected the traditional dhow-based trading system, the long-distance Arab trading routes as well as the intra-Gulf ones. They disrupted but did not destroy the dhow trade, creating a 'dualism' of systems. While steamers carried imports and exports to and from the main Gulf ports, dhows were used for connecting and trading with remoter parts, and for carrying materials such as tiles and timber. As well as local traffic, there remained a few profitable long-distance routes for the dhow traders: in the late 1930s Kuwaiti merchants were still investing income from their date plantations in the construction of dhows for the deep-sea trades to Africa and India.

Initially, the steamship routes between Bombay and Basrah followed the Persian coast, leaving eastern Arabia off the beaten track. The British India Steam Navigation Company Ltd (also known as the British India Line, or BI), set up in 1862, dominated the Gulf trade in the nineteenth century. A six-weekly mail service to the Gulf began in February 1863, running from Karachi to Gwadar, Muscat, Bandar Abbas, Bushire, Basra and 'any intermediate port required by government'.[12] According to a BI handbook of 1866, there were additional stops at Lingah and Bahrain. The Gulf service was one of eight that year.

The London–India telegraph cables, laid along the line of the Persian coast between 1865 and 1869, reinforced the strategic importance of the Gulf. The opening of the Suez Canal in 1869 also marked a new priority and, although the Euphrates Valley mail route fell into disuse, the Arabian peninsula formed an important part of British plans to protect the main sea route to India. Although the Gulf saw a massive increase in foreign shipping, it was not until the turn of the century that the Arabian ports of the lower Gulf saw any benefit. In 1903 the 'fast' weekly mail service calling at the Persian ports was supplemented by a 'slow' mail service which took thirteen to fifteen days and visited the smaller ports of the Gulf – Sharjah was added to the run.

The shah of Persia was determined to extend his authority over the southern ports of Bushire and Lingah – the Qawasim had lost control of the latter in 1902 – and his government imposed tariffs on exports and imports. As a result the Persian shore became more attractive to the extensive smuggling network of the Trucial Coast and Oman, and less so to Persian traders who were increasingly drawn to Dubai. In 1904 Sheikh Maktoum II bin Hasher of Dubai persuaded BI to switch its main port of call in the lower Gulf from Lingah to Dubai, thus enhancing the latter's status as a trading hub: goods from India were re-exported to Persia while goods to and from the Al Ain/Buraimi Oasis and the interior were directed through Dubai. It is said that, in the early days of the Dubai run, a boy was sent up a date palm to signal when the BI steamer came into sight; but he was not too troubled since, in 1905–6, only 34 steamers visited Dubai, unloading some 70,000 tons.

But it was a start; and although the amount of trade with the Arabian ports would remain relatively small for many years, Dubai also benefited from an influx of wealthy Persian merchants to the town, many of them settling in the Bastakiya district, bringing with them money, skills and the distinctive architecture of the wind tower. With the commercial nous of the Al Maktoum, these events marked the birth of Dubai's position as the main port of the area, strengthened by trading ties with India and Pakistan and enhanced by a lucrative trade in smuggled goods.

The BI Line steamship *Chindwara* at sea.

At a time when the area's economy was declining, Dubai remained a busy and thriving port; and when oil brought unimagined wealth, its future as an important player in the political and economic development of the region was assured. Indeed, Dubai's success has proved to be the most lasting legacy of the maritime struggles of the nineteenth century.

4

Jewels of the Sea: The Rise and Fall of the Pearling Industry, 1508–1949

AWAY FROM THE skyscrapers and bustle of the city, as waves lap quietly on the beach and the day is still and bright, there is nothing to show for the fleets that used to depart these shores each year for the great pearl banks of the lower Gulf, only stories from another age. In one legend, the pearl is the daughter of the rain, Bint al-Matar, created from a single drop of rain. In another, she is the daughter of the moon, Bint al-Qamar, fashioned from a dew drop in the silvery light of a full moon. In the ancient Sumerian fable of Gilgamesh, the hero plucks from the seabed the flower of immortality, which some writers have suggested is the pearl oyster. Perhaps the most evocative image arises in the fable of a thick mist that drifts down from the Caspian Sea, from which oysters extract large drops of liquid and shape them into a pearl.

If these legends are seen as little more than salesman's puff in the modern world, it is worth remembering that the pearling industry is threaded through the historical narrative, like a tapestry with a recurring theme. Pearl oysters were being harvested in the region around 5000 BC, as revealed by buttons made from mother-of-pearl found at Marawah, and there is evidence from Dalma Island that oysters were being used for food a few centuries earlier. Pearls have been found in Neolithic burials dating back to 4000 BC, for example at Buhais and in Umm al-Qaiwain. And there are signs of an early pearling industry in the discoveries from the first-century AD site at ed-Dur, which included a bell-shaped diver's weight and stack of pearl oyster shells.

Roman writers were well aware of pearl diving around Bahrain dating back to the fourth century BC and, according to Pliny the Elder, pearls from the Arabian Gulf were highly valued in the Roman Empire. Pearls were also used as ornaments in the Byzantine Empire, as evidenced by coins showing the emperor Justinian I (AD 482–565) wearing strings of pearls around his head. The lower Gulf appears in the historical texts at a time when Julfar was establishing itself as the second pearling centre of the Gulf to Bahrain, a status later confirmed by Portuguese writers. An early description of pearl divers is found in the *Travels of Lodovico di Barthema* from 1508, in which the Italian traveller Lodovico di Barthema describes a voyage of three days from Hormuz to a pearl bank which has 'the largest pearls . . . found in the world'.[1] Julfar was clearly an important pearling centre in the sixteenth century when a Portuguese traveller, Pedro Teixeira, described 200 *terradas* gathered around the Qatar pearling grounds for the summer season, of which 50 came from Julfar.

The appeal of pearls in medieval Europe is demonstrated by the many portraits of royal figures wearing pearls of various designs and elaborations. In 1580 the Venetian court jeweller Gasparo Balbi visited the region in order to find the sources of the pearls he was using to make jewellery, possibly with a view to creating a direct trading link between Venice and the pearling centres. He noted that the best pearls came from Bahrain and Julfar. By the mid-eighteenth century, pearling was the main industry of the Gulf and continued to be so until the twentieth century. As Sheikh Mohammed bin Thani of Qatar famously remarked to the English traveller William Palgrave in 1863: 'We are all from the highest to the lowest slaves of one master, pearl.'[2]

A dhow returning to harbour. At the height of the pearling industry, fleets of up to 1,200 vessels used to leave the ports of the Trucial Coast for the pearl beds in the Arabian Gulf.

There were other exports of course, such as dried fish and dates, and Ras al-Khaimah and Rams shared a thriving deep-sea trade, but it was pearls that increasingly provided the foundation of the region's growing prosperity, despite the seasonal nature of the industry. In 1866 the value of pearls exported from the Arabian Gulf was estimated at £400,000 (approximately £41.5 million today) and in 1905–6, the sum of £1,434,399 (£152 million) plus £30,439 for mother-of-pearl. Such were the profits of pearling in the early twentieth century that the shores of the lower Gulf towns were strewn with boats being built by men brought in from as far away as India and East Africa. New oyster beds were harvested, more foreign workers arrived to man the extra boats and the diving season was extended by a month.

The main pearling season, known as *ghaus al-kabir* ('the great dive'), ran from May to September. It was a time when the shallow sea was warm enough to allow for longer dives, essential if sufficient oyster shells were to be retrieved from the seabed. In the winter, when it was too cold to dive, pearling was confined to wading into creeks and shallows. In May, then, men would assemble in the main Gulf ports on the Arabian side of the Gulf, such as Abu Dhabi, Dubai and Ras al-Khaimah. These places were like magnets, attracting men from the interior to join the pearling dhows. They came not only from the Liwa Oasis, but from villages in the mountains and smaller towns along the coast, and farther afield, from the Batinah coast of Oman, too.

Their world revolved around the pearl. The extent to which the pearling industry engaged communities is illustrated by the statement in Lorimer's *Gazetteer* that noted how it employed 22,000 men on the Trucial Coast, more than 50 per cent of the male population, in the early 1900s. There was an annual migration to and from the sea, since a number of these pearl workers were tribesmen. But it was not a universal trend: one section of the Bani Yas, the Rumaithat tribe, were fishermen and pearlers who inhabited the coast and islands, often moving between one and the other, while others such as the Qubaisat owned 10,000 date palms and 185 houses in Liwa (according to Lorimer) and moved to the coast for the pearling season.

Pearling was a strictly male occupation, apart from certain coastal areas where women would also wade for pearls in the creeks and along the shore. Most pearling families of Dubai lived in the town, but in Abu Dhabi men travelled to the coast from places in the interior, such as the villages of the Liwa Oasis. They left their animals and date plantations in the care of their womenfolk, who herded the animals and harvested the dates, distributing fresh dates to families, friends and the needy, preserving or boiling the rest to create a syrup; and all while performing many other household duties and bringing up their own families. Many women travelled to the ports to see off their loved ones and to help with preparations for the voyage. They stocked the dhows with fresh water, an activity that included finding and digging out wells, scooping out the water and carrying it to the boats. Then, having watched the dhows depart for the pearling banks, they would return to their homes, in some cases an overland journey of many miles. The men on their boats would dream of the day when they would be reunited with their loved ones, reciting poems and singing songs in their honour.

The great fleets headed for the pearling banks that were strung along the curve of the southern Gulf, each with their own name: Umm al-Shaif, Abu Hasir, Abu al-Bukush and Ariela, for example. Some dhows ventured an even greater distance: Ceylon (Sri Lanka) was considered a lucrative source of pearls, and Socotra too during a poor Gulf season, the voyage taking up to 40 days. In 1926 it was reported from Sharjah that a number of Arab divers of the Trucial Coast, having earned little in the summer season, had arranged to dive on the pearl banks of Socotra Island and the Dahlak Archipelago off the coast of Eritrea – on 21 December, fourteen pearling boats left Dubai for the Red Sea.

A typical fleet ranged from the regular *jalbout* and *sambuq* to a variety of other boats. The average boat had eighteen to twenty men on board, although *sambuqs* would have up to 40 men on board, with more than one-third of the crew comprising divers. In the early 1900s, at the height of the pearling era, 1,200 boats were setting out from the ports of the Trucial Coast for stints of up to three and a half months on the pearling banks. The boats would leave the ports together, their crews rowing out of the harbour before setting sail, their pearling songs punctuated by the swish and pull of oars. The fleet was usually led by an 'admiral', who was an experienced captain or navigator, known as the *sirdal al-ghaus*.

On each vessel, there was a hierarchy of clearly defined roles: captain (*nakhudha*, plural *nawakhidah*), mate, cook, divers, a singer, rope pullers and apprentices. The *nakhudha* was the master of the enterprise; while some crews might have harsh, despotic captains who drove them hard and were quick to beat divers who refused to go down, others inspired loyalty without recourse to threats or violence. An average boat might have a crew of eighteen to twenty men, comprising ten divers, eight haulers and an apprentice. On the larger boats, there might be a *nahham* to coordinate the singing. On the smaller boats, the duties of cook were performed by the apprentice, who would also clean the boat and take care of the coffee pot and hookah pipe. Living conditions were so cramped that some men were forced to sleep on piles of discarded oyster shells on the deck.

Older Emiratis still remember the days when they worked the pearling dhows. The *nakhudha* navigated by whatever means were available to him – the sun, the stars or any visible features on the shore – and by 'reading' sand samples brought up from the seabed in order to determine whether a particular pearling bed had been reached. The dhow would remain on station while the work carried on, only moving closer to the shore in the event of a *shamal*, the northwest wind that could blow ceaselessly for three to four days, or to return to harbour for Ramadan. Some dhows would stay on one particular bank for the whole 120-day season, others would move from bank to bank. There were a few havens, such as Dalma Island, which served as supply bases and small markets during the pearling season. The diving took place from day-break to sunset, with the divers working in teams. One team would work for an hour or so and then rest in the water while the second team took over.

The *nakhudha* would position his boat above the edge of a pearl bank, drop anchor and let the boat drift across the bank, paying out the anchor rope as they went. The divers would dive for pearls and, if only a few pearls were retrieved, the boat would be allowed to drift some more. Every bank was different and even the same bank could differ from year to year: a good ýield might be followed by several barren ones, but it was reckoned that the best pearls came from the deepest waters. The boat, having drifted over bank, was then taken to a new position for the process to start all over again.

In the daylight, the sight of these dhows with their lateen rigging under a still blue sky on an emerald sea conveyed a deceptively tranquil scene: the diver waiting on the lowest side of the hull, wearing a tor-toiseshell nose clip to prevent water entering his nostrils, his body covered with moisturising oil, his ears plugged with wax, his hands protected from the rough edges of the oyster shells and rocks by leather finger caps; then the creak of timber interspersed with gulps of air and prayers to God before he dives overboard. The trick was to expel all the

The *nakhudha* of a dhow off the south Arabian coast in 1947.

air in his lungs before taking the plunge and – attached to a rope with a rough weight of some 6 kilograms (14 lb) to pull him down – make the jump with a basket in hand and dive to the bottom as quickly as possible, then to be pulled to the surface by the rope puller, the *saib*, on board the boat.

After *Fajr* prayers before sunrise, the diving began and continued for three hours, when the divers would return to the deck to eat a few dates and drink some coffee. Throughout the day, they made many dives, breaking only for *Dhuhr* and *Asr* prayers. The diver stayed in the water between dives, and the average depth of a dive was 10 metres (33 ft), but some went deeper, holding their breaths for up to a minute and a half and diving up to 40 times a day. The physical demands were intense, and it was said there were few divers in the Gulf who lived beyond the age of 50. Sawfish, rather than sharks, jellyfish or sea snakes, were considered the most dangerous form of marine life, and there were stories of men cut in half by these creatures. In the evening, they had their main meal and rested; some men said their *Maghrib* and *Isha* prayers together so they could they could go to sleep earlier.

The pearl was a hard master. Many divers experienced hallucinations through lack of oxygen, seeing weird shapes and figures such as headless camels and cutlass-wielding women on the seabed. And yet these were the least of a diver's worries: a diver might suffer blindness, deafness or brain damage later in life or, at worst, die at sea. It was said that in about 1885 some 250 pearl divers died in the course of their work. By custom, the diver's body would be retrieved from the sea, washed, wrapped in a sheet and tied with rope, with prayers being said, and then quickly dispatched to its watery tomb. If they were near land, the diver might be buried in a place set aside for that purpose; there are many small Muslim cemeteries that might have been used to bury divers and fishermen on uninhabited islands west of Abu Dhabi town.

Divers were a mixture of free men and slaves, Arabs, Baluchis and Africans. Those slave divers who could dive in deep or muddy waters commanded a high premium, but they could remain poor, owing debts to their *nakhudha* and paying a portion of their wages to their owner. And yet many slaves were treated as members of their owner's family, eating and working with family members, and could even become a *nakhudha* on one of the family vessels. But a sailor who joined a boat in the belief that he had escaped his troubles on the shore might be quickly disillusioned for, as we have seen from the events off the coast of Abu Dhabi in the early 1850s, roving debt collectors pursued debtors and seized dhows in satisfaction of debts even while they were at sea.

Local dealers recognized about 24 varieties of pearl but the large spherical pearl – white, rose-white or of a rose-yellow hue – was among the rarest of all; the black pearl (known to Arabs as the 'dead' pearl) was also seldom found and therefore highly valued. They differed in shape, from spherical or pear-shaped to button-shaped where the pearl had been pressed by the shell. Increasingly, mother-of-pearl, the smooth, shiny lining of the oyster shell used for ornamentation, was retrieved. The discovery of an especially valuable pearl would cause a sensation among the fleet. Even as the dhows were on the banks, the occasional merchant in his *sambuq* might be cruising between the boats haggling for any pearls he could get; but the chances were that the *nakhudha* would keep back the most valuable pearls for more serious bargaining ashore. At night, the crews would get together for a meal and to discuss the day's events, swapping stories and discussing the most valuable finds.

The *sirdal al-ghaus* would signal the end of the diving season by raising a flag for all the other boats to see. Homecoming was a joyous occasion as the fleets returned from the pearling beds, their crews rowing into harbour with the beat of a drum to accompany a pearling song and, in the darkness, the cooking fires on the dhows lighting up the horizon for the watching crowds, friends and family lined up on the shore waiting for their loved ones to step onto dry land. The crew would then lift up the boat, carry it onto the beach and clean it before dispersing. Those who lived in the oases would return there in order to tend their herds and plantations, often using part of their share of the profits to buy their own date plantations, or extend existing ones. Some would take up different employment until the next season arrived, finding work in the towns or even returning to sea, taking a place on the deep-sea dhows that traded between the Gulf and East Africa, or simply joining local fishing fleets. Towards the end of the pearling era, a number of divers became so specialized that during the winter they moved to places like Ceylon where the warmer waters allowed them to continue diving all year round. However, according to Lorimer, most pearlers spent their winters at home in 'idleness'.[3]

In his *Gazetteer* of 1908, Lorimer described a Trucial Coast that was highly dependent on the pearl trade. The people of Abu Dhabi lived almost entirely by pearl diving and fishing, the revenues of Dubai largely derived from the pearl fisheries and, in Sharjah and Ras al-Khaimah, 70 per cent of the sheikh's income came from taxes of the pearl industry. Behind the facade of dhows and divers was a network of investors, brokers and boat owners, all with a financial interest in the fortunes of the pearling trade. Tribesmen from Liwa sub-tribes formed cooperatives to purchase boats and share the net profits at the end of a season. The share was not an equal share between the crew but determined by the crew member's particular role, with the *nakhudha* receiving the largest share. Under the *amil* system, the boat was owned and fitted out by a businessman who took a large share of the profits and shared the remainder among the *nakhudha* and his crew.

Debt could be a problem, particularly for the crews of the *amila* boats, who had to borrow money to support themselves and their families until they received their share of the profits; sometimes, in a bad season, repayment was deferred to the next season. It was customary for a debtor with a share in the season's haul to offer the creditor pearls at a discounted price and then, if they were not accepted, to discharge the debt from the proceeds of sale on the open market. Debt became more of a problem when the pearl industry went into decline; in the good years there were ample rewards for one and all, but even those years were marked by occasional bad patches. In 1911, at a time when the industry was considered to be at its height, it was reported that the 'take' was poor and the market low.

It was not only in pearling that a man could run up debts, since debt was a feature of other occupations such as agriculture. Moneylenders might be other members of the community, *jama'a*, who were generally more sympathetic towards the debtor than the professional lenders, who tended to be small shopkeepers and merchants. The overall picture was not entirely negative, however, since their investments made a number of enterprises possible that otherwise would have been too expensive for an individual to bear. The ruling family of Dubai, the Maktoum, were considered fair lenders, allowing time to pay and even writing off debts in some cases; but there were a number of unscrupulous creditors. If a debtor defaulted, half his land would be forfeited but he would be allowed to continue working there. In some cases, the more ruthless creditor took possession of the whole land, forcing the debtor's descendants to buy it back at a much higher price.

For the divers debt was a fact of life, as they borrowed money from their *nawakhidah* to see them through the lean times. It was not unknown for debt-ridden divers to try to escape from their *nawakhidah*; indeed, the problem of runaway divers would occasionally come to the notice of the British authorities. In the spring of 1920, two runaway divers from separate Abu Dhabi boats escaped to Bahrain. The *nawakhidah* followed them and complained to the Political Agent, Harold Dickson, about the men, who had taken refuge in the agency building. Dickson managed to secure the men's freedom after a local businessman, Abd

Pearl divers at work in the Arabian Gulf.

al Rahma al-Zayani, offered to pay their debts. Dickson was clearly unimpressed by the *nawakhidah*'s conduct, remarking that he would 'gorge at having to return a runaway diver to anyone on the Trucial Coast. A more cruel and blood thirsty set of ruffians would be difficult to find. Once back in their hands a wretched negro would have a very thin time of it.'[4] This seems a harsh judgement based on a limited experience of pearling in the lower Gulf – there were good *nawakhidah* just as there were bad. But divers were often bound to their *nawakhidah* by debt, and, if the season was not a good one, the divers would have to borrow money from them in order to live. Debts could mount up over successive seasons, creating a greater incentive for the diver to escape and the *nakhudha* to pursue him.

Among the Trucial sheikhs, there was an agreement to facilitate the surrender of absconding debtors between one sheikhdom and another, making a sheikh liable for the debt and a fine of 50 Maria Theresa dollars if he refused to return a debtor. In this regard, any disputes were settled by a council of sheikhs, with the agreement of the British representative, the Political Resident. For disputes about individual debts, each of the main ports had a panel of men experienced in the pearling trade appointed by the ruler to sit as a divers' court, ensuring that local codes and regulations were enforced in a fair and systematic manner.

Once the diver had returned his basket of shells to the boat, the *nakhudha* would gather all the shells together, leave them to decay and weaken overnight and then supervise their opening in the morning, looking for the more valuable pearls and locking up the haul in a wooden box. Those pearls he did not sell to the itinerant merchants, he would take to the pearl dealer (*tawwash*) in the home port and the bargaining would begin. The quality of the pearls would be assessed according to size, weight, lustre and colour. For the unscrupulous *tawwash*, the object was to buy a pearl whose great value was not apparent to the *nakhudha* and thus make a great profit; but this tended to be a futile play, since the *nawakhidah* were usually well acquainted with pearls and their value.

And so, the haggling would go on. Much would depend on the haul, the quality of the pearls and the state of the market; sometimes the *tawwash* held the whip hand, other times the *nakhudha*. In a typical year, the *tawwash* might pitch his opening bid at about half the amount the *nakhudha* had asked for, then a series of offers would follow until the *tawwash* turned to his assistant and asked him what he thought they were worth; by a system of secret hand signals, these two could communicate with each other until an acceptable offer was made. Payment was made in silver rupees, and the pearls were then taken by the *tawwash* or his representative to a big pearl merchant in Bombay, where they were sold to Indians who might make necklaces that were sent to Paris and then on to New York.

Indeed, pearls were distributed to various markets, with many being sent to the West – its demand for pearls derived from a growing fascination with the Orient, not only in Europe but in the United States, where New York had a thriving pearl market. Some pearls were sent to Baghdad, where traders preferred the white pearl and took large quantities of the smaller seed pearl; yellow pearls were sold in India and Turkey, while ones of poorer quality were disposed of in Persia.

As well as sustaining its workers, merchants, bankers and traders, the pearling industry also provided the rulers with a lucrative source of revenue. In the early 1800s, rulers took the lead of the sheikh of Bahrain by imposing a tax first on pearling boats and then on crews, divers, merchants and pearls. This was good business, giving them a regular cash income with which to maintain their households, armed retainers and all the necessary trappings of power. In this way, the industry helped them to consolidate their power and confirm the tribal structures that had developed over hundreds of years while ensuring that, instead of presiding over subsistence economies, they ruled over the rich, thriving centres of the pearling business.

As one would expect for an industry so deeply embedded in the fabric of life, there was a political aspect to it all. In October 1911, as part of its regular duties, HMS *Sphinx* visited the pearling banks. On sighting the ship, the dhows hoisted their Qasimi flags, with the exception of a *sambuq* owned by an individual named Juma bin Rashid, a resident of Khan (a village near Sharjah), who flew a different flag. Another *sambuq* belonging to one Bin Obeidullah, a resident of Ajman, flew the Turkish flag. Since foreign boats were forbidden from fishing the pearling banks, the *Sphinx* sent a jolly boat to both these *sambuqs*, spoke to their *nawakhidah*, confiscated their flags and left the scene. There were a large number of Persians employed as seamen, divers and boat builders, and East Africans made good divers, but pearling on the Arabian side of the Gulf was strictly limited to local boats.

In the same year as the *Sphinx*'s visit to the pearling banks, news reached the Political Resident that the inhabitants of Qatar and Tangistan (a district of Bushire) were planning to attack the Dubai pearling dhows, with the result that a great number of the vessels kept a strict night watch until the end of the pearling season. A British presence in the Gulf, and the protection they offered under the maritime truces, added an element of security that had been absent in the past, allowing the pearl industry as a whole to thrive. The Political Resident, in his role as *hakkam*, was the final arbiter of pearling disputes between the Trucial sheikhs, and the navy prevented a recurrence of the days when the pearling beds were the scene of occasional battles.

There were many other factors that could affect pearling, such as local epidemics, overfishing, wars or a slump in the global demand for pearls. The pearl market was particularly affected by international events. In October 1912 the pearling season closed with an excellent take and good earnings for the divers, but the declaration of war between Turkey and the Balkan states virtually paralysed the pearl market, with the result that many Trucial Coast dealers faced bankruptcy. Those consignments already sent to India had not been sold and it was reported that the banks in Bombay had declined to make payments or undertake the dispatch of pearls to London or elsewhere while the war continued.

The threat of plague remained real well into the twentieth century. On 5 March 1913, owing to an outbreak of the plague at Dubai, the sheikh with his family repaired to the interior, together with the wealthier inhabitants and tradesmen of the town. Among the poorer people left behind there were around eighteen deaths a day and, in six weeks, it was estimated that as many as 1,300 had died from the epidemic. There were frequent burglaries in the houses which had been evacuated and, in one instance, 30,000 rupees in cash and household effects were stolen from three separate houses. In Sharjah four to five deaths from the plague were reported daily. In April it appeared that the plague was subsiding, with only one or two deaths a day. In July the sheikh of Sharjah recovered from the plague, although the next month it was reported that Sheikh Butti bin Rashid, an influential member of the ruling family of Dubai, had died from it. These events brought a downward spiral: a shortage of manpower led to a smaller catch, a decline in income and financial hardship for one and all. The following year, after the pearling season had been suspended in September on account of Ramadan, the catch was very poor and barely covered 10 per cent of the advances made to the fleets. The merchants, who were still waiting to recover their claims from the previous year, were at a loss to know how they were going to finance the pearl boats when the season resumed at the close of Ramadan.

Far from bringing a steady, year-on-year increase in profits, the industry was a roller-coaster ride of uncertainty. On 6 May 1916 it was reported from Bombay that the pearl market was reviving. There was much excitement among the pearl merchants of the Trucial Coast at the arrival of Ali bin Ibrahim al-Zayani of Bahrain, a broker to Rosenthal Frerès, pearl merchants of Paris. The firm's broker would normally visit Bahrain every year to buy pearls, but visiting the pearling towns lower down the Gulf was an exceptional event. He came to Dubai and Sharjah and bought pearls from several merchants at high prices, in some cases clearing out their stock. He also arranged with the local merchants that they should gather as many pearls as they could at the end of the pearl fishing season so that another representative of the firm might return to buy them at high prices for cash. For the pearl merchants, it was a win-win situation: by cutting out the middle men, the merchants sold the pearls themselves and not through the *banyan* Hindu of Bombay, saving the risk of transport and avoiding the 1 per

Pearl merchants in
Dubai, March 1960.

cent brokerage and other remittance fees. But the fickleness of the market was soon apparent – by the time pearl diving stopped again for Ramadan in August, earnings had improved but prices in Bombay had dropped.

Four years later, the pearling season was very dull and the merchants, not being able to sell their pearls, were unable to pay the *nawakhidah*, with the result that the divers were not inclined to dive. The pearling fleets were still struggling to recover from a storm earlier in the year which had wrecked many boats and drowned a number of divers and crew members. In November, however, when the pearling boats returned to Dubai, Sharjah and Ras al-Khaimah it was reported that the season had been a good one. Later concerns that the pearling beds were declining were never fully investigated; the *nawakhidah* blamed the popularity of mother-of-pearl, which led to fewer oyster shells being discarded into the sea with the result that fewer oysters were being 'fertilised'; others suggested that it was a simple case of over-fishing.[5]

Although Britain held back from becoming involved in the sheikh-doms' internal affairs, pearling could impact her interests in a variety of ways. The sheikhs of Hamriyah had secessionist tendencies, seeking to break away from Sharjah. Wedged between Ajman and Umm al-Qaiwain, Hamriyah was a coastal village that had a population of about 400 and each year sent a small fleet of 50 boats to the pearl fisheries. But in 1917, when fighting broke out between Sharjah and the sheikh of Hamriyah, Abdul Rahman, a large number of pearl divers were pressed into the fighting forces of both sides, disrupting the pearling season and preventing the captains and boat owners from repaying advances made to them by British Indian merchants.

The vagaries of pearling continued well into the 1920s. In July 1927 it was reported that Arab merchants of the coast engaged in the pearl trade were in a difficult position for lack of capital, and were forced to borrow at high rates of interest from Indian or Persian merchants; however, the pearl boats were yielding a better return that year than the previous one, the market for pearls was much improved both locally and in Europe and a brisk trade was anticipated. In August Dickson wrote that pearling operations were in full swing and the yield appeared to be good everywhere. In 1928, when pearling operations closed for the season and the diving boats all returned to port, it was reported that the catch had been better than for several years, but the market was not brisk.

In fact, the Dubai pearling fleet returned from the banks to find not a single merchant waiting for them on the harbourside. Next year it was reported that about 60 diving ships of the same fleet had failed to put out to sea owing to financial difficulties; the number of pearling boats had increased out of all proportion to the catch, and the pearl merchants were unable to subsidize all the boats. One of the prominent pearlers of Dubai, Mohammed bin Boyat, had gone bankrupt, owing money to British, Persian and Arab subjects to the tune of six *lakh*s of rupees. The Ruler of Dubai tried to persuade his creditors to make new advances, but without success. Another important pearler, Sheikh Muhammed bin Ahmad al-Dalmuk of Dubai, was also in difficulty. The year before, he had sold pearls worth several *lakh*s of rupees to Haji Muhammad Ali Zainal of Bombay, but had not yet received his money on account of delays in disposing of the pearls in Paris. In order to equip his pearling fleet for the next diving season, he borrowed 200,000 rupees from a Hindu money lender at an exorbitant interest of 36 per cent per annum.

In September, although there was much talk among the pearling crews of a pearl of great value having been sold in Bahrain, the catch was generally inferior and earnings low. In March 1930 a leading merchant of Dubai, Sheikh Muhammad bin Ahmad, returned from Bombay after selling his stock of pearls at a loss. In an attempt to cut his overheads, he reduced his establishment, dismissing bedouins and selling camels. His son Abdullah, being displeased with this drastic action, carried 60 camels off into the desert with the help of bedouin tribesmen. The ruler dispatched his brother, Jumah bin Maktoum, in hot pursuit.

In May 1930 there was excitement in Dubai at news from Bombay that Abdullah, son of Yusuf bin Abdullah, a respectable pearl merchant of Dubai, had been detained in Bombay by the High Court after certain Hindu businesses filed a suit against him for claims against his father. Abdullah had apparently brought his fathers' pearls to Bombay for sale but found the market dull. Being pressed by the Hindus, however, he sold the pearls at a loss for 150,000 rupees and out of this paid 80,000 rupees to his father's creditors. When Abdullah was about to return to Dubai with the remaining money to pay his Arab creditors and to finance pearling operations for the current year, the Hindus filed a suit in the High Court for the unpaid portion of their claims, about 31,500 rupees, and secured his arrest and detention. In reprisal, the ruler of Dubai threatened to arrest all the Hindus in Dubai. The Political Resident asked HMS *Lupin* to watch developments and, eventually, Abdullah was released on bail and returned to Dubai in July.

The arrival of an important buyer brought expectancy and pageantry to the coast. In November 1931 the famous pearl trader and business-man Abdur Raham Qusaibi arrived at Ajman, having travelled on his launch from Bahrain with the express intention of buying some pearls. The ruler of Ajman fired two guns and displayed horses in his honour – Qusaibi bought one pearl for 7,000 rupees and another for 17,000, paying in cash, but gave no presents to the sheikh. Qusaibi then pro-ceeded to Sharjah, where the ruler laid on a reception of three cannon rounds and a display of horses – but the ruler received no presents from the esteemed visitor. By now, word must have spread about the visitor's parsimony. In Dubai, the ruler neither fired guns nor gave a show of horses, nor even met him on horseback on the shore – Qusaibi bought no pearls and gave nothing in return. No doubt the story of the visitor's breach of etiquette was told along the coast for many years after.

———

THE NEMESIS OF the pearl industry arrived in the form of a bowler-hatted, kimono-clad son of a Japanese noodle-seller by the name of Kokichi Mikimoto. Although he is often credited with inventing it, the cultured pearl was in fact first grown by the Chinese in the thirteenth century, or even earlier. The pearl is created in nature by introducing an irritant, such as a grain of sand, into the oyster shell, which then reacts by producing layers of nacre to cover the intruder and to form the small (hopefully) spherical shape that we know as a pearl. The Chinese realized that, by putting artificial objects into the shell, they could replicate the natural process. Hence they inserted tiny statuettes of Buddha into oysters to create small blister pearls.

But producing spherical pearls was not an easy task, since pearls tended to form a variety of shapes: flat, semi-circular, dented and the like. In 1748 the Swedish naturalist Carl Linnaeus developed a method for culturing pearls, similar to the Chinese way, but it was not until 1900 that the first round pearls were produced by an Australian, William Saville-Kent. This involved inserting a small piece of mother-of-pearl into the shell in order to trick the oyster into producing more precious nacre, thus mimicking nature. Two Japanese men, Tatsuhei Mise and Tokishi Nishikawa, learnt the technique in Australia and brought it back to Japan, filing their own patents.

A *shahouf*, a smaller type of dhow used in the Arabian Gulf for fishing and pearling.

Mikimoto was born in 1858 in Toba, in the Mie Prefecture of Japan, a pearl trading area, and began selling natural pearls in his twenties, at a time when pearl powder was used to treat a variety of ailments such as eye disease, fever, measles and insomnia. After leasing a farm at Ago Bay, Japan, he began his own experiments in creating blister pearls using the Chinese technique. But his search for the perfectly formed cultured pearl would bring years of disappointment: it took five years to produce his first harvest of semi-spherical pearls, and he only found success by using the methods developed by Mise and Nishikawa. His cultured pearls, known as 'Mikimoto Pearls', were a great success in the European markets, offering a 25 per cent discount on the price of natural pearls.

By the 1930s the Japanese industry was humming, with hundreds of farms producing millions of pearls each year, more than matching Gulf pearls in terms of price and (to the untrained eye) quality. It was difficult to fool the Gulf pearl traders, however, and anyone caught trying to pass off cultured pearls for the real thing was quickly exposed. One story that did the rounds of the Trucial Coast in 1928 was of a Bahraini merchant who had sold a Japanese cultured pearl to a Qatari merchant as a natural pearl. The ruler of Qatar, Sheikh Abdullah bin Qasim Al Thani, took up the case and fined the perpetrator 20,000 rupees in order to settle the matter. The case served as a warning to smugglers of artificial pearls, perhaps, but the real threat came not from smuggling but from competition in the open market. While the Arabian fleets were setting out for the pearling banks of the Gulf, Mikimoto was quietly winning over the global markets with his artificial creations and undermining the market for natural pearls.

For the Trucial Coast, this was a disaster in the making. Japanese production of cultured pearls began to bite in 1925, with a slump in prices and several poor seasons to follow. By 1927 the pearling merchants were struggling, having to borrow at high rates of interest and, despite a good season in 1928, the underlying trend was downwards. Not only this, but the Great Depression starting in 1929 further reduced demand for natural pearls, and by 1931 the price of pearls had dropped by 75 per cent from two years previously. The advent of the Second World War was another blow, and the coup de grâce was delivered in 1947–8 when the new Indian government imposed taxes on pearls imported from the Gulf. The last major fleet set out from Dubai in 1949.

Although a few captains, the last of a dying breed, continued to set out for many years to come, the main pearling fleets lay idle, their crews forced to seek their living elsewhere at a time when opportunities were severely limited. The slump hit the pearl merchants hard. Unable to turn their hand to other forms of business, many became interested in politics, such as in Dubai where members of the ruling family, formerly indifferent to politics, also became involved. These events marked a subtle shift in the balance of power between rulers and merchants: the merchants were no longer willing to subsidize rulers while some rulers had a cushion of payments for oil and mineral concessions and air landing rights to fall back on. In the post-war years, these rulers would take a greater interest in projects that otherwise might have been the province of the merchant classes.

For ordinary people, it was a time when they looked after themselves and each other. Where cash was short, people resorted to bartering goods in lieu of payment. The emphasis was on family and the community. If they could not sort out their differences, they would go to a sheikh as *hakkam* for arbitration, or the ruler as *hukm*. Although the collapse of the pearl trade devastated the economies of the Trucial Coast, more so for the lack of central government or welfare system to cushion the blow, people helped each other and dealt with the consequences.

It is difficult to exaggerate the importance of the pearl industry to the development of the Trucial Coast and, ultimately, to the configuration of the UAE. As Lorimer pointed out, without the wealth generated by the industry, many ports of the Trucial Coast would have ceased to exist. It made Abu Dhabi a viable settlement and transformed Dubai from a small community into one of the leading ports and pearling centres of the Gulf. The pearl trade's collapse led to a corresponding decline in those towns to the extent that their populations were lower in the 1950s than they had been at the start of the century. But, just as the pearl workers were beginning to seek work elsewhere, the first oil men began arriving in the area. By a curious symmetry, the oil came on stream after the pearls had declined, restoring the wealth of the previous era, and then exceeding it beyond all expectations.

There are parallels between the pearl and oil industries of the Gulf. Both brought an element of globalization to the region, although in vastly different ways. In their heyday, Gulf pearls were traded across the world and its workers responded and were vulnerable to the fickleness of the global markets just as the modern emirates are to global oil prices. While the Trucial Coast sheikhdoms were not exactly single-product economies, they did rely to a large extent on the wealth generated by the pearling industry, a fact that only became a major problem when the industry went into decline from the 1920s – surely an object lesson in the need to diversify that is highly pertinent to the UAE's oil-fuelled economy of today.

There is one final twist in this story: the UAE might become a centre of the pearl trade once more. Modern predictions that pearling is set to make a comeback sound hollow in comparison with the past when some 95 per cent of the region's export trade was attributed to the pearl industry, but there is a certain irony in the fact that the Japanese have collaborated with Emiratis to build a pearl-cultivation farm in the sea off Rams.

The Emirates & Japan Pearl Cultivation and Trading Company in Ras al-Khaimah has set up the pearl farm for producing cultured pearls rather than natural ones. Each year 40,000 oysters are harvested with about 20 per cent discarded, but only 5 to 10 per cent of the pearls are good enough for the specialist market, with the remainder sold on the wholesale market. The creation of the Dubai Pearl Exchange marks the UAE's firm commitment to becoming a trade centre for both the natural and cultured pearling industry. In 2009 about 99.6 million dirhams (U.S.$27.1 million) worth of pearls was traded through Dubai, a small proportion of the $3 billion global market, but nevertheless a first step in attempting to re-establish the region's pre-eminence in pearls.

And what of natural pearls? Today, they share a small proportion of the global market, about 0.5 per cent. Pollution, dredging and shore developments such as the residential and industrial complexes have altered the marine environment, and the predominance of the cultured pearl shows no sign of weakening. But a government-backed committee, the Pearl Revival Committee, is aiming to reverse the decline of the natural pearl industry through a system of certification, which will differentiate between natural and cultured pearls and research into making oysters more resilient in their natural habitat. All this is to the good, saving the pearl industry from being consigned to a curiosity akin to a modern-day theme park or museum.

Perhaps more facts and figures will soon come tumbling out of the sky, together with shiny brochures and press releases to confirm that the UAE is a major player in the global market again. But at the heart of this revival is another irony. Kokichi Mikimoto cultivated the *Pinctada radiata* pearl-oyster in his Japanese farms, and this is the same species that is being used to create the new Gulf pearls – the same species that was a mainstay of the Gulf pearling industry in the past and the one that was used in Japan to kill it off.

And so, the new age of the pearl rises phoenix-like from the ashes of the old. Surely the pearlers of old, setting out in the summer haze and rowing out of the harbour with their families looking on, all enwrapped in the events of the time, would have given little thought to a future without pearls; but then, it has always been in the Emirati blood to seek new opportunities and adapt to a changing world.

5

Something in the Air: Dubai and the Northern Sheikhdoms, 1901–39

IN DECEMBER 1901 the 6,500-ton Russian cruiser *Varyag* was cruising through Gulf waters, French merchants were active in Muscat and the German firm of Wönckhaus was trading in Lingah. The British authorities, wary of these and other inroads being made by other nations, decided it was time to show their flag. In June 1902 the 11,000-ton HMS *Amphitrite*, the largest ship ever seen in the Gulf, visited its ports. As if this was not ample proof of Britain's supremacy in the region, the Viceroy of India, Lord Curzon, came calling the following year.

On 21 November 1903 Curzon visited Sharjah and, in the afternoon, held a grand durbar in a decorated pavilion on the quarter deck of HMS *Argonaut*. It was, apparently, a splendid occasion – the rulers of Abu Dhabi, Dubai, Sharjah, Ajman and the son of the aged ruler of Umm al-Qaiwain were all there. An Arabic translation of the address was read aloud but exactly what the rulers made of it is not recorded. Imperiously, Curzon declared:

> We were here before any other power, in modern times, had shown its face in these waters. We found strife and we have created order. It was our commerce as well as your security that was threatened and called for protection. At every port along these coasts the subjects of the king of England still reside and trade. The great Empire of India, which it is our duty to defend, lies almost at your gates. We saved you from extinction at the hands of your neighbours. We opened these seas to the ships of all nations, and enabled their flags to fly in peace. We have not seized or held your territory. We have not destroyed your independence, but have preserved it.[1]

A curious bystander might have queried the notion of 'independence' that Curzon espoused, since the rulers of the Trucial Coast were prevented by treaty from entering into agreements with any other foreign power. What Curzon meant, of course, was that his government was not interested in the internal affairs of the sheikhdoms as long as they did not impact on trade and communications in the Gulf.

But for the people of the tribes, the de facto ruler was not the British, the Portuguese or Persians before them; it was their paramount sheikh. He was the proud government (*hukm*) and wise arbitrator (*hakkam*). People were expected to settle their disputes between themselves and only when all else had failed did they approach their ruler or other notable – in this regard, rulers did not have a monopoly over the title of 'sheikh', which could denote any man of importance in a community or family. Rulers also adjudicated between tribes, in their own area and elsewhere, mediating between their fellow sheikhs and people. As well as making peace, they were required to make war and protect their people when necessary. This brought with it the right to levy tax (*zakat*) upon the community in order to raise money to maintain themselves, their families and their armed retainers, together with a degree of accountability.

A ruler did not exercise absolute power, nor was he elected by his people. As we have seen, he was chosen by family members and tribal elders, retaining his position as long as he maintained their respect and that of his tribe. Issues were discussed within his inner circle, and a canny ruler would take the views of family members into account. Loss of face was often a mortal blow and assassination an occupational hazard. A weakness at the head of a tribe could disable its body, making it susceptible to feuds and outside threats. The tradition of *hijra*, whereby one tribe or sub-section would break away to seek independence or the protection of another sheikh, was one way of settling matters, at least in the short term; but it could also lay the fault lines of more enduring tribal disputes.

Tribes had differences that kept them apart, and customs that bound them together. Underpinning their way of life was a given set of mutually understood, unwritten rules. Perhaps most familiar to Westerners is the saying 'an eye for an eye, a tooth for a tooth', a dramatic expression of the rather more prosaic concept of compensation that lies at the heart of tribal law. It often worked like this: 'My grandfather was killed by someone; compensation and reconciliation were arranged, and the sheikh came to the feast which ratified the agreement between the two

An image of the nomadic tribal life: a bedouin with camels.

families.'[2] This was not a hard and fast rule, however, and bedouin raiders were still prosecuting blood feuds into the twentieth century.

Away from the shore, the great wilderness that stretched into the distance barely touched the likes of Lord Curzon, who was not greatly interested in the internal affairs of the ruling sheikhs. Although Europeans had left a legacy of maps, many of which were jealously guarded as trade secrets, there were many blanks. The Danish cartographer Carsten Niebuhr sketchily described the Bani Yas in his eighteenth-century travels, and a number of British travellers had provided accounts since then. These included Captain Atkins Hamerton, who was ordered to visit the Al Ain/Buraimi Oasis in 1840 because of a scare about a possible Egyptian attack; Colonel Samuel Miles, who visited the oasis in 1876 and saw there, among other things, an American cannon that the Sultan of Muscat had brought back from New York in 1842; Reverend Samuel Zwemer, who took the first photographs of the area and travelled to Abu Dhabi, Sharjah and Buraimi in 1901; and Percy Cox, who travelled to Buraimi in 1902 and 1905. Reverend J. H. Bacon, who was planning to cross the Rub al-Khali by balloon, might also have appeared on this distinguished list, had he accomplished his mission. There were also various India Office records, such as the administration reports of the British political agency in Muscat, which helped to build up a picture of the inland tribes.

Only when other European powers began showing a renewed interest in the region in the later part of the nineteenth century did British officials make serious efforts to gather information about the inland tribes, towns and territories of the Arabian Gulf. One result was John Gordon Lorimer's *Gazetteer of the Persian Gulf, Oman and Central Arabia.* This encyclopaedia, in two volumes, of colonial intelligence, surveying the history and geography of the region, took ten years to complete and was published in reverse order: volume two in 1908, volume one in 1915. Descriptions of the areas forming today's UAE were collected by the Native Agent in Sharjah, Khan Bahadur Abdal al-Latif (1890–1907).

The old ways carried on: tribesmen of the Bani Yas and Manasir divided their time between the Liwa Oasis and the pearling fleets in the Gulf. The Manasir also herded their camels across their tribal range, as did the Duru, Al bu Shamis, Bani Kitab and Awamir – the latter were also renowned as *falaj* builders in and around Al Ain. The mysterious Shihuh, keeping apart from the others, came down from the mountains in the summer for the date harvest and fishing. A tribesman's attachment to his friends and enemies, and his predilection for alliances and feuds, were carried proudly into the twentieth century. The Sharqiyin, the second largest tribe after the Bani Yas and based in Fujairah on the east coast, cleaved from the Qasimi sheikhs of Sharjah and would eventually achieve recognition as an independent sheikhdom; the Naim inhabited parts of the Buraimi Oasis and their offshoot, the Al bu Shamis, remained allies of the Bani Yas. And so it went on.

For those living on islands such as Dalma, Sir Bani Yas and Sir Bu Nair, fishing or pearling, or both, brought a living, while those on Abu Musa also worked a red-oxide mine. For the inland villages, the availability of water was the determining factor, thus agricultural settlements tended to cluster around mountain springs, wells and *aflaj*; farming and the selling of wood, charcoal and dates were among the main occupations. As the coastal towns of the lower Gulf thrived through the pearl trade, they grew more wealthy than the inland communities, and acquired significant Indian, Persian and Baluchi populations.

At the start of the twentieth century, then, these towns were enjoying a period of prosperity. The maritime peace was lasting and the tribal situation was mostly calm. Each major town was dominated by a particular tribal faction, comprising the ruling family and its supporters. Sheikh Zayed the Great of Abu Dhabi had extended his rule to six of the nine villages of the Al Ain/Buraimi Oasis. In Ras al-Khaimah, the

troubles of the 'piratical' past were a distant memory and its fleet had
built up a valuable overseas trade. Nonetheless, the sheikhdom would
never recover its nineteenth-century maritime power, and its ruler, Sheikh
Sultan bin Salim Al Qasimi (ruled 1921–48), would grow increasingly
concerned about the decline of his prestige and authority in the hinterland. As we have seen, the Qawasim had already lost their hold on
parts of the east coast, the Shamailiyah.

In Dubai, the fishing village which had been transformed in 1838
by the arrival of some 800 members of the Al Bu Falasah from Abu
Dhabi, other changes were taking place. Sandwiched between the
competing Qawasim and Al bu Falah groupings, their independence
had been tenuous in the early days. However, through a prudent policy
of encouraging trade, astute alliances and keeping on good terms with
the British, the small sheikhdom survived and, indeed, thrived under the
Al Maktoum. In 1835 Maktoum bin Buti was a signatory of the Maritime
Truce, which paved the way to the permanent truce. When his co-ruler
Obaid died in 1836, Maktoum continued alone, thus establishing the
modern Maktoum dynasty that has ruled to the present day. Above all
the Trucial sheikhs, the Al Maktoum had a certain commercial nous,
which would be the making of Dubai.

Dubai sits on a curving creek, which in the mid-nineteenth century
comprised several settlements that clustered along its banks – Bur Dubai
on the western side of the creek, Deira on the eastern side and Shindaghah
on the spit of land at its entrance. The Bastakiya, named after the Bastika
region of Persia whence merchants had come and settled, was situated
on the Bur Dubai side of the creek. Many of these merchants had come
from places like Lingah to escape punitive customs dues, attracted to
Dubai by its more liberal trading regime. By the turn of the century,
the town had a cosmopolitan population of 19,000. Although the Bani
Yas were still in the majority, their numbers were supplemented by
other *Khaliji*, Persians, Baluchis and Indians. By 1903 it was a centre
of trade and pearling, a port of call for steamers, a town bustling with
merchants and entrepreneurs who prospered accordingly. Their presence
saw a number of modern schools being opened in the town, starting with
the Al Ahmadiyyah, founded by pearl merchant Sheikh Muhammed
bin Ahmad al-Dalmuk, where pupils sat at desks instead of squatting
on the ground under a palm tree.

There was also arms smuggling, which often exercised the minds
of the British authorities. As *The Times* pointed out, the rifle was the

tribesman's 'most cherished possession'.[3] In the past, sulphur mines at Jebel Dhanna may have supplied the gunpowder for his rudimentary flintlock. However, in the late nineteenth century more modern rifles such as the Martini-Henry came to be used. Although the arms trade was based in Muscat, where several French merchants sold European weapons on the open market, there was a brisk traffic of arms and ammunition to the rebellious tribes of the North West Frontier of India through the Arabian Gulf, and rifles inevitably found their way to the Trucial Coast.

In 1902 treaties had been made with Trucial sheikhs prohibiting the import and export of arms from their territories, but by 1909 the government of India was so alarmed by the influx of arms into Afghanistan that it instigated a naval blockade of the Mekran coast. On 27 December 1910, in an operation to find illicit arms in Dubai, HMS *Hyacinth* appeared off the coast and its commander ordered the town to be raided. However, in a major faux pas, he began the operation without first consulting the ruler, Sheikh Buti bin Suhail. As a result, people awoke to find armed British soldiers in their midst and, thinking they were under attack, fought back. In the ensuing firefight, 37 Arabs and four British sailors were killed, with another ten people wounded or

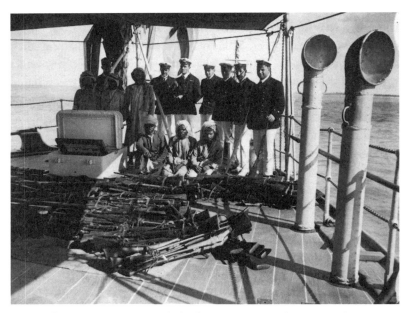

A haul of seized weapons on the deck of HMS *Fox*, 1910, when it was taking part in a naval blockade in the Gulf of Oman.

reported missing. To add insult to injury, the Political Resident Sir Percy Cox delivered an ultimatum to Sheikh Buti demanding compensation of 50,000 rupees, 400 rifles and the right to have a British agent, a guard, a sub-post office and a radio transmission station installed in Dubai. At this point, cooler heads in the India Office took over, and although the ruler paid the guns and money the other demands were quietly dropped.

If anything, the British remained divided on the degree of intervention in local affairs. A few years later the next ruler of Dubai, Sheikh Saeed bin Maktoum, ordered a freed slave to be forcibly removed from a British ship, the ss *Palitana*. The British authorities were not impressed, but although there were mutterings about establishing a permanent representative in Dubai or placing Dubai and Abu Dhabi under closer supervision, they took no further action.

A policy of supporting the status quo carried risks of its own. In bolstering Sheikh Saeed against his opponents, the Political Resident was liable to be sucked into the erratic currents of Dubai politics. Disaffection centred on the sons of former ruler Rashid bin Maktoum (reigned 1886–94), who formed a rival family group that considered their branch had a better claim to the succession. They were known as the Bani Rashid, or the 'Sons of Rashid'. As we shall see, from the late 1920s the history of Dubai crystallized in a series of conflicts between Sheikh Saeed and these Bani Rashid cousins.

———

BY NOW, the British officially recognized six sheikhs and their sheikhdoms – Abu Dhabi, Dubai and the northern sheikhdoms of Sharjah, Ajman, Umm al-Qaiwain and Ras al-Khaimah – but there still remained a number of smaller territories of uncertain status. While they all felt the fluctuations and ultimate decline of the pearl trade, it was the sheikhs of these lesser domains who found it increasingly difficult to maintain their independence against a background of economic decline. Power struggles within ruling families and disputes between local sheikhs created wide ripples, set tribe against tribe, and further undermined them.

There was little predictability about the process: they were all governed by the uncertain gravity of tribal politics. Hamriyah was semi-independent until it was incorporated into Sharjah in 1922. For brief periods, the Qawasim were split over Hira, Dibba and Kalba. The British recognized the latter as an independent sheikhdom in 1936 in order to build an airstrip there, but it was reabsorbed into Sharjah in 1952. Part of the east coast known as the Shamailiyah was controlled by the Sharqiyin tribe – everyone had regarded their territory as autonomous, apart from the British authorities, but even they recognized it as the independent sheikhdom of Fujairah in the same year.

There were some interesting moments. Hira was a small coastal village of 250 houses occupied by a sub-section of the Al bu Shamis. In June 1920 its headman, Abdul Rahman bin Muhammed, invaded the town of Ajman. Like other territories along the coast, Ajman was the name of both a town and a sheikhdom. It was small – today it is the smallest of the seven emirates that make up the UAE – with a hinterland of separate enclaves and different tribes under the rule of the Al Nuaimi dynasty. Abdul Rahman occupied its fort, only to be persuaded to leave by the Native Agent, Isa bin Abd al-Latif (1919–35). Since Abdul Rahman owed money to a number of people including British subjects, he was allowed to return to Hira on a promise not to cause any more trouble. In fact, he continued to intrigue in the area but remained in Hira until his death in 1942.

With shorelines on both sides of the Trucial Coast, the Qasimi ruler of Sharjah was an important figure in the politics of the area. His port of the same name was pre-eminent on the lower Gulf, but this would be challenged by Dubai, and weakened by the vicissitudes of the pearling industry and the later silting of its creek. The glory days of the Qawasim in the Gulf were long gone, and a succession of weak rulers had destabilized the sheikhdom, leaving it vulnerable to bedouin attack and secessionist claims. Sheikh Sultan bin Saqr al-Qasimi had come to power in a coup, having deposed his uncle Khalid in November 1924. Then, having agreed to respect his uncle's private property, Sheikh Sultan resiled from his promise and confiscated it, refusing to pay compensation. By 1927 a state of armed neutrality existed between them. Sheikh Khalid enlisted the support of other family members, together with the sheikhs of Umm al-Qaiwain and Hamriyah, and the Bani Kitab, two members of which had allegedly been ill-treated by Sheikh Sultan.

At the end of Ramadan in April, Khalid and his allies launched an attack on Sharjah, but failed to dislodge the ruler. A British warship, HMS *Triad*, appeared off the coast followed by HMS *Lupin* four days later. The Senior Naval Officer Persian Gulf, assisted by the Native Agent of Sharjah and Sheikh Saeed of Dubai, persuaded both sides to end hostilities and settle the dispute. Sheikh Khalid was to be compensated for losing part of his property, paid an annual allowance of 2,500 rupees and allowed to live unmolested at his date gardens in Dhaid. To enforce payment, no native boats were allowed to leave Sharjah for the pearl banks until Sheikh Sultan had made the first payment.

As it happened, Khalid preferred to reside in Umm al-Qaiwain, a fact that may have triggered the next upheaval. This was another small sheikhdom – the second smallest in the UAE today – largely populated by members of the Al Ali tribe and ruled by the Al Mualla dynasty. In February 1929 its ruler, Sheikh Hamad bin Ibrahim, was shot and killed in his fort by a slave, supposedly at the instigation of Hamad's blind uncle, Abdul Rahman bin Ahmed. The next day the fort was attacked by an outraged mob, who breached its wall and set the building ablaze. The bodies of both the slave and Abdul Rahman bin Ahmed were burnt and eighteen-year-old Ahmad bin Rashid, cousin of the murdered Sheikh Hamad, was proclaimed ruler.

The British authorities saw the hand of Sharjah in these events. As soon as he heard the news, Sheikh Sultan dispatched 60 of his men to Umm al-Qaiwain by sea, officially to offer his condolences and – probably – to secure the removal of his uncle Khalid from the sheikhdom. In fact, Khalid survived and went on to become the regent of Kalba. The new sheikh of Umm al-Qaiwain proved to be durable, too. Despite being described as a 'heavy, irresolute-looking individual', he confirmed all the treaties and agreements with the British and went on to reign until his death in 1981.[4]

Watching all these developments closely was Isa bin Abd al-Latif, the Native Agent. Described as a 'big man' with a 'somewhat crafty expression to his face', he was a British subject and owned houses in Sharjah and Ras al-Khaimah, living in the former during winter and the latter during the summer, enjoying his extensive date gardens there.[5] The agency post had become a hereditary office, with his father and grandfather preceding him in the role. Like his forebears, Isa was a successful businessman as well as an effective agent, intervening in local affairs and supplying intelligence to the Political Resident, translating documents and enforcing debts. But he was more than a simple British stooge. He made enemies such as Sheikh Sultan bin Salim of Ras al-Khaimah, and occasionally played a double game, manipulating the British against his opponents when it suited him. He was a powerful figure by any standard, and remained at the centre of events on the Trucial Coast from his appointment in 1919 until he retired in 1935.

Certainly the Indian merchants of Dubai feared him, more than they feared the ruler, with whom Isa bin Abd al-Latif remained on good terms. Sheikh Saeed bin Maktoum was a statesman and mediator, his round spectacles and ascetic appearance conveying a kindly and bookish air, and he was never happier than when he was out in the desert hunting with his salukis and falcons. But in the late 1920s, against a background of deteriorating pearling revenues and rising hardship, the Bani Rashid and disaffected merchants conspired to unsettle Dubai. Saeed faced several attempts to unseat him and, as time went on, he delegated much of the government to his son Rashid and his advisers. Another influential figure was his wife and confidant, Sheikha Hassa bint al-Mur, a businesswoman in her own right who conducted business from behind a drawn curtain in her own *majlis* comprising men, not women. In an age when women were strictly confined to domestic roles, the sheikha was truly remarkable. By the time of her death in 1947, it was reported that she had acquired considerable property in Dubai and abroad, as well as many businesses that she ran through agents.

In 1928, however, when the difficult years still lay ahead, it was the actions of Reza Shah Pahlavi (Shah of Persia/Iran from 1925 to 1941) and his government that caused the most disquiet in Dubai. The Persians had been asserting their presence in the Gulf. Although Hengam Island belonged to Persia, the local ruler was Ahmed bin Obaid bin Juma, father-in-law of Sheikh Saeed of Dubai. In May, Sheikh Ahmed and his followers were expelled and a customs post established on the island. This was an affront to Dubai, and his arrival in the town was greeted with outrage and dismay. In the event, British efforts behind the scenes led to the Persian government agreeing to Sheikh Ahmed's reinstatement in September.

By then the episode had been eclipsed by a more serious disturbance. Two months earlier a Persian customs boat had seized a Dubai-flagged *jalbut* as it travelled to the island of Greater Tunb. The passengers, mainly women and children, were taken into custody at the port of Lingah, with the women being deprived of their jewellery. The incident inflamed the Trucial Coast, especially Dubai, where there were several attacks on Persian businesses and talk of raising an armed force to attack Lingah and rescue the passengers. Isa bin Abd al-Latif intervened and the arrival of HMS *Lupin* helped to quell the town. For the Persians, the threat of a British gunboat appearing off Lingah, together with

British diplomatic pressure, seemed to do the trick. The passengers were released and the *jalbut* returned to Dubai.

But the matter of compensation remained. There was disagreement within the British government: some officials wanted punitive action against the Persians, others preferred a softly-softly approach while negotiations for a new treaty were underway – the Foreign Office wanted to pay compensation, but this was rejected by the Treasury. In the end, the government of India paid 5,000 rupees to the families of the passengers. But the failure of the British government to resolve the issue of compensation in a timely manner reflected badly on Sheikh Saeed – caught between *al-daulah* and his own people, Sheikh Saeed appeared to have done nothing and looked vulnerable.

There were other matters, such as repeated bedouin attacks on the town and Saeed's insistence that debts owed to Indians be honoured, which angered local merchants. There were some stormy sessions in the *majlis* as disaffected family members demanded a greater role in government, leading to an offer by Sheikh Saeed to resign. It was April 1929 and the disgruntled cousins, the Bani Rashid, were in the ascendant. One of their number, Mani bin Rashid, a highly educated merchant whose income had been hit hard by the decline of the pearl trade, was

The Dubai *suq*, the main market and meeting place for people to drink coffee and share stories, a place where the interplay of light and shadow provided the perfect setting for rumour and speculation.

proclaimed ruler. But the moment was short-lived, and the new arrangement was given short shrift by the Political Resident. Sheikh Saeed was restored to his former position – indeed, his absence was so brief that it was no more than a blink of the eye in his lengthy reign.

British policy in these circumstances was summed up in a message from the Resident in Bushire, written in that terse style of official telegrams:

> Although our policy is one of non-interference in internal affairs of Trucial Chiefs Government would not be prepared to recognise one Sheikh coming forward in circumstances so unsatisfactory as those detailed in your telegram. *Majlis* may therefore be informed that [the British] Government cannot recognise any change of this nature unless and until effected by will of the people and that [a] very serious view will be taken of any disturbance affecting British subjects. Sheikh should be able to reassert his position if he really has majority behind him. Otherwise to bolster him up would be against the policy of Government.[6]

Undeterred by their setbacks, a group of Bani Rashid notables and others demanded a *sharia* court to impose traditional sentences on offenders. In one case, the court sentenced a thief to have his right hand cut off, despite Sheikh Saeed's policy to commute such sentences. The Political Resident informed the sheikh that a 'savage and cruel punishment' had been inflicted, and that the appropriate disposal for this offence was a term of imprisonment. The sheikh responded that the man was a habitual offender and that the Trucial sheikhs could not afford the luxury of maintaining such men in prison.[7] His words were probably spoken through gritted teeth; Saeed was a compassionate man, having once dealt with a thief he found stealing a palace carpet with a simple warning. But his manner was perceived by his opponents as weakness. On one occasion, after a local boat was damaged and a threat made to beat up an agent of the British India Line, Saeed was powerless to extract an immediate apology from the perpetrators of the threat, who were affiliated to the Bani Rashid. It seemed that every confrontation diminished his power a little more.

These were restless years. The towns offered easy pickings for the bedouin in times of hardship: in 1931 there were many reports of raids on the outskirts of Dubai, Sharjah and Ras al-Khaimah. A few examples give a flavour of the times: a caravan travelling from Dubai was attacked and three people killed; a twelve-year-old boy was going to fetch water from a well about 3 kilometres (2 miles) outside Sharjah when three bedouins attacked and kidnapped him; bedouins of the Bani Kitab carried off a woman belonging to the household of a Sharjah merchant; three bedouins of the Awamir tribe took away three camels from Ras al-Khaimah; the Awamir looted the suburbs of Umm al-Qaiwain, and so on. Some of these incidents were probably part of tit-for-tat feuds between particular tribes, while others were settled with the payment of money to the raiders for the return of the stolen property or kidnapped person. The sheikhs were sufficiently worried about the situation to talk about forming an alliance against the inland tribes but, as it happened, their discussions came to nothing.

———

THERE WAS another development of a rather different kind. In the early 1930s the British government sought to build airfields for aircraft flying to and from the Far East. Today, when passenger jets regularly make the journey between Britain and Australia with only one refuelling stop, the tedium of early flights is easily forgotten. Aircraft of the time were slow and had a relatively short range, travelling 300–400 kilometres (200–250 miles) between fuel stops; the journey between London and Darwin took 27 stops and ten days to complete and was expensive – civilian air travel was the preserve of a wealthy elite. But for strategic reasons, the air route was vital.

Originally, flights followed a narrow corridor along the Persian coast, but when Tehran served notice that it wished to divert aircraft across the 4,200-metre (14,000-ft) Bakhtiari range, British officials had second thoughts. The proposed route provided little scope for emergency landing strips and the mountains played havoc with radio, therefore alternative routes along the Arabian side of the Gulf were explored. Places such as Dibba, Khor Fakkan and Muscat were ruled out because of their surrounding mountains, but Kalba was identified as an emergency airfield, and Ras al-Khaimah, Sharjah, Dubai and Sir Bani Yas as locations for both flying boat landings and airfields. There were other considerations, of course.

At first Ras al-Khaimah seemed ideal for the airfield. The sheikhdom had once been united with Sharjah; it was now firmly independent, though the British had been reluctant at first to accept this. Its ruler, Sheikh Sultan bin Salim al-Qasimi, who had succeeded his father in

1919 and been recognized by the British in 1921, was against the idea of an airfield. He was more preoccupied with the tribes of the Ruus al-Jibal, rebuilding his forts and extending his agricultural holdings. It was only after a naval blockade and the seizure of his pearling dhows that he relented and allowed a refuelling barge for flying boats to be anchored in the creek for a year; in the longer term, however, the British had to find a permanent airbase.

All along the coast, the rulers refused to grant landing rights, fearing that aeroplanes might bring more British meddling in their affairs. The ruler of Sharjah, Sheikh Sultan bin Saqr, was amenable to the idea but was challenged by his forceful brother Muhammed. While some British officials sympathized with his dilemma, there were others, such as the Political Resident Sir Hugh Biscoe, who favoured the use of force to impose a solution. As it happened, the outcome was successful, though not exactly in the way envisaged. HMS *Triad* appeared off Sharjah and another ship, HMS *Bideford*, was sent to Ajman and Ras al-Khaimah in order to quell the opposition. Biscoe boarded a ship at Bushire for his voyage down the Gulf but suffered a severe heart attack and died, leaving the Political Agent Harold Dickson to take over negotiations. On 22 July 1932, after three days of discussion with the sheikh, an agreement was reached for the establishment of a landing ground and rest house in Sharjah on payment of 500 rupees per month from the British government. After the final agreement was signed on board HMS *Bideford*, the captain was asked to fire a one-gun salute in honour of the ruler. This the captain declined to do, since regulations forbade a gun salute after sunset, but Dickson was able to persuade him. In the event, the captain fired a live shell that went off with such a loud roar that it almost sank the departing ruler's launch.

As for the project's economic benefits to Sharjah, the monthly payments to the ruler were only a part. The construction, maintenance and manning of the airfield and rest house brought jobs to the town, and a host of trading opportunities opened up: pearl traders, for example, could now send their pearls to Karachi with a courier by air. Postal and wireless services were established. Sharjah was accessible: air travel was price-competitive with shipping, and much faster. Far from being a desert 'backwater', the sheikhdom was connected to the outside world in ways that the others could not match.

The British officials who thought that the air route might 'civilize' the Trucial Coast were to be disappointed, since Arab life went on much

Imperial Airways Handley Page (HP) 42 aircraft, like this example, *Hanno*, were regular visitors to the Sharjah airfield while on their way to and from the Far East.

as before. A report in 1936 of two Awamir raiders being chased into the desert by the sheikh of Hamriyah, caught and dealt with in the traditional way – one surrendered his booty, the other was mortally wounded – led the Resident to reflect that, in spite of the air route, 'the people are still primitive there, and have their own ways, peculiar perhaps in our eyes but satisfactory in theirs, of settling their own affairs.'[8] For the bedouin, the aeroplane was simply another *Nasrani* folly. Why, after all, would a man need to travel by aeroplane when he had a perfectly good camel for the journey?

The flights certainly brought the West closer to the town of Sharjah, but for some traditionalists it was too close for comfort, as the Political Officer Trucial Coast, Martin Buckmaster, reported in the post-war years:

> A party of 38 French, mainly women, whose plane belonging to the Aigle Azur Line was grounded in Sharjah for an engine change. The ladies in the party caused the political officer considerable embarrassment by insisting, despite all his entreaties, on visiting the towns of Sharjah and Dubai in the scantiest of two-piece bathing suits, to the evident delight of the younger members of the two towns and the equally evident disapproval of their elders.[9]

While his fellow rulers could only look on with mixed emotions, perhaps envy and distaste, the airfield greatly enhanced Sheikh Sultan's coffers and status. By November, a British official was writing:

> What with the Royal Air Force and Imperial Airways as frequent visitants and the money coming in on account of the construction of the Rest House, Sharjah is gaining importance in the eyes of her neighbours and also a fame abroad.

Three years later, such was the number of aeroplanes in the sky that a rueful Sheikh Sultan of Ras al-Khaimah wondered if war had broken out anywhere. It was a prescient remark. Aeroplanes would remain a fact of life on the Trucial Coast and, with them, the presence of Westerners. Likewise, for the British, it brought a measure of permanence. In the past the British had tried to stay aloof, leaving the rulers to deal with their own affairs, but now it was a different matter when their own interests were engaged, such as the flights to and from the Far East, which could be disrupted by local wars.

Elsewhere, the regent of Kalba agreed to allow an emergency landing field and flying boat moorings if the British recognized him as an independent ruler, which they did. Under pressure from the British, Sheikh Shakhbut agreed RAF landing grounds in Abu Dhabi and on Sir Bani Yas, and Sheikh Saeed agreed an Imperial Airways flying boat anchorage for Dubai. In 1937 Sheikh Saeed granted an oil concession to Petroleum Development (Trucial Coast) Ltd, but his view that the concession payments were his own personal income did not win him any friends among the merchant community. Money was his Achilles heel, and when it came to an open conflict with his opponents, his income was the target of their campaign.

———

IN DUBAI, the economic woes of the 1930s created a growing class of impoverished and disaffected merchants and businessmen to add to the discontented sheikhly cousins. In 1934 an assassination plot saw the arrival of a British warship and two British warplanes in the sky above Dubai, intended as a sign that the British supported Saeed. Eight hundred loyal bedouin camped on the outskirts also helped to concentrate minds; the British promised guns and support in the event of outright warfare. Sheikh Saeed, who had briefly sought refuge on the

British ship, returned to dry land and immediately called a *majlis* of leading citizens to demand their loyalty, a move that appeared to have the desired effect.

Slavery was another contentious issue. Although it was legal on the Trucial Coast, trading in slaves was prohibited and the British authorities had promised to free any slave who reached the flagpole of the British Agency in Sharjah – a process known as manumission. Slaves escaping from cruel owners, divers running from creditors or slave families fleeing from insecurity: these were the people who most commonly sought release. But cases of cruelty were less common than might be supposed and divers pretending to be runaway slaves were questioned and often refused a manumission certificate; by far the largest numbers were slaves whose owners had fallen on hard times. In one example, a family of six slaves appeared at the Agency in Sharjah. The parents were Africans who had been kidnapped from Mukalla in the Aden Protectorate (today's Yemen) some 35 years before. They had been sold to a Dubai resident, who had used the men as divers until he fell on hard times and made arrangements to sell them. Uncertain about their future, the family fled their owner and sought manumission. Once certificates had been granted, the divers could undertake employment as free men.

Manumission as practised by the British was generally unpopular on the coast, giving rise to much feeling against them, especially in Dubai. In 1937, probably as a result of the economic downturn, the number of manumitted slaves rose to alarming levels, causing great consternation among the town's merchants. This, together with a British proposal to deport two gun runners, created such tension that HMS *Bideford* had to make an appearance. The Political Agent Hugh Weightman visited and refused to back down over the deportations. Eventually, Sheikh Saeed was forced to endorse Weightman's decision; but it was apparent that the ruler was under the sway of some powerful voices on the *majlis*.

In contrast to Sheikh Saeed, his son Rashid was a more dynamic character, always with an eye for the main chance. The first car to arrive in Dubai was a gift to the ruler in 1930 but it was Sheikh Rashid's efforts that created a virtual monopoly of the taxi business in Dubai. When a cousin, Sheikh Maktoum bin Rashid, began running a rival service between Sharjah and Dubai, Sheikh Rashid took a dim view. He gathered 30 armed men who wounded the taxi driver and put some of Maktoum's men in the stocks until midnight, when they were released. In an apparent tit-for-tat, Sheikh Maktoum threatened to stop all cars belonging to the ruler and an ugly situation developed – local opinion was against Sheikh Rashid, it was said. At this point, Sheikh Saeed intervened, ineffectually as it happened, and the situation quickly escalated as the Al bu Falasah united in opposition to the ruler; it required the intervention of the Political Resident to calm the town.

It was a complex situation, for there was more at stake than running a few taxis across town. Once again the real issue was control. Although Sheikh Saeed agreed to abolish the monopolies held by his close family, a Pandora's Box had been opened. It was a time of uncertainty in the Gulf: the reform cry had already been taken up in Kuwait and news of disturbances in Bahrain would not have gone unnoticed in Dubai. Merchants, members of the ruler's extended family and expatriate influences came to bear on the reform movement, whose demands centred on controlling the wealth of sheikhdom, such as it was, through the establishment of a *majlis* to allocate money towards projects in the community, diverting it away from the sheikh's coffers.

In the late 1930s, Dubai was a tinderbox. The ruler and his supporters occupied the Bur Dubai side of the creek and his opponents were on the other side at Deira, all fully armed and spoiling for a fight. On 6 October 1938, the sheikh's brother, Juma bin Maktoum, informed the Political Agent that the situation in Dubai was tense and that

A Dubai street scene, March 1960.

hostilities were likely to break out at any moment. There were reports of firing in the town. A Royal Navy sloop was dispatched to ensure the safety of British subjects and, if necessary, to provide a refuge for them. There were various offers from other rulers to mediate in the dispute.

Although the movement's demands were constructive, they also represented a serious threat to the sheikh's rule. In essence, its members wanted a council on the same lines as one established in Kuwait to take over administrative and executive functions, leaving the sheikh as a figurehead. After much discussion, the council agreed that the ruler's share of the state's revenue was to be fixed at one-eighth. A *majlis* of fifteen members, under the chairmanship of Sheikh Saeed but with the power of veto over his decisions, was formed. It held its first meeting on 22 October, with apparent cooperation between the conflicting parties. The sheikh attended a few meetings and then stayed away, making plain his feelings about the reform movement. In this, he had the tacit support of the British, since the Political Resident considered that the prospect of reform was rather more alarming than a simple change of sheikh.

Ultimately, the Dubai Reform Movement divided opinion. Although dismissed by its opponents as a group of self-seeking notables, others considered the movement as a democratic phenomenon. Its achievements included a municipal council, plans for a welfare system for the elderly, the employment of customs officials by the state rather than the ruler, an education department and the reopening of schools. Ambitions extended to improving the town's appearance and enlarging the port. In fact, the movement probably fell between the two stools, not being wide enough to claim democratic legitimacy but a serious attempt at reform nonetheless. In recent times, it has all too easily been dismissed as 'pork barrel' politics or a simple family squabble.[10]

Matters came to a head when the *majlis* under its leader Hasher bin Rashid restricted the ruler to 10,000 rupees of the state's revenues for his personal use. By this time, Sheikh Saeed was ignoring its decisions and the people of Dubai were becoming disillusioned. On 29 March 1939 Saeed disbanded the *majlis* and took advantage of his son's wedding to Latifa bint Hamdan of Abu Dhabi to settle the argument once and for all. Saeed's loyal bedouin, who were in town for the wedding, attacked and killed a number of prominent Bani Rashid – Hasher bin Rashid, his son and eight others – while the remainder escaped to Sharjah. In the wake of this calamity, the reform movement collapsed.

Among those put to flight was Mani bin Rashid, the Bani Rashid notable who had briefly replaced Sheikh Saeed as ruler in 1929. He too managed to find refuge in Sharjah, where he plotted to overthrow Sheikh Saeed. What followed can only be described as a war of attrition between his supporters and those of Sheikh Saeed, with Mani acting as the figurehead of the Bani Rashid rump. Sheikh Saeed offered to restore the latter's property if the Bani Rashid agreed to reside well away from Dubai – in Abu Dhabi or Ras al-Khaimah for example. But they were unable to find sanctuary in either place, going instead to live with the Bani Kitab southeast of Jebel Hafit. This was acceptable to Saeed, provided that guarantees of Mani's good conduct and control of his weapons were given. This arrangement soon fell through, however, leaving Mani and his party to return to Sharjah town, against the wishes of Saeed, who felt they were too close to Dubai for comfort.

Things had gone too far for Saeed to back down. The whole Mani affair had challenged his authority and any loss of face would have damaged his standing, possibly beyond repair. But what should he do? Saeed was not a belligerent man and, like many of his fellow rulers, he was always receptive to a peaceful solution. In the event, he threatened to attack Sharjah, but delayed his offensive by a week in an attempt to persuade Sheikh Sultan bin Saqr al-Qasimi and Sheikh Mani to agree terms with him. Eventually, both sides stepped back from the brink and the processes of sheikhly mediation took over.

By July 1939 discussions were still revolving around the thorny issue of finding a new home for Sheikh Mani and his followers. The village of Hamasa in the Buraimi Oasis seemed to be an acceptable choice. Mani arranged the removal of his womenfolk and disposal of his property from Sharjah under guarantees of protection from the Al bu Shamis tribe and the sheikh of Abu Dhabi. Sheikh Saeed thoughtfully advanced the sum of 500 rupees to help Mani with his removal expenses. On 10 August the recalcitrant sheikh and his party left Sharjah and, three days later, the last of Mani's possessions were handed over to an Al bu Shamis intermediary.

But thoughts of Sheikh Mani were still preying on Saeed's mind. As his brother, Juma, and son, Rashid, kept reminding him, Mani remained a threat: he was supported by a section of the Bani Kitab and had followers in Dubai. Saeed was left in a state of nervous anxiety, constantly worrying that an attack on Dubai was imminent. In this febrile atmosphere, as rumours of plots flitted along the dark alleyways and through the chatter of the busy *suq*, anything was possible. And when a plot against the ruler was uncovered, the reaction was severe – five conspirators were arrested and had their eyes put out with red-hot irons. 'There is general disgust at this act of savagery, although everything is quiet so far', reported the Political Agent Hugh Weightman.[11]

The British kept their distance. At this time, there was a Native Agent in Sharjah, and a British political officer who stayed on the coast during the winter months. He reported to the Political Agent based in Bahrain, who in turn reported to the Political Resident in Bushire. Weightman would occasionally visit the Trucial States and, on his next trip to Dubai, he found a moment of humour amid the gloom. He was approached by a servant of Sheikh Saeed's wife, the sheikha, and asked to supply her with a little rat poison because, she claimed, rats had been gnawing her vegetables. Weightman politely declined, noting that he did not know what 'rats' the sheikha had in mind for the poison: 'I thought it inadvisable to hasten the workings of Providence in this way', he wryly observed.[12]

6

The Hungry Years: The Trucial Coast in the Second World War, 1939–45

THE TENTACLES OF the Second World War spread far and wide, even to the Trucial Coast. Sharjah airfield became an important stage in the strategic air route as officials, troops and equipment were ferried to and from Britain and the East. The base itself was expanded: an RAF camp was complemented in 1944 by a unit of the United States Army Air Forces (USAAF) that stayed for eighteen months. The location of the Rest House reflected the ruler's concerns about keeping the British at arm's length, and its design echoed the fears of some British officials of bedouin attack. The result was a building on the edge of town that resembled a fort rather than a hotel. In fact, as we shall see, its defences were to be tested by the bedouin later in the war.

Although the conflict did not visit the Trucial Coast directly, and the sound of gunfire was not heard from over the horizon, it nonetheless left its mark on the people. The period is recalled locally as the 'time of hunger' and one year in particular is referred to as *sanat al-ji*, the 'year of hunger', although no one is entirely sure which year that was. Years were named after outstanding events, so there were other memorable years apart from the war years: the 'year of starvation and poverty' when food was so short that children were killed in a stampede to reach dhows that had just docked with sugar supplies; the 'year of fire' in Dubai when townspeople lost everything in a fire that ripped through their houses. The war years were also known as the 'years of cards' for the ration cards that the British authorities issued for sugar, rice and tea.

It is often forgotten that, a month after Britain declared war on Germany on 3 September 1939, Dubai and Sharjah were on the brink of their own war. The tension was almost palpable when Hugh Weightman visited Dubai in October, returning to Sharjah by camel with an escort of four mounted guards. As they rode around the head of Dubai creek, he noticed that one of the camels was carrying enough water to withstand a week's siege, and gave his guards some banter to this effect. Eventually a guard explained: 'Wallah, the sheikh is afraid and we are afraid with his fear.' A veritable 'Maginot Line' had been erected at Deira to stop cars coming from Sharjah, and another tower was about to be built by the creek. Men were out all night in the sand between the towers, keeping watch. That evening, Sheikhs Rashid and Obaid bin Juma were unable to join Weightman at a sunset dinner because they had 'important business' to attend to, namely supervising a stand-to-arms at their respective forts; they trusted no one, not even their retainers.[1]

Added to the mix was the figure of Sheikh Mani, the erstwhile reformer of Dubai. Far from abandoning his ambition to seize power in the sheikhdom, he pressed on with his cause. It was said that Mani was still popular in Dubai, and had re-established alliances with Umm al-Qaiwain, Ajman and the leader of the Bani Kitab. In December, it was reported that he had made a reconnaissance of the town as a preliminary to mounting a coup. Not only was he upbeat, but he claimed that he had friends 'even in Sheikh Saeed's towers'.[2]

Sheikh Mani was not easily deflected, but he found a major obstacle in the figure of John Howes, the political officer. On a visit to Sharjah to distribute cash among his friends, Mani asked Howes for British support for his plans for political reform. But Howes was unimpressed, plainly telling the sheikh that his presence in the sheikhdom was unwelcome. He warned Mani that he was breaking his undertaking to Sheikh Saeed to stay away, and that the sooner he abandoned his intrigues and left Sharjah, the better it would be for everyone. Mani needed no second bidding and departed quickly, having lost the argument but not his ambition. In January 1940, it was reported that he was still planning a coup, and that an attack on Dubai was expected soon.

For Sheikh Saeed, there was another distraction. His brother, Sheikh Juma, suddenly left Dubai for Abu Dhabi, travelling at night by camel. The cause of his leaving was a dispute over the impending marriage of Saeed's daughter to Juma's son, Maktoum. At this point the ruler's eldest son, Rashid, who had a good reputation for retrieving camel thieves and absconders, caught up with Juma and his entourage, bringing them back to Dubai. But the rumours still persisted that Juma wanted to emigrate, possibly to Iraq. Howes suspected that his actual motive was probably a 'haunting fear of assassination, which prompts him to sleep at nights locked up by himself at the top of his new private tower in Shindaghah'.[3]

But this was merely a sideshow when compared to the Sheikh Mani affair, which was more than a simple family squabble. Mani's next move was to leave Sharjah and move towards Khawanij in a preamble to an attack on Dubai. His men carried a large supply of empty gunny bags on their camels, possibly intending to fill them and impress the bedouin with their large quantities of rice, thus winning their support. It was also reported that they had been buying arms from as far afield as Rams.

And yet Sheikh Saeed remained conciliatory towards his opponent, promising him an allowance if he went to live in Bahrain or India – this despite spending up to 2,000 rupees a month on the defence of Dubai. Mani was not easily placated, of course, and he was said to be 'out for vengeance or nothing'.[4] Rumours of his strength grew wilder with each day that passed: first 200 men gathered at Khawanij, then 350, then 500. In fact a better estimate was garnered from the number of goats that were killed for the *Eid al-Fitr* feast; and no doubt Sheikh Saeed was somewhat reassured to hear that they had only slaughtered three.

By now, Sheikh Rashid was acting as regent for his ailing father. He left Deira with approximately 150 men to meet a group of tribesmen led by Rashid bin Mani a few kilometres outside the town. A gun battle ensued, with the latter being forced back to Khawanij with three men wounded, including Rashid bin Mani himself. When the Bani Kitab refused to detach themselves from Mani's cause, there was talk among those in Sheikh Saeed's circle of attacking Mani's supply base, Sharjah. Emotions were running high: on the night of 27 January, trigger-happy guards fired at a couple of innocent fishing boats in Sharjah creek, suspecting an attempt to attack the town.

In the end, it was tribal pressure that put paid to Mani's campaign. Sheikh Shakhbut of Abu Dhabi came down firmly in favour of Sheikh Saeed, causing the Bani Kitab to desert Mani's cause. On 31 January the defeated sheikh arrived at the political officer's house in Sharjah and asked him to settle the dispute. Although Sheikh Saeed refused to negotiate directly with Mani, he again confirmed that he would pay him an allowance to leave the Trucial Coast. Mani kept up his demands until it became clear that he would not succeed, and at last he accepted defeat. With his family he went to Bahrain and Bombay before finally settling in the village of Hira in April 1941, living there in exile until his death in January 1947. People held him in such esteem that the *suqs* in Dubai were closed for three days in mourning.

View across the creek at Sharjah.

With hindsight, although we might view Sheikh Mani's exploits as little more than a skirmish and a war of nerves, his threat to Sheikh Saeed's rule was a real one, and there was always a risk that, in the turmoil of tribal politics, he might gain an irresistible momentum. In the event, it never happened. The danger of war breaking out lay elsewhere, in the strained relations between Sharjah and Dubai. In this instance, even Sheikh Shakhbut was powerless to stop the two rulers from reaching their own fateful conclusion.

Despite a truce, Sheikh Sultan of Sharjah decided to send his men to occupy a sangar on the Dubai side of Khan creek, a provocative act that had predictable consequences. Sheikh Saeed declared war. Sheikh Rashid bin Saeed placed men across the Dubai to Sharjah road some 6.5 kilometres (4 miles) miles from Sharjah, and Sheikh Sultan established quarter-mile posts from the creek towards the airfield. Hostilities broke out and bullets flew, but none with any great accuracy – as was customary – and there were a few men wounded on both sides, with one Sharjah man killed and two Dubai men taken prisoner. Also in the customary manner, the Trucial sheikhs offered their services as mediators. Ammunition was running low in both camps with the bullet belts of the Sharjah men only half full, while in Dubai they were using old nails in gunny bags as cannon balls. In the absence of a ready supply of fresh stock, the shooting came to a halt and, on 9 March, Sheikh Sultan of Ras al-Khaimah duly arranged a three-month truce.

There was still time for a little intrigue. Sheikh Sultan of Sharjah arranged for his secretary to meet Sheikh Saeed on the evening of 22 March. When the secretary arrived, he said he had no important message to deliver to Sheikh Saeed, but wished to collect a tin of nails from a house in Dubai. The sheikh, somewhat suspicious of his intentions, issued a permit allowing him to return to Sharjah with the tin of nails, but then secretly instructed his men to disregard the permit and search the secretary on the outskirts of Deira. When the unfortunate secretary was apprehended and searched, the tin was found to contain a few nails on top of 400 rounds of ammunition. The plot had failed, leaving Sheikh Sultan to consider the whys and wherefores of the situation.

———

ONE MIGHT SUPPOSE that the Trucial sheikhs were so wrapped up in their own affairs that the Second World War passed by unnoticed, but this was not the case. The Political Resident visited all the rulers to remind them of their obligations under the Exclusive Agreements of 1892 to hand over enemy subjects and not to have any dealings with the Axis powers. The events of the war were followed closely in the sheikhly circles. A common question they asked was whether there was any hope of peace, a concern that sprang from the hardships they were experiencing, with high prices and food shortages, and the postponement of oil development caused by the war.

As for ending the war, Sheikh Sultan of Ras al-Khaimah put forward a typically bedouin solution, namely that Great Britain should negotiate a truce with Germany, arm herself rapidly during the period of the truce and then reopen the war with renewed vigour. He also proposed that peace might be negotiated through the mediation of the king of Saudi Arabia or the Turks. Otherwise, some bedouins suggested that the Trucial sheikhs might act as mediators in brokering a peace treaty.

As loyal as the sheikhs appeared to be, the Native Agent remained a key figure in protecting British interests. Between 1936 and 1945, the post was held by Khan Bahadur (formerly Sahib) Sayyid Abdur Razzaq. He was a Kuwaiti who, like his predecessors, combined his business interests with his political role. He has a curious claim to fame. In the 1920s the British gave gramophones as presents to the ruling sheikhs. It is said that Abdur Razzaq was one of the first to import a gramophone for his own use, and to start a business selling them. When others heard of his success, the idea quickly caught on. As more people acquired them, gramophones began appearing in cafés where customers would sip tea, smoke *shisha* and listen to music. Local singers began recording their songs, and those like Ali bin Hazim and his daughter from Dubai became increasingly popular.

But that is another story. It was as Native Agent that Abdur Razzaq's most important work was done, acting as the eyes and ears of the Political Resident and, like his predecessors, running a network of spies. Raymond O'Shea, who was seconded to the RAF airbase at Sharjah during the war, considered Abdur Razzaq's influence so pervasive that no tribal war would break out while he was on the scene because he had spies in 'every town, village and camp'.[5] O'Shea recounted how these spies had alerted the Sharjah airbase to an impending bedouin attack, allowing personnel to make preparations before the fighting broke out. As soon as the shooting started, a powerful aircraft beacon was switched on, causing the bedouin to flee in disarray.

During Britain's darkest hour in June 1940 – France had been invaded the month before – Abdur Razzaq learned that Sheikh Sultan bin Saqr of Sharjah was playing German government radio broadcasts in Arabic so loudly that they could be heard a couple of hundred metres from his palace. Donning a disguise, Abdur Razzaq walked to the palace to see if the rumours were true. On his arrival, he discovered a large crowd gathered round a wireless set to hear the German news. Apparently, a number of people had been talking freely in the town about the 'mighty power of Germany and the collapse of France which would soon be followed by the complete crush of Britain'. Slogans such as 'Long live Hitler!' and 'Right is with Germany!' had been chalked on walls in the town. Abdur Razzaq suspected the main troublemaker to be the sheikh's secretary, Abdullah bin Faris, who although seemingly loyal to the British, was thought to be spreading dissent among the townsfolk 'behind the curtain'.[6]

It was a time of intense German propaganda in the Middle East, with radio broadcasts in Arabic being broadcast seven days a week. When challenged by Hugh Weightman, the sheikh put in a robust defence, enclosing with his letter a document signed by 48 notables supporting Faris's innocence – which Faris had in fact obtained by deception, substituting one document for another when the signatures were taken.

Although Weightman's hands were tied, being unable to force Faris from office, nothing more was heard of the broadcasts, and the ruler put on a show of loyalty to the British government, avoiding all talk of German or Italian progress in the war. It was also reported that Faris was similarly avoiding any mention of the Nazis and was careful to spread only 'good' news about the war.

The Arabian Gulf was strategically important for the Allies as they shipped arms and equipment to the USSR through the northern Gulf ports, and the airfield at Sharjah was an important link in the east–west air route. In this respect, the war did impact upon the people of the Trucial Coast in some unconventional ways. In March 1940, an HP 42 aircraft, *Hannibal*, was flying from Jask to Sharjah when it was lost, possibly ditching in the Gulf of Oman. No wreckage was ever recovered although speculation that the aircraft might have landed in the mountains of the Ruus al-Jibal endured for many years. In 1971 a Royal Geographical Society expedition to the Musandam Peninsula was asked to look for any aircraft debris, such as struts that local people might have retrieved and incorporated into their buildings, but none was found.

In contrast, the war and its aftermath provided enough aircraft wreckage to supply a cottage industry of panel beaters. This prompted a political officer to remark later that 'There is quite a brisk trade springing up on the Trucial Coast of beating out trays from "pranged" aircraft.'[7] In February 1943 an RAF Wellington bomber was forced to turn back due to an oil leak off the coast of Fujairah. It crash-landed near Dhadnah, coming in over the sea, colliding with date palms and coming to rest in a huge cloud of dust, scattering local people in terror. A propellor came off in the process, killing one of the crew. Sheikh Mohammed bin Hamad al-Sharqi of Fujairah placed a guard by the plane and the remaining crew were evacuated by sea three days later, after the deceased member had been buried *in situ*. Since then, the present ruler has erected a memorial there.

On 22 April 1944 two anti-locust Anson aircraft were forced to make emergency landings on Sir Bani Yas, where they were met by local people seeking money and firearms. Despite the wartime deprivations, the people were able to give the crew gifts of flour and peas in return. The crew was airlifted out by an Imperial Airways flying boat to Bahrain, with the abandoned aircraft also being recovered. A few days later, a Flying Fortress crash-landed near Jebel Dhanna on the opposing shore, the crew having parachuted out and landed some

79 kilometres (49 miles) east of the crash site. In July 1945 an American Curtiss Commando aircraft crashed southeast of Dubai with the loss of all three crew members. The wreckage was found by tribesmen of the Bani Yas, but the damage was so bad that nothing was recoverable, apart from the bodies, which were taken to Abadan in Iran for burial.

Otherwise, the Trucial Coast was generally quiet, with 1941 reported as being a year of 'almost perfect peace'.[8] All the same, Abdur Razzaq's clandestine skills were always handy. In February 1942 an Iraqi suspect in a Basra bombing conspiracy, Abdul Karim Mahmud, landed in Dubai. He was kept under surveillance for several weeks, and plans were drawn up to remove him, but this was considered too difficult by conventional means. There was no extradition treaty in force and an informal 'extradition' would break the Arab tradition of hospitality, since Abdul Karim was a guest of the ruler. While Karim became restive and threatened to leave for Qatar or Saudi Arabia, the British authorities hatched a plan.

On 21 May a British vessel arrived off Sharjah and Abdur Razzaq went aboard. He arranged for the ship's launch to lie off a deserted part of the beach between Sharjah and the Hira. Meanwhile, Sheikh Rashid bin Saeed told Abdul Karim that Abdur Razzaq wanted to see him urgently. The Iraqi was dispatched in a taxi with a driver who knew exactly where to take his passenger. Immediately after the taxi had left, Karim's belongings were bundled into a second taxi and sent after

The ruler's palace at Sharjah, 1958.

him. When his taxi arrived at the beach, Karim found Abdur Razzaq waiting for him.

It was a dramatic moment. Abdur Razzaq told Karim that he was being sent back to Iraq. Karim, no doubt shocked by this news, demanded to see his host, the sheikh of Dubai. Abdur Razzaq refused, adding that the affair had nothing to do with the sheikh. At this point, Abdul Karim became abusive but not violent, which in any event would have been futile since Abdur Razzaq was flanked by two men armed with cudgels and a third armed with a rifle. Karim's parting remarks left little to the imagination: 'After four months I shall come to this place when your masters are no longer in existence, and I shall then hang you by the neck with hooks.' Karim was then taken on the launch to the waiting naval ship and duly delivered to the police at Basra.[9] Karim was never able to fulfil his promise, and the affair passed quickly into history.

Above all, the period is remembered as a time of hunger. The Political Resident received regular reports that people on the Trucial Coast were experiencing food shortages. To make things worse, there was a severe drought, as reported in January 1941:

> There has been no rain except for a few drops, since last year, and the situation is serious. In fact cattle and camels are in such an emaciated condition that if rain occurs within the next few weeks, it is more than likely that they will be unable to withstand the consequent cold and exposure and will perish.[10]

A month later still no rain had fallen. No doubt local people followed the custom of gathering branches from the desert trees and burning them in order to encourage the clouds to bring rain but, when it did fall in March, it was too little, too late.

Everywhere along the coast, people suffered. In Ras al-Khaimah, rice and sugar were in such short supply that people boiled and squeezed date sacks in order to extract the last drops of goodness from them; prices rose and many departed, trying to find a better life elsewhere. Mazari traders, for example, left with their families and went to Kenya, where they stayed until they died, their graves a testament to the harsh realities of the hungry years in the Gulf.

And yet, although wartime hardship is embossed on the collective memory, not everyone starved. It is said that the people of the mountains had everything and the coastal people and bedouin had nothing. Certainly, for the mountain tribes, this was relatively true, for they did not experience the peaks of the pearl trade or the troughs of the war. They remained poor, but were unchanged by the war, while the coastal people grew poorer. Wheat was grown in the mountains, but was difficult to store on the coast.

In some parts, the pre-war migration of young men to the oilfields of the northern Gulf had led to date gardens being neglected. One story told, perhaps euphemistically, how the women of a village used to wait for a date to drop into a circle drawn in the sand before eating it. On the coast, the men with boats sailed to Iraq in order to collect supplies of wheat; but generally the situation was dire. All the while, bedouins of the desert would still offer the customary hospitality, serving a date and a coffee cup to any passing traveller even though there was no coffee to pour into the cup. Conversations would usually began with 'what's the news?' followed by 'there is no news' and then an earnest discussion about all news under the sun.

In the 1930, most goods were imported from Iran and India, with small quantities of wheat imported from Australia into Dubai. In 1943 the Government of India announced that it was stopping the export of cereals, leaving the Trucial Coast to look for other sources of supply. The British government arranged to ship cereals from Basra to the lower Gulf and, since Iraqi wheat was more expensive than the earlier Australian imports, effectively subsidized the shipments. For a people largely used to eating rice, it was difficult enough to adapt to the new diet. When white flour began arriving most people did not have the facilities to make bread, and those that did complained that it produced a low-quality loaf. Meanwhile, the ruling families helped out as much as they could; the Qasimi family, for instance, handed out emergency supplies to their people during the hardest times.

As ever in wartime, hoarding and smuggling were a fact of life. On a visit to Ras al-Khaimah in May 1944, the Political Agent found evidence of both activities. Rationed sugar and rice were reaching the Dubai black market and being exported to Qatar and Bahrain – the sheikh of Bahrain was often complaining to the Political Resident about these commodities being smuggled onto his island. At one point, in order to address the problem, the Resident proposed cutting the quota to the Trucial States by 500 tons.

Along the coast, the shortages were impacting on the dwindling pearl trade. The difficulty of baking bread on small, overcrowded sailing vessels meant that many captains were unable to provide cooked meals for their crews. As a result, fewer boats were put out. Trade was also affected by the war: a lack of steamers prevented local traders from exporting goods to India, a problem exacerbated by the seasonal monsoon, which made sailing to Indian ports impossible. The shortages led to rising prices, which no amount of subsidizing could suppress. Muscat prices provide something of a guide: the price of rice rose from around 11 rupees per bag in February 1941 to 31 rupees per bag by March 1943, when imports ceased; wheat rose from about 10 rupees in February 1941 to 45 rupees in November 1943; and ghee rose from just below 4 rupees for 4 kilograms (9 lb) in weight in February 1941 to 31 rupees in August 1944.

Another consequence of the war years was the redeployment of the old pearling fleets. As many of the old diving boats had lain at anchor while the industry contracted, other uses were found for them in fishing or on the Gulf trading routes, taking dates or smuggling surplus war rations to Iran. Some ex-pearlers took to the deep-sea routes, sailing to East Africa in the course of occasionally clandestine trade. Dubai resident Saif Ahmed al-Ghurair recalled that they used to transport dates from Iraq to East Africa and return with textiles, teak and – on one occasion – boxes of ammunition. These were purchased in Mombasa from African soldiers under British command, 40 boxes with about 1,000 rounds in each box. After some reluctance, the crew agreed to handle the illicit cargo and return to Dubai, where the ammunition was sold at a handsome profit.

But it was in the realm of gold smuggling that Dubai came into its own. At one time, virtually all the gold entering India came through Dubai. Local merchants would buy gold on the open market and then sell it to customers who made the arrangements to smuggle it into India. There had been a trade in gold since before the war, through Kuwait and other places, but the hardships of the hungry years forced individuals to seek a living in new and different ways. As they learned the business of smuggling gold, a growing number of Dubai boat owners took up the trade, carrying cheap gold from the port to the Indian coast where they waited offshore for fishing boats to collect their shipments. In time, as the Kuwait trade declined, more smugglers moved to Dubai, together with the carpenters to build the boats – eventually, the smugglers abandoned their old diving boats in favour of faster ones with engines obtained from Pakistan.

Fishermen hauling in a catch. Fishing provided valuable food during hard times, although a shortage of firewood in Abu Dhabi meant people occasionally had to eat their fish raw.

Saif Mohammed al-Qaizi was a dhow builder who, among other things, fixed the engines of the gold-smuggling boats. He described how the smugglers tended to come regularly from Deira to make the secret journey to India. The trade was not illegal in Dubai, but spies in the port might report boats to the Indian authorities, so the smugglers had to be careful. Certain days were chosen to ship the gold into the country, such as festival days when the Indian police and coastguard would be preoccupied with other matters. Upon reaching the coast, the smugglers would transfer the gold from boxes to belts strapped around their waists. If the boat collecting the gold failed to show at the rendezvous, the smugglers would wait a few days before returning to Dubai.

In the post-war years, gold smuggling was to become a staple trade of Dubai to the extent that *nawakhidah* regularly carried consignments of gold hidden in their ordinary cargoes. In 1959 the Indian government was so concerned about the impact of this activity on its economy that it withdrew Indian rupees from the region and issued Gulf rupees instead. Needless to say, the gold smugglers found ways around this, receiving payments in smaller denominations or in kind, using valuables such as watches. As one observer noted in the 1960s, judging by the number of gold watches for sale in Dubai in that decade, the smugglers must have built up a healthy trade. Today, its legacy can be found in the city's famous gold *suq*, among the largest gold markets in the world.

And so, although many people remember the war years as hard times, some good things did emerge from the period. Perhaps its common hardships also brought the rulers closer together. Towards the end of the war, the Political Resident called a meeting of the Trucial sheikhs – the first meeting of its kind since Sheikh Zayed the Great's meeting 40 years before. They came together on 7 March 1945: the rulers and Sheikh Mohammed bin Ali bin Huwaidin of the Bani Kitab met for lunch with Charles Prior, the Resident, at Dhaid, about 65 kilometres (40 miles) inland from Dubai. The only notable absentee was Sheikh Shakhbut of Abu Dhabi, who had not received sufficient notice of the meeting. Although Prior had a reputation for explosive outbursts and, in the customary manner, the sheikhs came 'armed to the teeth', the meeting was cordial enough. Indeed, the most warlike of them all, Sheikh Mohammed, arrived with his followers unarmed out of courtesy to Prior.

It was a milestone in Gulf affairs to get the tribal leaders together in this way, albeit without the pomp and circumstance of Curzon's visit in 1903. It created a precedent, leading to regular meetings that prefaced the formation of the Trucial States Council in the 1950s. These were the first tentative steps towards creating a modern state, although the sight of Arab chieftains squatting around a traditional feast spread on a carpet on the ground might have conveyed a less solemn intent. The meeting also confirmed that relations between British officials and the Trucial sheikhs had survived, and been strengthened by, a difficult period in the area's history. A suspicion of the British that once prevailed among local people was beginning to dissolve.

Indeed, the Allied victory in Europe in May was greeted with a spontaneity and enthusiasm that took even British officials by surprise. As soon as Germany's unconditional surrender was officially announced, all public buildings and private houses in Sharjah were decorated, even down to the humblest *'arish*. The sheikhs of Dubai and Ajman joined in the festivities, firing their ancient cannons. There followed three days of celebrations as the streets were thronged with large crowds and many dancing parties, all performing the only Arab dance they knew – a war dance.

The three sheikhs sent congratulatory messages to the Political Agent, and a deputation of merchants visited the political officer,

Raymond Murphy, and offered similar felicitations. On 11 May a crowd of about 2,000 people gathered outside the agency office in Sharjah and dancing continued until sunset. On 12 May Murphy threw an official dinner party for the sheikhs of Dubai, Sharjah, Ras al-Khaimah, Umm al-Qaiwain and Ajman, the regent of Kalba, their relatives and followers, local notables and fourteen British and American officers from the RAF camp in Sharjah – in total, about 250 people attended. The guests assembled on the inner veranda of the Agency and, after coffee had been served, Murphy gave a short speech which was translated into Arabic. Dinner was served in the agency compound. The feast was, according to British sources, the biggest of its kind ever to have been given on the Trucial Coast and much appreciated by the rulers.

And so the war ended on a high – but the festivities belied the true state of the Trucial Coast, which would take years to recover. Despite all the feasting and celebrations, and the end of rationing, the wartime years would not be easily forgotten.

7

Sweet Crude: Abu Dhabi and the Discovery of Oil, 1909–71

LITTLE DID THE feasting sheikhs know, but the key to the region's future prosperity lay under their feet. Not directly of course, since the oilfields waiting to be discovered were mainly beneath the seabed and deserts of Abu Dhabi, yet near enough. There was no indication of the prosperity to come: the town of Abu Dhabi was a straggling line of *'arish*, a few stone buildings and palm trees backing on to a flat, barren island, all dominated by the sheikh's palace, Qasr al-Hosn. Not much had changed since the early 1900s, when it was a modest settlement with a population of some 5,000 souls, occasionally swelled by the tribesmen who came in from the Liwa villages to join the pearling fleet.

By then the Bani Yas had become the most formidable tribal group in the region, due in no small part to the achievements of Sheikh Zayed the Great. But his death in 1909 threatened to awaken old ghosts as the succession was thrown into confusion. Zayed's eldest son and heir apparent, Khalifa, refused to succeed his father, probably because he wanted to avoid the grisly fate of other Al Nahyan rulers in the past. For Khalifa, this may have been a wise decision but it left Zayed's second son, the weak and ailing Tahnoun, to take up the reins. When Tahnoun died in 1912 and Khalifa again declined to rule, the succession fell to another of Zayed's sons by a different mother, Sheikh Hamdan bin Zayed al-Nahyan.

Sheikh Hamdan's rule began well enough. He enjoyed good tribal connections, being linked to the Al Bu Falasah and Sudan sections of the Bani Yas, and the Dhawahir, by marriage. In the arena of tribal politics, he proved to be a firm ruler, settling feuds in the Buraimi villages and negotiating a peace between the tribes and the sultan of Muscat and Oman. In 1913, when the emir of the Nejd, Ibn Saud, took the province of Al Hasa from the Turks, Hamdan tried to obtain arms and ammunition in order to repel a Wahhabi advance into his territory –

in the event, it never happened. He also joined an alliance with the ruler of Umm al-Qaiwain against Sharjah but stopped short of taking military action, thus avoiding British intervention. That happened when Hamdan supported Ibn Saud's dissident cousins by allowing them to reside in Abu Dhabi. In 1915 the British authorities regarded his action as a clear breach of their treaties with the Gulf sheikhs and Ibn Saud, and sent a warship to Abu Dhabi in order to enforce the cousins' departure. Any enmity between the two rulers appears to have been short-lived: by 1920 Sheikh Hamdan was exchanging presents with Ibn Saud and the emir of Al Hasa, Abdullah bin Jiluwi, sending camels and horses and receiving gifts to the value of about 24,000 rupees in return.

In another time, Hamdan might have reigned for a good many years, but the Al Nahyan were about to embark on another upheaval. Against the backdrop of a declining economy, Hamdan struggled to stay in favour with his relatives. He could no longer afford to assist them financially and was forced to raise taxes, alienating local merchants in the process. A number of disaffected notables left Abu Dhabi, forcing Hamdan to visit them in Dubai in order to persuade them to return, promising to waive any uncollected taxes. But it was too late to retrieve the situation, and Hamdan paid the ultimate price. In August 1922 Hamdan was assassinated and his brother Sultan succeeded to the sheikhdom. Hamdan's family fled to Dubai, where seventeen years later his daughter Latifa would become the wife of the ruler's eldest son, Sheikh Rashid bin Saeed.

For the moment, Sultan's accession was welcomed by the Al Nahyan and the Bani Yas at large. Having declared himself willing to abide by all the treaties and agreements in force with the British government, Sultan's rule seemed to be assured. But tribal disturbances in the Dhafrah and Al Ain/Buraimi area, together with the appearance of Wahhabi tax collectors in the area, brought new challenges. And, like Hamdan before him, Sultan's rule suffered from a shortfall of revenue, leaving nothing for family members, who turned against him. On 4 August 1926 Sheikh Sultan invited his half brother Sheikh Saqr to supper. On arrival at Sultan's house, Saqr immediately shot Sultan dead and wounded one of his sons, Khalid.

As the new ruler, Saqr inherited a legacy of dread and mistrust. The British Resident reported that he had never seen a man with fear so written on his face and gave him a year at most to live. Indeed, Saqr's hold on power remained precarious. The past was not forgotten, especially since he had been involved in the assassinations of both Hamdan and Sultan. His links with the Al Bu Falasah of Dubai were a liability, his attempt to enlist the support of the Bani Yas's traditional enemy, the Wahhabis, lost him support and a dispute with the Manasir tribe further weakened him. A failed attempt to capture two of Sultan's sons on Dalma Island led to stern rebuke from the Political Resident for transporting troops by sea. In the midst of these adversities, it emerged that Saqr was planning to murder the esteemed Sheikh Khalifa bin Zayed and two other family members. Acting on the premise that it was preferable to kill than be killed, Khalifa hatched a counter plot with the Manasir sheikhs. On 1 January 1928 one of Khalifa's servants attacked Saqr but did not kill him; however, he was soon caught by a band of Manasir tribesmen and finished off.

Khalifa, with his Manasir supporters, now held the upper hand. Saqr's family was expelled and went to live in Dubai, where they would be a source of discontent for many years to come – the assassination of a sheikh could cast a long shadow, even in the twentieth century. Since Khalifa was offered and again declined the invitation to succeed, the elders chose the eldest of Sheikh Sultan's four sons, the 25-year-old Shakhbut, to succeed. As well as having the advantage of his father's well-connected bloodline, Shakhbut had the support of the British authorities, although they remained pessimistic about his chances of survival. However, Shakhbut's mother, the formidable Sheikha Salama, drew an oath from her sons not to kill each other, a simple vow that

The ruler of Abu Dhabi, Sheikh Saqr bin Zayed (bearded with bowed head and sword in the back row), 1927.

served the sheikhdom well. Generally, Shakhbut appeared to be a popular ruler, and the Native Agent visiting Abu Dhabi four months after Saqr's demise noted that the people 'liked' and 'praised' him.[1]

But by the 1930s Abu Dhabi was in trouble. The sight of the fleet returning from the pearl banks, drums beating and oarsmen chanting, was fading into memory. The ruler had to rely more on the taxes on date plantations and bedouin cattle collected by his agents, and revenue from fishing permits, than anything from the pearl trade. The pearl industry was doomed and there was no immediate prospect of any new sources of income to replace it. Sheikh Shakhbut's tentative rule needed time to establish itself and there was certainly plenty of that but the town was poor and tired and needed a miracle to survive. Then, against all odds, a miracle seemed to happen.

———

THERE WERE NO OBVIOUS clues to Abu Dhabi's oil-rich future. Unlike parts of Iraq, where oil seepages abound, there were no surface indications of oil in the sand-covered sheikhdom. In the Arabian Gulf, there were occasional signs, such as bitumen discharges in the sea or washed up on the shore. But a 1908 report by geologist Guy Pilgrim, Deputy Superintendent of the Geological Survey of India, had put a dampener on any serious exploration. He concluded that northern Persia was a more favourable petroleum prospect than southern Persia or the Arabian Gulf.

The Trucial sheikhs were already tied into the British commercial network through the Exclusive Agreements of 1892, which were reinforced by more specific accords. In 1906 the appearance of a Greek merchant seeking access to the pearling beds prompted Abd al-Latif, the Native Agent, to warn the sheikhs not to make agreements without British consent. This was followed in 1911 by local undertakings not to grant pearl and sponge fishing rights to foreigners, and similar undertakings given in 1922 in respect of oil concessions. Here, the intention was to exclude non-British firms from oil exploration in the Gulf:

> On general political grounds it appears very desirable that all oil concessions in these territories should be in the hands of a single British company and the activity shown by foreign oil companies in obtaining a foothold in undeveloped lands seems to indicate that some action should be taken in this direction in the near future.[2]

But the oil companies were not seriously interested in the area until 1932, when Standard Oil of California (SoCal) struck oil on the island of Bahrain. SoCal went on to gain a concession for the Eastern Province (Al Hasa) of Saudi Arabia a year later. In theory, the agreements struck with the Trucial sheikhs should have allowed the British to exclude SoCal and other non-British firms with ease; in practice, this was difficult. The Americans had already gained footholds in Iraq and Bahrain against British opposition, demonstrating that some accommodation was inevitable. The British government had a 51 per cent stake in the Anglo-Persian Oil Company, but the company was legally bound to act with its international partners in the Iraq Petroleum Company (IPC): these were American, Anglo-Dutch and French oil majors and a private shareholder, Calouste Gulbenkian.[3] It was more a question of damage limitation than complete exclusion; and the fact that IPC had its head office in London gave British officials a measure of reassurance.

The Trucial Coast was a petroleum backwater at this time. For oil company executives in London, Paris or New York, it might as well have been on the moon, so remote and strange did it seem. Conversely, among the rulers, there were suspicions that IPC was only interested in the region in order to keep competitors out. Indeed, IPC's haste to sign up the rulers did betray a certain fear that SoCal would steal a march on them as they had done elsewhere. Acting through its associate company, Petroleum Concessions Ltd (PCL), IPC sent representatives to negotiate with the sheikhs and geologists to carry out surveys, subject to a proviso that only British personnel would be used.

Sheikh Shakhbut was an intelligent and conservative man, a keen proponent of oil exploration who told the oilmen that oil had been seen in the sea and bitumen washed up on the coast; but his most pressing problem was a shortage of drinking water. In Abu Dhabi town, wells were being dug about 1 kilometre (less than a mile) inland as shallow pits, which had to be scooped out again each day because their sides kept falling in. The sheikh wanted a good water supply for his people and had heard about the exploits of one Major Frank Holmes, a New Zealand mining engineer who had made a name for himself by drilling water wells on the island of Bahrain. When the Political Agent suggested that the sheikhdom might benefit from a water survey, Shakhbut readily agreed.

The Anglo-Persian geologist Peter Cox visited Abu Dhabi in 1934, but owing to the difficult terrain he was unable to carry out a full survey,

An aerial photograph of Qasr al-Hosn – 'White Fort' – in 1959. The darker walls of the original fort can be seen inside the white walls of the later construction.

returning a year later to accomplish the task. This time Cox was surprised to find Shakhbut lukewarm towards the prospect of a water survey – he was now preoccupied with oil. The rains had provided a temporary solution to the water problem, and the cost of drilling a water well (30,000 rupees, about £135,000 today) was more than he was prepared to pay – the sheikh had always taken a close interest in preserving his meagre finances. Also, he had heard about oil negotiations which had recently concluded in Qatar, and knew how much his fellow rulers had received for their oil rights.

Elsewhere, Sheikh Sultan bin Salim of Ras al-Khaimah caused some excitement by asking the French to provide geologists to explore for oil. The Political Resident, Trenchard Fowle, discovered that the sheikh had approached the commander of a French naval ship, *Bougainville*, on its visit to the coast. Although it appeared that the French had not acceded to his request, Anglo-Iranian (as Anglo-Persian was now known) was quick to respond. Two geologists and a guide, 'Haji' Williamson, were sent to the sheikhdom in order to sign a two-year option to explore for oil. At this stage, IPC was content for Anglo-Iranian to make the first moves and transfer the concessions to PCL at a later date.

Meanwhile, progress was being made in Abu Dhabi. On 5 January 1936, Haji Williamson obtained a two-year option from Sheikh

Shakhbut on a down payment of 7,000 rupees plus 3,000 rupees a month (£30,500 and £13,000 today). On 30 September, another IPC associate company – Petroleum Development (Trucial Coast) Ltd (PDTC) – was incorporated to operate oil concessions in the area.

Now, for the first time, *Nasrani*s were able to travel about the sheikhdoms with a certain degree of freedom. Quite what the local people made of them can only be surmised; generally the geologists were well received, but for a people who had had seen few Westerners apart from the occasional British representative, these strange characters must have been a great curiosity. For the oil company, there was Haji Williamson, an Englishman 'gone native', who had variously been (among other things) a British spy, gun runner and dhow owner, and now a negotiator and guide for the oil company; Frank Holmes, who was now employed by PCL to negotiate agreements with the Trucial sheikhs; and the aloof Stephen Longrigg, a leading negotiator for the oil company.

Things did not go well. There is nothing like the scent of oil to bring out the proverbial knives, and in May 1937 Haji Williamson fell victim to local intrigue and was banned from the Trucial Coast. Meanwhile Holmes managed to secure an oil concession for Dubai before having to retire through ill-health two months later. With the departure of PCL's two chief negotiators, it fell to Longrigg to continue talks with the remaining Trucial rulers. He was assisted by the unassuming but quietly effective Basil Lermitte, also an IPC man, whose travels often raised eyebrows up and down the coast. Charles Pelly, the Political Officer Trucial Coast (1941–2), noted Lermitte's 'furtive peregrinations' and 'sudden and obscure' movements, together with a 'natural secretiveness' which concealed 'nothing in particular'.[4] Sheikh Saeed of Dubai nicknamed his son Rashid 'Lermitte' because he never told his father what he was up to. In fact, Basil Lermitte was highly respected on the Trucial Coast, being a fluent speaker of Arabic and often donning Arab robes for his visits to the rulers.

And then there were the geologists, Jock Williamson and David Glynn-Jones, who landed at Dubai in November 1936. Sheikh Saeed took them into the desert to enjoy some hunting before they went on to Abu Dhabi. Although parts of the sheikhdom were difficult to access, they did manage to visit jebels Hafit and Dhanna, and Sir Bani Yas, which informed them about the structure, type and age of the rocks they might expect to find under the vast and impenetrable sands.

In November 1938 they travelled to Buraimi to meet up with two colleagues who had travelled from the Omani coast. By now, the option to explore for oil in Abu Dhabi had expired, and their surveys were hampered by logistical problems, local politics and trigger-happy tribesmen on the Omani side. After his survey had finished, Williamson wrote a geological report on the Buraimi area in which he advised against any further geological work on account of a lack of oil and gas indications in the area.

To imagine the conditions they faced, we should picture a land devoid of the modern conveniences and infrastructure: no roads, no telephones, no satellite navigation. For local people, the most alarming aspect of the geologists' appearance on the scene was probably the sight of their vehicles since, apart from a few dilapidated examples in the towns of the coast, cars rarely ventured inland. People were familiar with aeroplanes from a distance but the sight of an approaching motor vehicle could instil considerable fear. Indeed, for those brave enough to touch a vehicle, the driver often had a particular treat, pressing the horn and causing them to fall over each other as they tried to run away.

All this paled when it came to signing the final concession agreements with the Trucial rulers. As negotiations dragged on up and down the coast, the British authorities took a hard line, insisting that they would not allow the sheikhs to enter into agreements with any other company apart from PCL. In September 1937 the sheikh of Sharjah signed up, although this agreement was not ratified for another eight months and access to the Bani Kitab territory remained out of bounds. The regent of Kalba followed in December 1938 but the sheikh of Abu Dhabi was proving intractable. Shakhbut was demanding the same terms as those granted to the sheikh of Kuwait, which the oil company was not prepared to meet.

This posed a dilemma for those officials who were anxious to restrict the oil business in the lower Gulf to British-led firms such as PCL. The Political Agent had already reminded Sheikh Shakhbut of his obligation to deal only with PCL but the days of sending warships to coerce a recalcitrant ruler were past; the most the British authorities might do was withdraw travel documents (for they controlled the issue of visas in the Gulf), impose fines and threaten what was left of the pearling fleet. It therefore came as a great surprise when the sheikh suddenly backed down and granted a 75-year concession on the oil company's terms. By a concession agreement signed on 11 January 1939, he would receive a down payment of 300,000 rupees (£1.2 million today) and annual payments of 100,000 rupees (£400,000), increasing by 25 per cent every four years. Upon the discovery of oil, a royalty of 3 rupees (£12) per ton would replace the annual payments. These terms reflected those agreed by other Gulf rulers, and took into account the size of Shakhbut's sheikhdom.

What persuaded him to change his mind? It is unlikely that we will ever know for certain, but no doubt his brothers were involved in private discussions with him, as was his uncle, Khalifa, from whom he always took advice; and perhaps he had genuinely believed he could get better terms from the oil company and now realized he would not. Whatever the explanation, there must have been great relief among those who sat and waited for news in the wintry gloom of London. Khalifa for his part was to remain on the scene for a few more years to come, expiring in October 1945 at the reputed age of 108. In due course Khalifa's son Mohammed would take over the role of adviser and confidant to Shakhbut. There were other advisers, such as Mohammed's father-in-law and the leading merchant Ahmed bin Khalaf Al-Otaiba, whose grandson, Mana bin Saeed al-Oteiba, would become Abu Dhabi's first oil minister and the UAE's as well.

All this lay in the distant future, of course; back in 1939 the oil company was yet to find oil. The spring and summer months were spent drawing up plans for the coming cool season but, as luck would have

Geologists meet a hunting party and falconer in the desert, 1967.

it, the advent of the Second World War put everything on hold. And so, while war raged in Europe and the Far East, life on the Trucial Coast went on. In 1942 Sheikh Shakhbut was able to put his concession payments to good use by extending Qasr al-Hosn, building new walls around the original fort and adding two residential wings. In the future, visitors would be impressed by the grand facade but not so much by its simple interior. Lermitte went quietly about his duties, shuttling to and fro, paying the sheikhs the money they were owed under their concession agreements. Certainly the hardships of wartime made the payments – and any increase – all the more welcome. In January 1943 Lermitte sailed from Bahrain to Abu Dhabi on a dhow with 25 boxes of silver rupees, Sheikh Shakhbut's annual payment. But the astute ruler had read the wording of the 1939 agreement, which entitled him to a 25 per cent uplift. When Lermitte arrived, he was astonished to find the sheikh refusing to accept the money offered and demanding more. In the event, Shakhbut won the argument and Lermitte had to return at a later date with the same amount, plus 25 per cent more.

It would still take a few years to sign up all the sheikhs: Ras al-Khaimah and Umm al-Qaiwain agreed full concessions in 1945, Ajman in 1951 and Fujairah in 1953. Even then, oil exploration was slow to restart after the war. The Trucial Coast did not commend itself to survey work. The heat was unbearable in the summer months, and basic facilities were still non-existent. Vast stretches of wind-blown sand and mudflats restricted the geologists' range of work to the more accessible areas, which mostly comprised scrub land, shores and mountain ranges; otherwise the company was forced to rely largely on geophysical surveys to gain a detailed picture of the underlying stratigraphy. At one point, when the huge sand dunes of the desert proved too difficult, helicopters were used. By the 1950s, however, gravity surveys of Abu Dhabi were being carried out with improved vehicles, such as Dodge Power Wagons equipped with low-profile balloon tyres.

There were other problems besides. Although the oil company paid for armed escorts, the interior could still be a dangerous place for its geologists as tribal conflicts endured. In 1945 war broke out between Abu Dhabi and Dubai over Khor Ghanadha, an inlet that Sheikh Saeed claimed marked the boundary between the two sheikhdoms. Once his son, Rashid, had landed there with 300 men, he was in breach of the terms of the Maritime Truce for transporting troops by sea, for which the British authorities imposed a fine of 200,000 rupees. This desultory war dragged on until 1948, engaging the tribes on both sides: the Awamir and Manasir siding with their traditional ally, Abu Dhabi, and the Bani Kitab with Dubai.

The real issue was oil, or at least the money that oil might bring. There were no formal boundaries until the oil men arrived; the presence of survey parties seemed to bring the whole territorial issue to life. On one occasion, members of a PDTC survey party visiting Jebel Ali prior to drilling were caught in a stand-off between opposing tribesmen across a rocky foreshore, each group claiming the area as their own. A parley ensued; the oilmen were sent away and returned a week later to find that the tribesmen had been mollified. Eventually, after arbitration, the frontier line was drawn from the coast west of Jebal Ali to a point some 48 kilometres (30 miles) inland; but Sheikh Shakhbut remained unhappy about the outcome.

There was also a political aspect to it all. The smaller sheikhdoms were of little petroleum interest – there was scant prospect of finding large quantities of oil in them. Yet failing to sign the rulers would have weakened Britain's predominance in the region and made it susceptible to other foreign, especially American, interference. In this way, those sheikhs with concession agreements acquired a degree of legitimacy. All manner of sheikhs had claimed jurisdiction over various parts of the Trucial Coast, together with the right to negotiate directly with the oil company, but now, with oil concession agreements in hand, the rulers were exclusively empowered.

But even when his position was formally recognized, a ruler's hold over his own people could be uncertain. As we have seen, the Bani Kitab refused access to the geologists even after their supposed overlord, the sheikh of Sharjah, had signed an oil concession. In 1947 the sheikh of Jazirah al-Hamra was negotiating with Sheikh Sultan of Ras al-Khaimah for a share of any income from oil found in 'his' territory. Certain tribes such as the Shihuh and Khawatir opposed the oil company's presence in parts of Ras al-Khaimah, claiming the territory as their own. In May 1949 Said bin Badi, the amir of Shimal, a date palm district of Ras al-Khaimah, sent a warning to the new ruler of Ras al-Khaimah, Sheikh Saqr bin Mohammed, informing him that on no account was he to allow oil company surveyors into 'his' area. When Said rallied to support the defence of a tower in Rams against Saqr's son and lost, Saqr had him and his cousins arrested and incarcerated. He then attempted to put out Said's eyes with a red-hot iron nail, leaving him with barely the sight of one eye. Said was a member of the Bidah tribe, which was so outraged that, with the Shihuh, they rose up against the ruler. The dispute was eventually settled on payment of 800 rupees and five *jilla* of dates per annum to the injured sheikh as compensation.

By the end of 1952 there were seven officially recognized sheikh-doms: Abu Dhabi, Ajman, Dubai, Ras al-Khaimah, Sharjah and Umm al-Qaiwain, with Fujairah being recognized as the seventh in March of that year. However, such were tribal memories that when PDTC liaison officer Ronald Codrai visited the sheikh of Fujairah some 25 years after his fort had been pummelled by a British gunboat, the sheikh demanded to know why Codrai had shelled his fort 'yesterday'. This tendency to truncate time was particularly noticeable when it came to settling the boundaries between the seven sheikhdoms and with the sultanate of Oman. It fell to Julian Walker, Assistant Political Agent, to carry out the painstaking work of drawing boundaries over a period of five years, interviewing local inhabitants, surveying the land and examining old documents, always alert to the possibility that an event described as 'recent' might have happened many decades before. It was as if time and place were all jumbled up and needed to be unravelled, like a tangled ball of string.

But the first effects of the Arabian oil boom were being felt long before the borders were settled. As oil had brought new wealth to Saudi Arabia, so there was a growing demand for slaves. In Oman, Buraimi was an important market for slaves brought from East Africa, Iran or the Coast, and slave traders were still based in the village of Hamasa well into the 1950s. Here slaves were purchased and taken to Dammam in the Al Hasa province of Saudi Arabia. With a rising demand for slaves came reports of women and children being abducted for the trade. As local people observed, however, this was not always such a bad fate. Slaves were employed as domestic servants, guards or work-ers, and the owner was required to look after them, even arranging their marriages. Many slaves were well treated and lived a better life than free men; indeed, some rose to positions of prominence, like Barut who was appointed acting regent of Kalba in 1937.

More apparent was the number of young men leaving their homes to seek work in the oilfields of Bahrain (oil discovered in 1932), Kuwait (1938), Al Hasa (1938) and Qatar (1940), thus abandoning traditional occupations, returning with money for their families and with experi-ence of life in an oil-based economy. In the early days, they went simply to earn enough money to get married, but then it would stretch to two or three spells. They brought back a host of items: diesel pumps for wells and engines for dhows, cement for local construction and nylon nets for fishing, for example. The oil sheikhs were happy to offer employment to poor Omanis as well but the Trucial sheikhs, desperate to raise revenue in any form, were issuing travel documents to anyone who wished to go to the oilfields, irrespective of where they came from, bringing an influx of workers from India and Pakistan. In one year, the number of visas issued in Ajman outnumbered the local population three-to-one. To avoid this situation, the Political Agency in Sharjah started issuing visas in person – by the early 1950s, these numbered at least 27,000 per year.

There was some work to be found locally on the few drilling rigs that were set up sequentially on the Trucial Coast. PDTC spudded in its first wildcat well at Ras Sadr in February 1950, but the signs were not encouraging. A political officer summed it up thus: '[A depth of] 7,500 feet has now been reached and the driller still confidently smokes.'5 The well was abandoned at 3,960 metres (13,000 ft) and cost the company £1 million (£25 million today). The next well at Jebel Ali also proved dry. Among the problems faced by the oil company were the fierce climate, the remoteness of the drilling sites and the difficulty in finding a good supply of labour. A local diet of fish and rice gave the local workmen little stamina and those workers who were former slaves found working on a rig far more strenuous than their former lifestyles.

The problem of boundaries erupted over the villages of the Al Ain/Buraimi Oasis and parts of Abu Dhabi. This so-called Buraimi dispute, which is considered in more detail in Chapter Eight, forced PDTC to abandon the western desert and drill its next well, Murban No. 1, several kilometres from the preferred location. The company set up a base camp at Tarif, some 113 kilometres (70 miles) southwest of Abu Dhabi town, and laid out a landing strip on a nearby stretch of *sabkha*, enabling aircraft to land. In the summer of 1954, the Murban well reached a depth of 3,837 metres (12,588 ft) but drilling ceased in tragic circumstances when a young Shell engineer and an assistant were killed by poisonous fumes. The well was apparently a dry hole, although later investigations revealed traces of oil. The company returned to western Abu Dhabi, where it had identified two more seismic structures, Gezira and Shuweihat.

Oil operations at Shuweihat in 1956.

A series of dry holes followed. Gezira was abandoned at a depth of 3,810 metres (12,500 ft) and Shuweihat at a depth of 3,767 metres (12,360 ft), both being abandoned as dry holes. The next well was at the other end of the territory, at Juweisa in the sheikhdom of Sharjah. Despite a huge logistical effort in transporting drilling equipment and material across a barren terrain, this well was also abandoned, at a depth of 3,936 metres (12,915 ft). Thus at the start of 1958 oilmen were having serious doubts about whether oil would ever be found beneath the sand and rocks of the Trucial Coast.

FOR MANY YEARS, there had always been a nagging suspicion that there was oil under the Arabian Gulf; perhaps Sheikh Shakhbut's reports of oil off the coast and islands of his sheikhdom were right after all. But offshore oil exploration was in its infancy and it was only recently that the Americans drillers had started drilling offshore on platforms in the Gulf of Mexico. These developments brought the whole issue of ownership of undersea resources into play, and a new concept in international law, the 'Continental Shelf', emerged in the late 1940s. Geologists used this term to denote an extension of the continental crust where the sea was relatively shallow, and where contemporary drilling techniques could be used. The Arabian Gulf appeared ideally suited to offshore drilling, being shallow and relatively benign; and it was likely that the oil-bearing rock formations of the mainland extended under the sea.

On 10 June 1949 Sheikh Shakhbut proclaimed jurisdiction over his seabed and eighteen months later granted an offshore concession to Superior Oil of California. PDTC, which was operating the 1939 onshore concession, claimed that they held the seabed rights and objected. With both sides refusing to back down, the matter went to arbitration. The sheikh travelled with his brother Zayed to Paris for the arbitration hearing in August 1951, when the tribunal decided in his favour.

Shakhbut was vindicated but any satisfaction he might have felt was short-lived. In May 1952 Superior Oil withdrew from the Gulf, citing 'financial, political and economic grounds' and leaving the concession open to suitable bidders.[6] Anglo-Iranian (soon to become British Petroleum), which had been watching from the wings, instructed their subsidiary, the D'Arcy Exploration Company, to apply for the concession. This was granted on 9 March 1953 on a down payment of 1.5 million rupees (about £2.7 million today) and an annual payment of 60,000 (£109,000). The 65-year offshore concession covered 30,370 square kilometres (11,726 sq miles) of Abu Dhabi's continental shelf and required the company to undertake a certain amount of exploration work before the end of March 1954. The starting point was a marine geological and hydrographic (mapping) survey of the seabed, followed by a geophysical/seismic survey. Drilling was to commence within five years. The company gave undertakings to the ruler to take precautions to protect navigation, pearling and fishing.

The first undersea geological survey was carried out by Jacques Cousteau and his crew on the research vessel *Calypso*. Divers managed to obtain 150 rock samples from the 400 stations where observations were made. The samples were examined on board by one of the geologists under a microscope then catalogued and bagged up for further examination in BP's laboratories in London. Palaeontologists could determine the age of the rocks from the fossils they obtained, and that information helped geologists to map a structure beneath the seabed.

On 18 May 1954 BP joined forces with Compagnie Française des Pétroles (CFP, later known as Total) to form an operating company, Abu Dhabi Marine Areas Ltd (ADMA), with CFP taking a one-third share in the company. The new company commissioned a geophysical/ seismic survey by Geomarine Survey International with their seismic ship, the MV *Sonic*, which was conducted between December and April the following year. In early 1956 the *Astrid Sven* was dispatched to the Gulf. This was an ageing 1,200-ton freighter that the Nazis had used during the war to refuel their U-boats in the Indian Ocean. The vessel was refitted with living quarters for 30 personnel and was equipped to carry out further survey work.

On the basis of these surveys, a decision was taken to drill the first exploratory well on an old pearl bank known as Umm Shaif. Plans were drawn up to establish a base at Das Island and to develop the use of helicopters for supply and transport purposes. Soon the island, once a barren, waterless, lonely place inhabited only by seabirds, scorpions and turtles, would become a thriving outpost of the oil industry. There were many other issues to consider, however, such as a lack of experienced local labour, infrastructure and data about sea conditions in the Arabian Gulf.

For the drilling platform, the company opted for a platform with jack-up legs and the drilling rig, the ADMA *Enterprise*, was specially built in Hamburg. In addition to the rig, the platform had assorted equipment and machinery, living accommodation for 50 men, an electricity plant, a distillation plant capable of producing nearly 800 imperial gallons of

Sheikhs Shakhbut (centre front) and Zayed (second row left) with family members and advisers at an arbitration meeting in Paris, 1951.

fresh water every hour from the sea, and a helicopter landing pad. It was towed to the Gulf, where it was berthed in a man-made harbour at the southern end of Das island. Drilling began in January 1958: the barge was moved some 32 kilometres (20 miles) to the location for ADMA Well No. l, the four legs, 50.3 metres (165 ft) long, were lowered onto the seabed, and the working deck was jacked up on these legs until it was clear of the sea. The Arabian Gulf suddenly had a new island.

The first oil was struck ten weeks later at a depth of about 2,668 metres (8,755 ft) in the Lower Cretaceous Thamama limestones. Described as a 'nice sweet crude', the oil quality of the Umm Shaif field was good (36° API) but – ironically – news of the discovery was greeted with 'general gloom' in BP's London headquarters on account of the global surplus of oil.[7] The oilfield, a super-giant about 300 square kilometres (116 sq miles) in size, came on stream in 1962. A year later, an even larger offshore field was discovered to the southeast of Das known as the Zakum field. Today there are many other oilfields off the coast of Abu Dhabi, not all of them developed.

Meanwhile events in the Dubai offshore concession had moved more slowly. After D'Arcy obtained the first offshore concession in 1954, matters were put on hold for several years. Finally, in 1966, oil was discovered in the Fateh ('Good Fortune') field. This brought particular challenges to the operating company, especially in solving the problem of storing oil in shallow waters. A solution was found by building and transporting large floating tanks known as *khazzans* to the oilfield where they were then grounded. More offshore fields followed: southwest Fateh (1970), Rashid (1976) and Falah (1976). These finds, though not on the same scale as Abu Dhabi's, enabled Dubai to finance a number of massive projects new to the Gulf – this was the start of the city as we know it today.

In 1974 the Mubarak offshore field was discovered, making the emirate of Sharjah the third producer of the UAE. While the northern part of the field is shared with Iran, Sharjah has the drilling and production, sharing its crude and revenue with the Iranians; 20 per cent of the remaining revenue goes to Ajman and Umm al-Qaiwain – the latter had conducted a lengthy dispute with Sharjah over maritime jurisdiction.

One consequence of offshore oil exploration was a rising interest in maritime boundaries. Adjoining oil concessions required that these boundaries should be clearly defined if disputes like that at Jebel Ali were

The ADMA *Enterprise*, which struck oil at Umm Shaif in 1958 – the first discovery of commercial oil in the UAE.

to be avoided. PDTC had already asked the Political Resident for a survey of seabed areas of the northern sheikhdoms to be carried out, which entailed boundary points being established along the Trucial Coast. Qatar and Abu Dhabi argued over Halul until two British experts determined that Halul belonged to Qatar, while Abu Dhabi retained several islands. Sheikh Shakhbut was unimpressed; he never forgave the British for the loss of Halul and remained at loggerheads with the ruler of Dubai over their common boundary.

APART FROM GIVING RISE to a myth that oil was only to be found under the pearling beds of the Gulf, the discovery at Umm Shaif provided a major clue to future onshore discoveries. Oil had been discovered in the Thamama formation which was also present in the Murban structure. The endgame now entered its most critical phase. Exploration of the western desert opened up again after Saudi troops were expelled from the Buraimi Oasis in 1955. PDTC spudded in a second Murban well on 18 October 1958, but this proved no more successful than the first. The well went as far as a gas zone at 3,230 metres (10,600 ft), having been tested for oil in several formations on the way down, but revealing nothing of commercial value.

In May 1960, when all hope of finding oil onshore seemed lost, Murban No. 3 struck oil. On testing, it produced good-quality oil at a strong flow from a reservoir that was later confirmed to be a giant oilfield. As with ADMA's offshore find, the oil came from several porous limestone zones of the Cretaceous Thamama group. In 1962 the company followed this discovery with another giant oilfield at Bu Hasa, which lay some 40 kilometres (25 miles) southwest of the Bab-Murban seismic dome. Although most of the partners in IPC already had enough oil, they nevertheless decided to export the crude oil from Abu Dhabi, provided the company could produce it at a competitive price; at the time, the global oil prices were low: $1.8 per barrel, or about $14 per barrel in today's money.

On 25 July 1962 PDTC abandoned its other concessions on the Trucial Coast and became the Abu Dhabi Petroleum Company (ADPC). A 112-kilometres (69.5-mile) pipeline was built from the Murban-Bab field to a storage and export terminal at Jebel Dhanna and on 14 December 1963 the first cargo of crude oil was exported on the *Esso Dublin* tanker. The company, recognizing the need to integrate nationals into the company, introduced apprentice training schemes for its personnel. In 1965 ADPC signed a 50-50 oil-sharing agreement with Sheikh Shakhbut, followed by a similar agreement with ADMA in 1966. As was customary, ADPC agreed to relinquish a certain amount of acreage over a fifteen-year period, thus allowing American, Italian and Japanese companies to participate in the search for oil.

The discovery of oil created great pressure on Sheikh Shakhbut to change his ways. But when the oilmen first proposed the 50-50 agreement, which was more favourable than the previous agreement, he was most reluctant to accept it. The Political Agent Donald Hawley suggested that Shakhbut was unwilling to accept the new agreement because he did not understand its terms or feared the changes oil wealth would bring. In the light of the sheikh's assiduous interest in earlier oil negotiations, the former claim seems unlikely, while the latter rings true; perhaps another explanation is that he was still smarting from what he perceived as a lack of British support for his territorial claims. Whatever the explanation, he remained a staunch opponent of development and resisted any attempt to improve the sheikhdom. It was perhaps inevitable that in 1966 Sheikh Zayed, with the support of his family, deposed his brother and ushered in a new age of rapid economic growth. The background to the coup, and the family's soul-searching dilemma that went with it, are considered in the next chapter.

All the while, the work of exploration went on. The emphasis was squarely on geophysical surveys on an industrial scale, with three seismic crews on contract from the General Geophysical Company comprising up to 120 people and 36 vehicles of various kinds, including six mobile shot-hole rigs. On a typical day, they drilled 1,500 shot holes and laid out over 1,000 geophones with cables that transmitted data to instruments in the field. The results were then sent to London for processing and interpretation.

The work was hard, the environment unremitting and it could be a lonely existence for the seismic crews when the only visitors were an ADPC supervisor or the occasional military patrol. Yet they enjoyed all the mod cons. Indeed, the camps resembled social clubs that had been dropped into the desert. Air-conditioned caravans were arranged in a semicircle around a central mess tent, which served as a dining room, bar, operations room, darts hall and general community centre. But even the heat of the summer months was too much and the field party would disband for their annual leave, departing the Gulf in high spirits, while mechanics were left to overhaul the vehicles back at base.

From 1960 the most famous field party, Party 19, surveyed the Murban-Bab and Bu Hasa areas, moved southeastwards and subsequently covered most parts of Abu Dhabi. As a result of these surveys, the company discovered large oilfields at Asab in 1965, Shah in 1966 and Sahil in 1967. The crews completed operations in 1971, and their equipment was shipped to Saudi Arabia.

In 1971 the Abu Dhabi National Oil Company (ADNOC) came into being. The government stopped short of full nationalization, Sheikh Zayed taking the view that the country would benefit from the oil companies' expertise and thus avoid all the difficulties that full nationalization had brought elsewhere in the Middle East. ADNOC went

Bedouin children posing against a background of smoke from a burning
gas flare at the Murban oilfield, 1962.

on to take a 60 per cent interest in the ADPC and ADMA concessions, and
the latter companies became the Abu Dhabi Company for Onshore
Operations (ADCO) and the ADMA Operating Company (ADMA-OPCO),
respectively. In 1977 the Zakum Development Company (ZADCO) was
formed to operate the Upper Zakum field. The original IPC partners
retained shares in Abu Dhabi oil in a concession that did not expire until
January 2014. Today you will see posters proclaiming the part played
by Total and Exxon-Mobil in the development of the UAE, which was
largely through their involvement in the company that started it all, the
long-since forgotten Iraq Petroleum Company.

8

Blueprint for a Nation:
The Trucial States, 1945–68

AT MIDNIGHT ON 14/15 August 1947 Britain's historical *raison d'être* in the Gulf came to an end, swept away by the independence of India and Pakistan. By then, of course, the region had other strategic uses, providing a corridor to British bases in the Far East and a buffer against Soviet expansion, but its oil-rich potential was perhaps the strongest reason for staying on. As we have seen in the previous chapter, a host of issues flowed from the matter of oil – internal security, the need to settle boundaries, immigration, logistics and labour – all of which threatened to suck Whitehall deeper into the internal affairs of the Trucial Coast.

A fresh breeze was blowing through *al-daulah*. The old Indian Civil Service had been disbanded and the supervision of British affairs in the Gulf transferred to the Foreign Office. The Residency transferred from Bushire to Bahrain. On the Trucial Coast, a Political Agent replaced the Residency Agent in 1949, followed five years later by a move of the Agency from Sharjah to Dubai, and the term of political appointments was extended from one year to three. A new breed of political officers appeared on the scene. These Foreign Office types might have been more flexible, more worldly wise than their Indian Office forebears, but they were a mixed blessing as far as the Trucial sheikhs were concerned. In the past, the India Office had resisted Foreign Office attempts to sacrifice its Gulf interests in favour of British policy in the wider world. Now, with the India Office disbanded, the sheikhs had no such champion for their cause.

Although there was a common interest in finding oil and a realization that social and economic changes had to be made, there would be little money to pay for development programmes until the oil was on tap. Even as late as the mid-1950s, apart from an occasional oil rig, survey vessel or Sheikh Shakhbut's yellow-finned Cadillac, there were no obvious clues to the future that lay ahead. Sharjah was a declining settlement around a silting creek with a sprawling hinterland that stretched from the northern coast to the eastern shore and was unruly in parts – the Bani Kitab refused to allow the ruler to visit his date gardens in Dhaid, some 48 kilometres (30 miles) inland. In Ras al-Khaimah, the call of the *muezzin* drifted between ancient towers set against a backdrop of mountains. Ajman, the smallest sheikhdom, was in three sections – coastal, desert and mountain – with a capital that was dominated by an impressive fort guarded by a rusting cannon, the epitome of an old Gulf town. Umm al-Qaiwain, 'the Mother of Two Powers', was, like its neighbours, built around a creek and in a state of gentle decay.

On the eastern coast, the newly recognized sheikhdom of Fujairah comprised the principal town of a mountainous territory. Its fort had been bombarded more than 25 years before, as the ruler liked to remind visiting British officials. Further up the coast, the town of Khor Fakkan belonged to Sharjah but was boxed in by the Fujairah sheikhdom. Its name, 'Creek of Two Jaws', is said to have derived from its natural harbour set between the mountains. Here you could still see at anchor the large trading dhows that plied the Indian Ocean to the East African coast. As is the custom in the Islamic world, people undertook the Haj pilgrimage from all over the Trucial States. One resident of Khor Fakkan, Umm Obaid, described how she travelled with her husband and son all on one passport – women never travelled alone – riding in a truck to Dubai, whence they sailed by dhow to Dammam on the coast of Saudi Arabia.

It took four days to reach land and most of the passengers ended up seasick. When we arrived, the police in Dammam checked our papers and our luggage and demanded we get vaccinated, which I refused. They then separated the women from the men, and we stayed in tents before we headed in big truck-like cars to Mecca. A difficult and long journey, but worth it in the end.[1]

The Dubai she passed through would have been a great contrast to her home town. It was a bustling port, the trading hub of the lower Gulf and a smuggling capital of the Middle East. Here dhows gently jostled in the middle of the creek as *abras* criss-crossed its congested waters, carrying passengers from one shore to other. The first bank on the Trucial Coast, the Imperial Bank of Iran, had opened a branch in 1946 in a building that had a lavatory which – for obvious reasons – protruded over the creek. In the *suq* that was situated on the Deira side, amid the smell of spices, incense and fish, and the din of traders calling out their wares, all manner of men did business: Arabs, Baluchis, Iranians, Africans, some in flimsy stalls, others sitting cross-legged with their wares around them. Merchants standing about discussing matters of the day, black-robed women with plump baskets on their heads, beggars reaching out for alms, men on trotting donkeys, these were the scenes of the market alleyways. *Bedu* from the interior, the *bedu* of old, still visited the *suq* with charcoal to sell and goods to buy, tethering their camels before going inside. On the other side of the creek, the towers of the Bastakiya and Shandaqa, built to catch the breezes, imparted a sense of fading elegance. A few boats setting sail for the pearl banks at the start of the season were reminiscent of an earlier age.

Western sensibilities were easily shocked by the state of the towns and villages that lay along the shore. Raymond O'Shea, writing during the hungry years of the Second World War, described houses lacking basic drainage or sanitation, with piles of rubbish left outside or on the beach, where vultures picked at, and flies congregated around, rotting carcasses of livestock. Even in the towns of the 1950s, there was no running water, and many houses had a salt-water well for washing plates, with supplies of sweet water brought in by donkey once a day. There were no roads, public electricity or public telephones, in fact no modern conveniences of any kind. In the absence of air conditioning, people would leave the coast in the summer and head for Al Ain or the desert in order to live in tents and *'arish*. Every two years or so, locusts would swarm in from Pakistan and across the Arabian mainland, darkening the sky and shredding the crops – one unlikely report had them eating babies. Disease, particularly eye disease, was common. In the absence of modern medical treatment, traditional remedies were still used and epidemics raged.

Education was rudimentary. In the villages, those children who could be spared from domestic duties or helping with the date harvest were educated in the Quran by an old *mutawwa*, usually in a makeshift classroom or under a tree. Mohammed al-Fahim describes his schooling in Abu Dhabi in the 1950s:

[The teacher] would position himself in the middle of the room facing the door while we, the pupils, sat in sand or on woven mats in a circle around him. Twenty-five or thirty of us, both boys and girls, sat silently reading, each of us struggling over a different page of the Quran. In fact, our entire education consisted entirely of reading the Holy Book.[2]

Those students who memorized the Quran would perform *Al Toumina*, visiting neighbourhoods with their teacher singing or reciting traditional verses from the holy book as they went, being welcomed by the residents who would offer dinner and small gifts in return. While the emphasis was on religious studies and learning to read, girls were not in the least encouraged to learn writing. In fact, so few could read or write well that people had to rely on the local *mutawwa* to inscribe their documents and letters. In the towns, children were also taught mathematics so they could help in the family business when they were older.

There was no formal state system of education, and no schools for higher religious learning such as a *madrasah*. Those wishing to become scholars had to travel farther afield. In the early 1920s, for example, Humaid bin Ahmed bin Falaw and thirteen fellow students boarded a dhow for a treacherous sea crossing to Qatar, the first batch of students to be sent from the coast to study under the renowned religious authority Sheikh Mohammed bin Abdulaziz. Two of the students caught smallpox and died; Humaid returned to Ajman and became a well-respected judge, teacher and imam. Such were the limited opportunities that a number of families left the Trucial Coast and settled in places like Kuwait, where the father could obtain well-paid work and educate his children in relatively modern schools. A number of schools that had opened during the height of the pearling industry, such as the Al-Mahmoudiya school in Sharjah, were forced to close with the decline of pearling in the 1930s.

In later years, some blamed the British for the poor conditions on the Trucial Coast. In fact the British government, although not responsible for the internal development of the seven states, was keen to persuade the sheikhs to improve the lot of their people. The British government itself lacked the financial resources to provide large-scale aid. The Second World War had seen Great Britain victorious yet bankrupt; successive runs on the pound had left the economy weak, and the

The creek at Dubai, March 1960.

post-war shift towards spending money on state programmes in the UK rather than abroad – the so-called 'welfare not warfare' debate – further eroded the government's ability to finance major projects on the Trucial Coast.

Much was done on an ad hoc basis: the occasional visiting doctor or missionary would provide basic treatment, drugs were distributed during epidemics. More permanent measures were possible, such as the appointment of a permanent medical officer for the coast, a clinic in Dubai in the late 1930s and the establishment of locust patrols in 1949. In the same year, the clinic was replaced by the Al Maktoum hospital with 38 beds and Chief Medical Officer Desmond McCaully in charge. Although welcome, these measures simply scratched the surface of a deeper problem.

Others blamed the sheikhs for failing to share their wealth more equitably among the local population. While sheikhs were expected to be generous providers, and often were, there was a limit to what they could achieve and for the most part people looked after themselves. Historically, there had been no welfare system apart from slavery. Sheikhs were constrained by the declining economic conditions and, although they now received an income from oil concessions, they were not exactly rolling in money. The Al Maktoum tended to run their sheikhdom as a business, but for many rulers running commercial enterprises was not an option because it was considered demeaning. If it was done, it was done quietly: one sheikh might discreetly open a business in a neighbouring sheikhdom in order to supplement his income, but for the most part it was a case of sitting back and waiting for the oil to flow – if it ever did.

How did the Trucial sheikhs view Britain's role? As one might expect, attitudes were mixed, ranging from Sheikh Shakhbut of Abu Dhabi's perennial distrust of the British to Sheikh Rashid of Dubai's willingness to work with them on development projects. There was a general acceptance among all of them that Britain was the final arbiter in disputes between them. The Political Resident – now based in Bahrain – was known in Arabic as *Fakhamat Ar Rais*, meaning 'His Big Excellency'. The local sheikhs and Arabs referred to him as *Rais Al Khalij*, the 'Head of the Gulf', as a matter of course, without any hint of sarcasm.[3] But, as we shall see, this did not imply an unqualified consent to Britain's political and economic monopoly in the region.

The Trucial States were not British colonies or protectorates, but through treaties enjoyed a protected status: the British managed their foreign affairs in consultation with the rulers, who retained an absolute jurisdiction over their internal affairs, apart from criminal offences committed by foreigners which were dealt with by a British magistrate – usually a political officer. The British government could only advise on internal matters, they could not dictate. Rulers were left to decide economic and social issues within their own sheikhdoms, provided these did not impact on their external relations. It was an archaic arrangement, and one that would struggle to survive the rapidly changing Middle East of the 1950s.

The British still liked to show the flag, of course, with aerial demonstrations bringing a new trick to the imperial repertoire. In June 1949, for example, Brigand bombers flew from Sharjah via Ras al-Khaimah and Rams to Al Ain, then to Dubai, Abu Dhabi and Liwa before returning to the airbase. Apart from scattering citizens as they flew over rooftops and attracting rifle fire over Al Ain – no doubt from local bedouin who regarded shooting at aircraft as the perfect sport – the flights passed without incident. The following day, Saeed bin Maktoum of Dubai was invited to join one of the flights but declined, apparently fearing a devious British plot to remove him from his sheikhdom.

The post-war Trucial States could hardly be described as a work in progress. They were traditional Arab societies, each one ruled by a sheikh with a few representatives, *qadis* and armed retainers according to tribal custom and *sharia* law. That they were a nation or nations in the modern sense was debatable. Tribal raiding by the Awamir and Manasir tribes was sporadic and the interior still dangerous in the late 1940s. The Saudi-run slave trade appeared to be flourishing and historic counter measures against it, such as maritime searches, blockades and bombardments, were no longer effective.

EVEN SO, there was a certain charm to the way of things. In May 1952, when people gathered for the feast marking the end of Ramadan, *Eid al-Fitr*, the British representative in Sharjah reported a picture of pastoral simplicity. The *majlis* was the centre of a sheikh's world, a meeting place where he could come face to face with his subjects and listen to their petitions. That of Sheikh Saqr III bin Sultan al-Qasimi, the ruler of Sharjah, far outshone those of the other rulers in its splendour. Opposite his palace was the main centre of attraction, a large banyan or *rolla* tree where three makeshift swings had been erected. Families from neighbouring towns came together here, meeting friends and renewing old acquaintances. Everyone down to the poorest and smallest was wearing new clothes, boys in robes like their fathers, girls in colourful dresses fringed with silver thread, playing on the swings.

The summer was known to British expatriates as the 'hundred days of hell'. August was the worst month, when high temperatures combined with a dripping humidity smothered the coast in a warm, wet blanket. At high noon in the quiet towns of the lower Gulf there was little sign of life. Many expatriates had returned to their homelands, while sheikhs were in their summer residences or taking vacations abroad. On the shore, many families moved out of their houses to live in the drier desert air or, in northern parts, headed for the hills or gardens of a nearby oasis.

By October, the mood had lightened. Everyone was back, the weather was cooling down and evenings were bearable again. In the winter, rain occasionally refreshed the land, and flash floods were a danger in the mountains. In March, a *shamal* might arrive, churning up the sea and bringing sand storms to the interior, briefly eclipsing the sun and choking the land; but the sun returned stronger each time, as if invigorated by these onslaughts. In June, hell began all over again. 'Hot and humid' or 'pleasant and cool': this was how the seasons were described as the year spun round.

No one imagined that this patchwork land would unite to become one of the richest countries in the world. Five of the seven sheikhdoms were split into smaller pieces and no one had a clear idea of where the various boundaries lay. There were several factors in favour of the rulers working together – the geographical proximity of their territories, a shared history and tribal traditions, and their Arab-Islamic roots – but Zayed the Great's meeting of 1905 with the other Trucial sheikhs had not been repeated. Bernard Burrows, an official in the Eastern Department of the Foreign Office (and later Political Resident in the Gulf) observed that, while there was a strong argument for federation, the obstacles were immense: the sheikhs were divided, communications poor and resources few.

It was apparent, on the other hand, that a measure of cooperation was required: a small military force to prevent raiding and protect political officers on their inland visits, for example. As a result, with the agreement of the rulers, the Trucial Oman Levies was created in 1951. Formed with a nucleus of British officers of the Arab Legion from Jordan, the Levies (known as the Trucial Oman Scouts (TOS) from 1956) had an eventful start. A shortage of local bedouin recruits led to the inclusion of Dhofari and ex-Aden Protectorate levies, a volatile mix which created more problems than it solved, including a mutiny after which the Adeni contingent was replaced. In September 1952, the Levies were pitched into the Buraimi dispute when the Saudi emir of Ras Tanura, Turki bin Abdullah al-Otaishan, arrived in the Omani village of Hamasa and declared himself *tarifa* to the surrounding tribes. The Levies were ordered to blockade the village.

The Saudi claim, if successful, would have squeezed Abu Dhabi into a narrow wedge of coastal territory. Moreover, by demanding to negotiate directly with the sheikhs of the Al Ain/Buraimi area, they threatened Abu Dhabi's position there. The villages around the north, west and south of the oasis – Al Ain, Hili, Jimi, Mutaradh, Muwaiqi and Qattarrah – were loyal to Abu Dhabi. The villages of Hamasa, Buraimi and Saara in the central east were notionally under the rule of the sultan of Muscat and Oman, but the principal sheikh of Hamasa, Sheikh Rashid bin Hamad al-Shamisi, was staunchly pro-Saudi and had connections with the Saudi slave trade.

The Saudi claim, based on the Wahhabi conquests of old, was fuelled by the prospect of finding oil in the desert of southeastern Arabia – not in and around Al Ain/Buraimi, but to the west. The Saudis also had an eye on Khor al-Udaid as a 'window on the Gulf', hoping to separate Abu Dhabi and Qatar by claiming a thin strip of territory running to the sea. But it was the oasis that really mattered, for whoever held it could influence the tribes of southeastern Arabia. The Saudi emir, Turki, set about distributing money and laying on many feasts for the local tribes-men, who were asked to sign declarations of allegiance to Saudi Arabia in return. Yet throughout all the threats and inducements, Sheikh Zayed, who was based in Al Ain, remained loyal to his brother, Sheikh Shakhbut, the ruler of Abu Dhabi.

The British government, acting on behalf of Abu Dhabi and Oman, opposed Turki's occupation of Hamasa and sent low-flying aircraft to harass and drop leaflets on the village. However, with entrenched positions on both sides, a stalemate ensued. The dispute consumed the diplomatic energies of the Foreign Office and dominated the affairs of Abu Dhabi for the next three years. The situation was not helped by Sheikh Shakhbut's attitude towards his own people. In November 1952, he refused loans for the pearling season, leading a large section of the population to threaten *hijra* by decamping to Qatar. As Sheikh Ali of

Fort Jahili, Al Ain, built for Zayed the Great in the 1890s and the family home of the Al Nahyan, until it became a base for the Trucial Oman Levies in the 1950s.

Qatar was offering money for them to settle there, Shakhbut saw no need to compete with him.

For a brief moment, the Buraimi dispute hit the international headlines and Westerners were reading about this small corner of the Arabian desert for the first time. In 1953 Sheikh Shakhbut happened to be in London receiving medical treatment at the time of Queen Elizabeth's coronation and he was invited to attend with a companion. But the sheikh, upon learning that the physician in charge of his treatment had been bribed by the Saudis to poison him, fled to Paris. His absence from the coronation was cleverly concealed from public gaze by giving his two empty seats to the ample Queen of Tonga, Sālote Tupou III.

Over the next three years, negotiations between Britain and Saudi Arabia failed to resolve the dispute, leading to an arbitration hearing in Geneva in September 1955. When the Saudi representative tried improperly to influence the tribunal, and the British delegation discovered they were about to lose the first round, Whitehall withdrew from the proceedings and ordered the Trucial Oman Levies to expel the Saudis from Hamasa. There was a short battle in October and Hamasa was retaken, with a number of Omani sheikhs exiled to Dammam afterwards.

The Buraimi dispute was by no means over and it would take another nineteen years before a settlement was reached. But it had a massive impact on the future of the region for, if the Saudi intervention had gone unopposed, there was a good chance that the area would have come under Riyadh's sway and the UAE would not exist as we know it today. It also confirmed the legitimacy of Sheikh Shakhbut as the ruler of Abu Dhabi and his authority over six villages of the Al Ain/Buraimi Oasis at a time when there were murmurings of dissent from within his own family. If anything, Shakhbut's rule emerged from the dispute stronger than ever before.

———

ALTHOUGH NOT trumpeted as a move towards federation, the creation of the Trucial States Council in 1952 was a tentative step towards a more coordinated approach. The council was comprised of the seven rulers and the Political Agent as chairman. Among the measures to be considered were the creation of essential services that most modern states take for granted today: police, customs, health and education. Although this is credited as a British initiative, it is often forgotten that the council could only function with the agreement of the rulers, who themselves displayed a commitment to work together; but, as was so often the case, it was a commitment of differing shades and intensities.

The council's first meeting, held on 23 March 1952, presented an interesting mixture of personalities around the table: Sheikh Shakhbut, ruler of the largest sheikhdom and the most cautious of the seven, did not attend and sent his son and secretary in his place; Sheikh Rashid, standing in for his father Saeed, the infirm ruler of Dubai, a proactive leader who supported a coordinated approach provided it did not blunt Dubai's competitive streak; Sheikh Saqr bin Sultan of Sharjah, a nationalist who had a strong interest in education; Sheikh Saqr bin Mohammed al-Qasimi of Ras al-Khaimah, who was keen to press ahead with development, particularly in agriculture; Sheikh Ahmad II bin Rashid al-Mualla of Umm al-Qaiwain, a respected mediator of disputes; Sheikh Rashid bin Humaid al-Nuaimi of Ajman, the venerable ruler of the smallest sheikhdom; and Sheikh Mohammed bin Hamad al-Sharqi of Fujairah, which had been recognized as an independent sheikhdom only two days before. In the chair was Christopher Pirie-Gordon, described as 'not particularly zealous in pursuit of his official duties but, when he had to be, very effective'.[4]

Its early meetings were symptomatic of the dilemma they faced: how to protect the traditional way of life and modernize, all within a meagre budget. Each ruler responded in his own idiosyncratic way, falling somewhere between Shakhbut's diffidence and Rashid's appetite for change. If the rulers were late for meetings, it was not intended as a discourtesy, only a gentle way of saying that they were not ready to accept Western methods of timekeeping quite yet; if they stayed away, it meant there had been a falling out with the Political Agent or another sheikh, but relations would soon mend; if the Agent discussed proposals with individual sheikhs outside the meeting, it was only because the sheikhs were more responsive in a one-to-one setting; if measures were agreed but not carried out, it simply confirmed that the council decisions were discretionary, not mandatory.

Of the participants, Sheikh Saqr bin Sultan was the most animated in discussion and Sheikh Rashid, once freed from the constraints of his ageing father, made useful contributions. For the most part, however, the meetings were marked by indifference and apathy. The smaller states, Ajman, Fujairah and Umm al-Qaiwain, usually passed the meetings in 'bearded silences' in contrast with the sheikh of Sharjah's frequent interjections.[5] In theory, the Trucial States Council was to meet twice a year and yet, in the spring of 1953, British officials were despairing that the council had not met for almost a year; eventually a meeting was held in April. The first meeting at which all seven rulers were present was the fourth one held in November 1953, at the height of the Buraimi dispute.

There were certain warning signs that matters could not be allowed to drift indefinitely. The events of 1951, when the Anglo-Iranian Oil Company was nationalized by the Iranian government, were shocking enough for the British authorities. All across the Middle East, the tide of Arab nationalism was a growing threat to their interests in the region, even along the Trucial Coast. In an attempt to improve their schools, the rulers of Sharjah and Dubai received financial help from Egypt, Kuwait and Qatar, and hired a number of Egyptian and Palestinian teachers. Egyptian teachers in Bahrain and Qatar were particularly active during the 1950s, leading nationalist sympathies in the Gulf. Many of these teachers had been attracted to the expanding economies of the Gulf and would later progress to higher posts in Arab education in the region. It was not only in the schools that the Egyptian influence was felt: Gulf students were travelling to Cairo for study, Egyptian technicians and professionals such as doctors were working in the Gulf, Cairo Radio was blaring its fiery brand of nationalism across the airwaves and newspapers were spreading a similar message throughout the Gulf. Through British eyes, these were all seen as dangerous connections.

The British and French invasion of the Suez Canal in November 1956 on the pretext of separating warring Egyptian and Israeli armies is often seen as the last post of British imperialism in the Middle East. Forced to withdraw under pressure from Washington, Britain suffered a massive loss of face among Arabs at large. The event was hailed as a great victory for the Egyptian president, Gamal Abdel Nasser, and Cairo Radio propagated his anti-imperialist message – though there were few radios on the Trucial Coast at that time. The Dubai National Front, a loose grouping of opponents to the British presence in the Gulf, was supported by Egypt. In the aftermath of Suez, there were a number of incidents: part of the Political Agent's house was burnt down and his car attacked, a TOS officer was attacked and an attempt was made to sabotage planes and radio transmitters, and to saw through a freshwater pipeline supplying the RAF base at Sharjah. In comparison with events in Bahrain and Qatar, however, these incidents were minor and

From the late 1950s, new schools were opened for local children such as these, photographed in Abu Dhabi, 1960.

the Suez Crisis passed without any mass demonstrations or outbreaks of violence in the region.

As it happened, the first slender outlines of a modern state were sketched during the early meetings of the council. Surveys of water resources and of the silted-up creeks of Dubai and Sharjah were commissioned. A well-boring programme was started in Ras al-Khaimah and the *aflaj* at Al Ain were repaired. The Al Maktoum hospital was improved, and the first modern school in the area was built in Sharjah. Peter Tripp, the Political Agent from 1955 to 1958, was so encouraged by the council's progress that he suggested a five-year plan, which was approved. More improvements were planned to the sheikhdoms' administration and education systems, and the establishment of police forces was agreed. Slavery, which the British suspected was ongoing but the rulers claimed had died out long ago, was officially declared abolished in 1958.

Various issues bedevilled the council, however. The legal concept of citizenship was non-existent: there were no citizenship laws and the council was unable to reach an agreement on the question of passports; the definition of a 'citizen' thus remained undefined. We have already seen the problems caused by the indiscriminate issuing of travel documents by rulers such as the sheikh of Ajman, but when the Political Agent proposed that passports be issued they were not accepted elsewhere in the Gulf. The sheikhs could not agree on a central location of a passport office, the fees to be paid or even the validity of the passports for travel between the sheikhdoms; it was not until a meeting of the council in 1965 that the issue was resolved. Another thorny issue that defied a solution for many years was that of locust control: initial resistance from the bedouin to the use of pesticides was overcome but locust swarms still continued into the 1960s, despite the work of locust control teams deep in the Arabian desert and elsewhere.

Until the oil revenues began, there was little money to pay for large-scale social programmes, although Arab states such as Kuwait made contributions to individual sheikhdoms. To move matters along, a number of sub-committees were formed under the aegis of the Trucial States Council. After the five-year plan was agreed, the Education Committee began its work under the chairmanship of the Political Agent. One of its first acts was to ban teachers from engaging in political activity. In 1957 the British funded an agricultural research station followed by an agricultural school at Digdaga in Ras al-Khaimah. In 1958 a school was opened in Abu Dhabi and a trade school in Sharjah. A programme to train local teachers in order to reduce the number of teachers being brought in from Egypt, Syria and elsewhere was initiated. But attempts to coordinate policy were disjointed: in 1960 Sheikh Rashid appointed an education manager for Dubai but Sheikh Shakhbut rejected the idea for Abu Dhabi.

The Health Committee also began in 1957. Its membership included a doctor and it appointed four travelling doctors for the Al Maktoum hospital, and small clinics were opened in the other sheikhdoms. In 1963 a small hospital was opened in Ras al-Khaimah and a general manager appointed to coordinate health services across the area. After the departure of Dr McCaully in 1964, the coordination of health services became a pressing issue as the number of health organizations in the Trucial States began to rise. In 1967 an Omani, Dr Asim Jamali, was appointed as medical administrator to coordinate and advise on these activities.

Progress in Abu Dhabi was slow. In 1960 Sheikhs Shakhbut and Zayed invited American missionaries, Pat and Marian Kennedy, to open a clinic in Al Ain, which was known as the Oasis Hospital or the Kennedy Hospital to locals. The accession of Sheikh Zayed in 1966 brought a new momentum. Dr Philip Horniblow was appointed director of health for the Abu Dhabi government. At first, there was only a healthcare centre in Abu Dhabi town, a small, square, concrete building next to the *suq*. It comprised two rooms for consultation, four other rooms into which only men were admitted, a small storeroom and a room used as a minor injury 'theatre'; open drains ran along the corridor.

A Syrian doctor, a Pakistani who administered medical care and a local orderly made up the Abu Dhabi medical team, treating only the male population. There were no facilities available for local females or children. Should any medical help be required for them, male members of the household would attend the clinic in order to collect medicines on their behalf. As it became known that there was an English female nurse working in the clinic, women (many of whom were pregnant) tentatively started to appear, together with their children, to seek treatment. When the storeroom was converted into a consulting/delivery room, medical and obstetric care for women in Abu Dhabi began to be provided.

After a few months, another room was converted into a ward, separated from the male rooms, thus providing a place where mothers and babies could be cared for in the days after delivery. This service rapidly developed into a form of community care, where an English nurse would attend deliveries at the clinic or in the desert. Often, during the night, a Land Rover would arrive at the nurse's house with a request to attend a pregnant woman in her *'arish* village. In time, the development plans for Abu Dhabi included a multi-purpose hospital on the outskirts of the town with services for women and children. Sheikh Zayed formally opened this hospital, known as the Central Hospital, in 1968.

TO MAKE MATTERS worse for the British, they had a rival for the hearts and minds of the Trucial rulers. The Arab League was an organization of Arab states created to foster cooperation and collaboration between fellow Arabs. Although formed in 1945 with British encouragement, Whitehall came to view it with great suspicion, seeing it as a vehicle for Nasser's brand of radical nationalism. One issue catching the eye of the Arab League was a dispute between Sharjah and Iran over the ownership of an island known as Abu Musa, which appeared to highlight a growing threat to the Arab character of the Gulf region.

Abu Musa was about 5 × 3 kilometres (3 × 2 miles), lying 65 kilometres (40 miles) off the coast of Dubai, the redness of its rocks broken by a few patches of green. Some 70 families lived on the island, which was rich in iron oxide deposits. They made their living from fishing and smuggling, being conveniently situated between the Trucial Coast and Iran, carrying items such as rice, carpets and raw opium to Dubai and returning with watches, tea, gold and refined opium. It was also a valuable source of income to the ruler of Sharjah on account of the iron oxide mine on the southeast coast of the island. In 1898 the ruler had granted a mining concession to three Arabs but, eight years later, two of them transferred their rights to the German firm of Wönckhaus, much to the dismay of the British authorities. Under pressure from the British, the ruler cancelled the concession and a British warship removed the company's workers from the island. From then on the concession was worked by a British company, Golden Valley Colours, until the mid-1950s.

Two other islands, the Greater and Lesser Tunbs, were part of the same problem. They lie in a strategic position at the entrance to the Arabian Gulf near the Strait of Hormuz. Until recently, all the oil exported from the Gulf countries passed through the strait, meaning that its protection from foreign control was vital; these islands were of considerable strategic importance. The British had seized these islands and Abu Musa in 1821, in the aftermath of their victory over the Qawasim, who had previously taken the islands from the kings of Hormuz. The British allocated Abu Musa to Sharjah and the Tunbs to Ras al-Khaimah.

Tension over ownership of the islands appeared in the late 1920s when Reza Shah began asserting his power over the islands of the Gulf. As we have seen, this resulted in the expulsion of Sheikh Ahmed bin Obaid bin Juma from Hengam Island and the Dubai dhow incident off the Tunbs. The British were reluctant to intervene on account of treaty negotiations they were conducting with Iran at the time.[6] It was hoped that the future of Abu Musa and the Tunbs might be settled as part of the treaty but negotiations broke down without an agreement. In the late 1950s the British erected a plaque on the Lesser Tunb to signify that it belonged to Ras al-Khaimah. There matters rested until 1963 when the u.s. and Iranian navies carried out joint manoeuvres in the Gulf, including a mock occupation of Abu Musa, which Iran claimed was within their territorial waters. This raised fears of an Iranian takeover of the Arabian coast, fuelled by the large number of immigrants crossing the Gulf to look for work in places like Dubai.

When the matter came before the Arab League, it agreed to send a delegation to the Trucial Coast in October 1964. The British had decided not to oppose the visit on the grounds that to do so would lay them open to a charge of anti-Arabism. The League representatives, led by Secretary General Abdul Khalek Hassouna, received a warm welcome, particularly in Sharjah where local merchants put up flags, on pain of a large fine if they refused, it was said; in fact an Egyptian influence was already well established there, with pictures of Nasser widely displayed and Sheikh Saqr's private secretary Gharib believed by the British to be an Egyptian agent. At their meetings with local rulers, the representatives discussed plans to provide development aid for the Trucial Coast, a suggestion that was apparently met with customary inscrutability from five of the seven rulers. The League also had plans to set up a development office in the area but only the two Saqrs – the sheikhs of Sharjah and Ras al-Khaimah – showed any enthusiasm for the idea.

The visit triggered a series of events that would prove critical to the destiny of the Trucial States. In an attempt to head off the Arab League, the British put a proposal to the Trucial States Council that all offers of aid should be channelled through a single fund, the Trucial States

From second left to right: Sheikh Saqr bin Sultan, ruler of Sharjah, with Sheikh Rashid of Dubai and the Political Agent Peter Tripp in 1956.

Development Fund, and its Development Office, thus avoiding the possibility of rulers entering separate agreements with the League. The two Saqrs initially resisted the idea but after much behind-the-scenes lobbying the Political Agent, Glencairn ('Glen') Balfour Paul, got his way at a council meeting on 1 March 1965. However, when the deputy secretary general of the League, Dr Sayed Nofal, visited the area in May, five of the seven sheikhs – of Ajman, Fujairah, Ras al-Khaimah, Sharjah and Umm al-Qaiwain – signed agreements, despite the council's earlier resolution.

The stage was set for a showdown. The five sheikhs appeared determined to cooperate with the Arab League, and there was a risk that they might break away from the others. After much deliberation, the British decided to ban League members from visiting the Trucial States altogether. The area was sufficiently remote to make this a practical measure and there was no unrestricted access, since foreign visitors had to obtain visas from the British authorities. The airports at Sharjah, Abu Dhabi and Dubai were closed for 'repair works', the latter two being re-opened a few days later.[7] Planes were only allowed to land if everyone on board had a visa. At this critical juncture, just when it seemed that the League's visit had been successfully avoided, word reached the Political Agent that Sheikh Saqr of Sharjah was planning to issue passports to League members, making them his citizens and thus negating the need for visas.

In some ways, Saqr was in a difficult position. He was the ruler of a relatively poor sheikhdom, with none of the resources of Abu Dhabi or Dubai, and was tempted to look for funding elsewhere. He was not alone in his sympathies with the Arab League, it was just that he was more impatient than others; but the British had grown impatient too. His overtures to Cairo were dangerous and threatened to undermine their position in the Gulf. It was a matter for the ruling family, of course, but the Political Agent kept a close eye on developments and liaised with the sheikh of Dubai so that, when the family made a decision, the British were in a position to assist. On 24 June 1965 Saqr was deposed, as described by Dubai businessman and banker Easa Saleh al-Gurg:

> The sheikh was invited to a meeting with the Political Agent. He set out, attended by various of his retainers and two armoured cars. On his arrival at the Agency a paper was waved in front of him which was alleged to be the record of the family council's

decision. The sheikh asked to see the paper; this was refused. In fact, it bore only one signature, that of the sheikh who was to succeed him as ruler . . . He was led out of the back door of the Agency, avoiding his armed retainers at the front, driven to the airport and put on a flight to Bahrain. He was said to have wept as he saw his emirate disappearing below him.[8]

It was not the last word from Sheikh Saqr. Exiled to Cairo, he remained angry and resentful towards his cousin and successor, Sheikh Khalid III bin Mohammed al-Qasimi, dreaming of the day when he might return to Sharjah and recover his sheikhdom. Khalid, a gentle man of letters, proceeded with plans to develop Sharjah and granted small plots of land for his people to build on, benefiting from Abu Dhabi's oil wealth and Dubai's rapid growth. But Saqr's dream – or nightmare – came true. On 25 January 1972 he returned to Sharjah with a group of armed men and shot his cousin dead. Nevertheless, the coup failed and Sheikh Khalid's brother, Sultan III bin Muhammad al-Qasimi, became ruler – leaving Saqr to remain under house arrest in Abu Dhabi.

This was a tragic aside: the essential point was that the entreaties of the Arab League had been rebuffed by the mid-1960s. It was agreed that the Political Agent would be replaced as chairman of the Trucial States Council by one of the rulers and a deliberative committee set up in order to bring a sharper focus to development; again, this would be under an Arab chairman. The Agent would still be represented at these meetings, but his removal as chairman was designed to remove any suggestion that the committee was simply a vehicle for British domination.

The British administrator in charge of the Development Office was replaced by Easa Saleh al-Gurg, with Sheikh Saqr of Ras al-Khaimah as chairman. Thus, although Britain provided financial support and advice, it was under the aegis of Arab-led institutions, dampening any criticism about the level of British involvement in the area. The few Trucial organizations were enough to provide a fig leaf of federalism – at least enough to repel any attempt to federate the sheikhdoms in another way.

Attempts were made to engage Saudi Arabia in the process. But the Suez Crisis had led to Saudi Arabia breaking off diplomatic relations with Britain, a state of affairs that was to continue until 1963; the Buraimi dispute also remained an obstacle between them. It was only through the intervention of Balfour Paul that a Saudi contribution was made to the Trucial States Development Fund. However, this breakthrough can be attributed to a mutual desire to outflank the Arab League rather than to any thaw in diplomatic relations between the two countries.

In 1965, therefore, Britain and Saudi Arabia each contributed £1 million to the fund, while Qatar gave £250,000, Abu Dhabi £100,000 and Bahrain £40,000. All the while, the British had been trying to encourage the rulers towards federation. Although they all had divergent views, it was the intransigence of Sheikh Shakhbut that posed the most serious stumbling block. Despite the fact that his oil revenues were beginning to flow, he remained deeply sceptical about change. In the past, the British might have dismissed his traits as the harmless idiosyncrasies of a bedouin sheikh but, as the 1960s unfolded, he was increasingly seen as a major obstacle to progress. On the matter of oil revenues, he was unyielding: in 1963/4 Abu Dhabi's oil revenue was a meagre £1.5 million, but it rose to £28.1 million in 1966 and yet expenditure on development projects remained pitifully small, amounting to only £2.7 million.

An air of decline seemed to cling to Abu Dhabi like the dripping heat of summer. Its people, most of whom were not engaged with Arab nationalism or the actions of the Arab League, were voting with their feet. The population had already been falling as people sought to escape from the decline of the pearl trade and the hardships of the Second World War, but the flow was not staunched, not even by the discovery of oil. Shakhbut's attitude did not help, in fact at times he seemed uninterested in their fate. We have seen how his refusal to advance loans during the pearling season – what was left of it – had led a section of the Bani Yas to threaten *hijra* in 1952; indeed, some carried out the threat. Members of the Mazari section moved to Dubai and those from the Qubaisat and Rumaithat went to Qatar. It is believed that, at one point, the population of the town fell to a mere 4,000 souls, a sad reflection of the despair at the economic situation in the sheikhdom. There was no public development, no municipal structure, no facilities or roads: when Shakhbut's son, Sultan, tried to establish a municipal office, his father had it burnt down. The oil company was forced to ship supplies from Dubai and a second power plant remained unfinished because Shakhbut would not provide the funding; a contract for a desalination plant was awarded to a Dubai firm because there was no equipment in Abu Dhabi to build it with.

For those who remained, life went on as before. Some lived in tents and *'arish* around Qasr al-Hosn, using goatskin buckets to scoop water from under the sand that was so salty that they called it 'creek water', only suitable for washing rice and laundry; fresh water was shipped in from the islands of Al Futaisi or Dalma in large boats. When a family cooked a meal, they would invite their friends and neighbours to join them, even if there was little food. Sheikh Shakhbut was not oblivious to their plight. In the evenings, he would leave the palace and meet his people, walking about and offering them help. His *majlis*, prayer meetings and meals also offered opportunities to meet people and discuss their problems. Visitors to the palace would each be offered a basket filled with bread, flour, dates, coffee and cardamom to take home.

There were a few flashes of hope in the gloom. In August 1954 a certain Major Lippet appeared at Qasr al-Hosn with a visionary scheme to improve roads, schools and a free port in Abu Dhabi. A draft contract was presented but Shakhbut, being unable to read the document, asked for the matter to be delayed while his clerk scrutinized it. But the major insisted on reading the contract aloud and then asking Shakhbut to sign. In ordinary circumstances, Shakhbut would have declined; in this instance, he had good reason for signing. For years, he had suspected PDTC of short-changing him over customs dues, which they assessed themselves. The chance to set up his own customs department was too tempting to resist. Besides, the venture would also bring him a profit without any strings. So he signed the agreement. Perhaps Abu Dhabi's situation would have improved if the schemes had gone ahead but, in the event, the discovery of oil was still some years off, and the Abu Dhabi Development Company went bankrupt. Lippet already had a dubious track record for his dealings with the red-oxide mine on Abu Musa, and it was with some relief that the Political Agent witnessed the demise of his ambitious scheme.

In Shakhbut, we see a ruler distrustful of the oil company, bitter towards the British for territorial decisions that had gone against him and resistant to change. It was not that he was greedy or gratuitously mean; austerity was simply in his blood. Most Westerners who met him for the first time liked him; he was charming and intelligent with a keen sense of humour. On one occasion, for example, when the American journalist, Wanda Jablonski, asked him about the slave trade in Abu Dhabi, he light-heartedly reassured her that she was too 'old and skinny' to be a slave.[9] On the other hand, he was sensitive and

Abu Dhabi in 1962.

quick to take offence. While he might have had good reason to disagree with the British on occasion, he took the decisions that went against him as personal slights.

But this was only part of the story; it should not be forgotten that the sheikh retained the respect of the tribal rulers for a large part of his reign, and paid subsidies to the Manasir and Awamir tribes well into the 1950s; his tribal base was relatively secure. And his resistance was not so outlandish as it might first appear, for the example of other Gulf countries had alerted him to the dangers of oil wealth: mass immigration, consumerism and the ruin of the traditional ways. It was an understandable point of view but, like King Canute of England, Shakhbut faced a relentless tide.

It fell to the inner circle of the Al Nahyan family to consider Shakhbut's fate. It was a heart-wrenching dilemma. Sheikha Salama, the matriarch of the family, was still alive and her sons were alert to the promise they had given her in 1928 not to kill each other. Of the four, Sheikh Zayed was the youngest and seemed the most likely to succeed his brother, if a way could be found of doing it without blood-shed. As the ruler's representative in Al Ain and the Eastern Province, he was highly respected among the local tribes and had played a key role in refusing bribes from Saudi agents at the height of the Buraimi dispute. Although he had shown only loyalty to Shakhbut, he had come round to thinking that Shakhbut had to go. Of his other brothers, Hazza died in 1958 and Khalid had not shown any particular inclination to become ruler; he would eventually support Zayed in an attempt to remove Shakhbut.

There were some troublesome moments for the family in the 1950s, but it was not until the early 1960s that matters came to a head. It is believed that the family discussed a coup against Shakhbut but twice held back; no doubt their promise to Sheikha Salama weighed heavily on their minds. In 1963 there was much dissatisfaction among the merchants of the town about the lack of progress, and despair in the ruling family that their allowances were being restricted. Shakhbut relented and the notables awaited the flow of the enlarged oil revenues in 1964 but, as it happened, their expectations were dashed and they found themselves in exactly the same position as before.

The British looked on with a rising sense of apprehension. A British political officer had been based in Abu Dhabi since 1955, and this post was upgraded to Political Agent in 1961 in recognition of Abu Dhabi's growing importance following the discovery of oil. The first agent, Colonel Hugh Boustead, was an experienced administrator who had held posts in Sudan, the Aden Protectorate (part of today's Yemen) and Muscat. He was faced with some interesting challenges in his new posting. Sheikh Shakhbut wanted to build a pipeline carrying water from Al Ain to Abu Dhabi town and, after some haggling, this was achieved. Meanwhile, Sheikh Zayed was keen on agricultural schemes for Al Ain and appointed a Pakistani agricultural officer, Abdul Hafeez Khan, initially paying him out of his own pocket. However, Shakhbut blocked a grander development scheme for Abu Dhabi.

When plans for a union of the seven Trucial sheikhdoms plus Qatar and Bahrain began to take shape, Shakhbut made it plain that he considered Abu Dhabi far too important to be included. He refused to allow Zayed to attend a meeting of deputy rulers and himself declined to attend a meeting of Gulf rulers. The Political Resident in Bahrain, Sir William Luce, was pessimistic about the prospects of federation while Shakhbut was ruler of Abu Dhabi; indeed, Luce had mooted the idea of removing him in favour of Zayed. In 1964 the British foreign secretary, Patrick Gordon Walker, rejected a plan to oust Shakhbut, but it was secretly agreed that the British would supply limited military support in the event of Zayed deposing his brother.

In mid-1966 Zayed, Khalid and their cousin Muhammed tried to persuade Shakhbut to set a proper budget but he declined, taking the view that it would be shameful because he would have to reveal his earnings to his people. Eventually, in August 1966, Zayed took his chance and Sheikh Shakhbut was escorted from his palace by the Trucial Oman Scouts and put on a plane to Bahrain. Reactions to the coup in Abu Dhabi were muted; a relieved acceptance of Zayed's rule, mixed with a personal respect for Shakhbut among family and tribesmen, so much so that he was able to return to Abu Dhabi three years later and live quietly in Al Ain.

Elsewhere on the Trucial Coast, it was reported that Sheikh Rashid of Dubai was outraged by the removal of a fellow ruler to the extent that it coloured his relations with Sheikh Zayed, with whom he had previously been on good terms. There were also British suspicions that Rashid was stirring up trouble in Ras-al Khaimah and Sharjah, possibly as a prelude to annexing them. In the end, Rashid and Zayed patched up their disagreements at a meeting with the Political Agent, Archie Lamb.

Sheikh Zayed boosted Abu Dhabi's contribution to the Trucial States Development Fund to 80 per cent of the total budget. He also set about catching up with his neighbours, bringing Abu Dhabi up to date with developments along the coast. He initiated a five-year development plan, abolished taxes and built free homes for his people. He made overtures to other tribes in the lower Gulf to settle in Abu Dhabi, leading to 3,000 members of the Zaab tribe of Jazirah al-Hamra relocating to the town. Zayed brought a new air of optimism and enthusiasm, but Abu Dhabi still lagged behind Dubai. This raised the problem of which city should be the capital of a federation: the town with the oil money or the city with the trading links? It would be a difficult choice.

Dubai was surging ahead. The decline of Sharjah had continued unabated since the 1930s, all to the benefit of its neighbour. A combination of Sheikh Saqr's reluctance to engage British help and a preference for Arab League aid had brought fatal indecision, with his town's creek silting to such an extent that it became virtually useless. Meanwhile, at the heart of Dubai's development was the figure of Sheikh Rashid, who, like the merchant princes of old, recognized trade as the key to future prosperity. He had an astute mind that would rapidly fix on the essential issues in a business case or at a meeting of the *majlis*. This was epitomized by the story of a Lebanese businessman who appeared before the sheikh with an ambitious drawing of buildings and palm trees that Rashid dissected in a matter of minutes, dismissing the hapless supplicant with a flea in his ear. And yet, Rashid was a most personable man with his roots in the bedouin ways and, when the work was done, there was nothing he liked better than training his falcons and relaxing with friends.

At Rashid's direction, Dubai's creek was dredged and a breakwater built to prevent sand bars forming, allowing larger ships to dock. While Sheikh Shakhbut was burning down Abu Dhabi's only municipal office, Dubai had the makings of a municipality in a modest organization of seven people set up in a single room above the customs building in Bur Dubai, charged with simple tasks such as street cleaning. In 1957 a municipal council (*Baladiya*) of 23 members was appointed from tribal elders and traders. Although it had limited powers, the *Baladiya* supervised matters of public health, street cleaning and construction, advising the government on a range of issues.

The banking sector grew, allowing credit to merchants who had previously relied on traditional payment systems such as the *hawala* network, thus enabling them to expand their trade and business. Slowly but surely, citizens who had once buried their money in the sand came to trust bankers enough to open up accounts, although the banks would still keep large amounts of cash in their vaults on account of some customers asking to count their money. The British Bank of the Middle East (the successor to the Imperial Bank of Iran) briefly had a monopoly on banking in Dubai but then other banks such as the Eastern Bank moved in. In 1962 the concept of a national bank was discussed in the *majlis*, leading to the establishment of the National Bank of Dubai the following year.

All the while, from his office in the customs house, Sheikh Rashid looked on. With an ear on discussions with his officials and an eye on shipping movements in the busy creek, Sheikh Rashid's mind was a crucible, distilling plans for the future. The opening of the Al Maktoum Bridge in 1962 marked a turning point in the town's history, connecting Bur Dubai with Deira and enabling cars to pass between the two at a charge of one rupee. Ever since the flying boats stopped calling in, Sheikh Rashid had nourished the idea of a new airport for Dubai. Initially, the

British authorities opposed it, taking the view that the airport 19 kilometres (12 miles) away in Sharjah was sufficient. However, with the support of the Political Agent, Donald Hawley, Rashid got his way and an international airport opened in 1965. At first, an ambitious plan to build a deep-water harbour met with scepticism from the British, who were not convinced of the scheme's financial viability, fearing it would bankrupt Dubai. In the event, a deep-water harbour called Mina Rashid was opened in 1972 with fifteen berths, which accelerated Dubai's economic growth and population. It was followed by a new port 35 kilometres (22 miles) from Dubai at Jebel Ali, which opened in 1983 with 65 berths. These enterprises paved the way for Dubai to become the Gulf's prime transit import and export centre.

Sheikh Rashid counted a number of officials such as Mahdi al-Tajir and Easa al-Gurg among his advisers. There were also a few prominent families whose merchants and traders in earlier times might have pressed for reforms but were now happily tethered to Rashid's vision of the future. Trade licences were granted to these commercially skilled families, preserving and perpetuating a system that is the foundation of Dubai's commercial success. From the 1960s, these business families began to emerge into the limelight: Futtaim for Toyota, Al Ghurair for real estate and shopping malls, Al Gaz for Pepsi. The Al Owais family who had been pearl merchants, Juma al Majid who was involved in trade, the Galadari brothers, Muhammad al-Mullah, Othman Sager – all these names are well known in Dubai today.

It is an oft-quoted cliché that the UAE has achieved in 50 years what it has taken other industrialized nations 300 years to achieve. This is where it all began: the first hints of a federal government were appearing in the departments of the Trucial Coast Development Fund; the first signs of an infrastructure and coordinated public programmes were materializing; banks were established and construction firms moving in; department stores opening, telephone systems and postal systems being installed. In the towns, the first concrete shells of apartment blocks and hotels were appearing. The new was jostling with the old: houses were replacing huts, roads overlaying tracks, and trucks squeezing out donkeys. Where indigenous tribesmen once slouched with their rifles, gangs of foreign workmen now shuffled by with their shovels and cement.

The whole mishmash was a confusion of tradition and ambition, tribal politics and corporate plans. In this period we see the blueprint

Dubai merchants drinking American soft drinks in 1960.

drawn and the building blocks laid for a modern state; something was emerging. Quite what was in store for the seven sheikhdoms was anyone's guess – federation, separation or revolution – but, whatever the outcome, it was clear that massive changes lay ahead. For a people who were *murtahiin bi qulubna*, comfortable in their hearts, the world was to be transformed beyond recognition.[10]

9

Divided We Stand: Unification and Beyond, 1964–80

AFFAIRS WOULD TAKE a strange course over the next few years. They started well enough – in 1964 the British prime minister, Harold Wilson, supported a UK military presence east of the Suez Canal, keeping bases in Singapore, Malaysia, Aden and the Arabian Gulf. But there was an element of wishful thinking in all of this. Wilson was not in a strong position, since his Labour government had a slender majority and his party was split over the issue. It was becoming increasingly difficult for the UK government to pay the costs of maintaining its armed forces abroad. The economy was declining and the balance of payments problem, with the value of imports consistently exceeding exports, was making devaluation of the currency more likely. At this stage Wilson still believed he could maintain British forces abroad while defending the pound. These were expensive delusions, for which the country would pay a heavy price.

In truth, Britain was acting in the dying light of empire and was simply unable to maintain its role as policeman of the world. Wilson was a realist and certainly knew that the economic situation would require stringent measures, but believed that Britain could still maintain its position in those countries that still welcomed it. Britain's position in Europe was equivocal – it would be another seven years before it was admitted to the EEC – and America was tied up in Vietnam, having refused to take over Britain's role in the Gulf. These factors, together with a sentimental attachment to the empire of the past, seemed to ensure a British presence in the Gulf for the foreseeable future. Although historians have since disputed the extent of Britain's commitment, arguing that the government was committed to withdrawing its forces eventually, it is clear that the British defence secretary, Denis Healey, was considering the possibility of increasing the armed forces in the Gulf as late as June 1965.

Pax Britannica, by which Britain guaranteed the peace of the region and looked after its interests, looked set to endure. As we have seen in the previous chapter, British officials were working to improve coordination between the sheikhdoms through the Trucial States Council and Development Office. At this stage, in the mid-1960s, the purpose of these was twofold: to counter allegations that the area was being 'ruled' by a colonial power and in the longer term to foster a sense of collective independence.

To begin with, the Gulf rulers were considering a union of the seven Trucial States with Qatar and Bahrain. Qatar, the richest state, employed an Egyptian lawyer, Dr Abdul Razak Sanhuri, to draft a constitution for a union of nine. Bahrain, to some extent hobbled by the shah of Iran's sovereignty claim over the island, had the largest educated population and administrative regime. The Trucial States, in contrast, were less developed and had various rivalries among themselves, such as those between Sharjah and Fujairah, and Ras al-Khaimah and Fujairah, dating back many years. Although Qatar and Bahrain had their own rivalries, most notably a territorial dispute over the Hawar Islands, it was understood in those early days that, if a union were to materialize, it would be under the leadership of Qatar and Bahrain rather than Abu Dhabi or Dubai.

It was clear that creating a union would by no means be an easy task. There were different currencies across the region – from 1966 Bahrain and Abu Dhabi were sharing the dinar while the northern sheikhdoms of Sharjah, Ajman, Umm al-Qaiwain, Ras al-Khaimah and Fujairah were using the riyal of the Qatar and Dubai Currency Board. Within the Trucial States there was the glaring disparity between the wealth of Abu Dhabi and Dubai on the one hand and the northern sheikhdoms on the other. When it had been suggested that the wealthier sheikhdoms should help the others, Sheikh Shakhbut retorted: 'Who do you think I am? Some sort of communist fellow?'[1] All that changed, of course, with the succession of Sheikh Zayed as ruler of Abu Dhabi.

For Whitehall, the deepening financial crisis was not the only factor at work, since there was an ongoing debate in Parliament about foreign policy priorities. The first official indication of a change of direction came with the Defence White Paper of 1966, which recommended the withdrawal of British forces from Aden. Here the position was becoming untenable: as an attempt was made to amalgamate a small colony with a sprawling hinterland, local resistance in the form of the

National Liberation Front was stiffening, and terrorist attacks were draining resources.

Even so, despite these developments, Britain's position in the Gulf remained unchallenged, and looked to benefit from the release of forces from the troubled Aden territories. Indeed, Sharjah seemed the perfect replacement for Aden as a regional military base. Although Sheikh Saqr bin Sultan had resisted any idea of expanding facilities in his sheikhdom, his successor Sheikh Khalid signed an agreement with the Political Resident in 1966. A number of troops leaving Aden the following year were accommodated in the camp at Al Mahatah in Sharjah, while the Trucial Oman Scouts were transferred to a camp at Al Murqab to make room for them.

Meanwhile, anti-British feeling in the Gulf was inflamed by the Arab–Israeli war of June 1967. There was much unrest in Bahrain, a few days of demonstrations in Dubai with shops being damaged and the British Agency surrounded, and in Sharjah a number of sailing boats at the British club were set alight in the night; but otherwise the situation remained calm. After Egypt's defeat, Nasser's pan-Arab dream began to fade, broadcasts from Radio Cairo's 'Voice of the Arab Gulf' ceased, while others looked for different ways to achieve a Gulf free of 'colonial' influences. There were ongoing guerrilla wars in Oman throughout the 1960s, which occasionally impacted elsewhere in the Gulf with incidents like the bombing of the British India ship *Dara* off the coast of Dubai in 1961. Marxist-Arab guerrillas tried to expand their revolutionary appeal to the whole peninsula, giving rise to the Popular Front for the Liberation of the Occupied Arab Gulf (PFLOAG), but their appeal on the Trucial Coast was strictly limited. In Yemen, a civil war rumbled on, with Egypt backing the republicans and Saudi Arabia the royalists.

In 1966 the Labour government's commitment to the Arabian Gulf remained strong. It had survived a severe buffeting from party members and a financial crisis. Wilson had won an overwhelming majority in the general election four months previously, and was still resisting a devaluation of the pound. Nonetheless, the warning signs were mounting as Malaysia and Aden were added to the confirmed list of military withdrawals in the East. It was now British policy to depart from the Gulf when conditions were 'satisfactory', but there was a subtle change in the wording of internal documents. A timescale of about eight years was being mentioned for withdrawal, and there was a suggestion that it might happen even if conditions were 'less than satisfactory'. There was a general acceptance that Britain would have to withdraw from the Gulf by the mid-1970s, possibly sooner if the situation deteriorated rapidly.

In the short term, however, the developments in Malaysia and Aden strengthened the case for keeping a military presence in the Gulf and prompted government ministers to reaffirm Britain's commitment to the rulers. The area was vulnerable after the retreat from Aden, and there was no need to add to the rulers' discomfiture by announcing an earlier withdrawal. Time was needed to get over the Aden episode and allow the sheikhs to stand on their own feet. In public, it was suggested that the possible consequences of withdrawal – the loss of oil, a run on sterling and damage to British interests in Iran – would be far worse than the alternative. But the Gulf rulers, detecting a change of tone in government pronouncements and fearing they were next in line after the retreat from Aden, were nervous. And so it fell to the minister of state at the Foreign Office, Goronwy Roberts, to visit the Gulf states in early November 1967 and reassure them that 'the British presence would continue as long as it is necessary to maintain peace and stability in the area.'[2]

It is worth pausing at this juncture to consider the situation in the Trucial States. As we have seen, the rulers were working towards a federation, although its precise form was not yet apparent. The accession of Sheikh Zayed had been a major boost to the cause of federation but there was a worrying aspect to his leadership. He was generous, insisting that Abu Dhabi would meet the costs of federation, but not keen on collaborating with his counterparts. His refusal to allow the Trucial States Council to make decisions affecting Abu Dhabi seemed to reveal where his real ambition lay. If it was speculated that he was driven by a desire to assume leadership over the whole Trucial States, this was probably true – and not unreasonable in view of his sheikhdom's vast financial resources.

Zayed still faced a major obstacle in the form of Sheikh Rashid of Dubai. It is often said that the essential difference between the two men was that Zayed was a bedouin chief while Rashid was an entrepreneur. It appeared that the two rulers had patched things up after Shakhbut's removal, but their commitment to working together remained in doubt. Rashid would surely oppose any move by Zayed to lead the seven sheikhdoms, himself also being a front-runner. Rashid had

Sheikh Zayed celebrating the anniversary of his accession with members
of the Zaab tribe in 1971.

attended meetings of the Trucial States Council since their inception
and had been a beacon of modernity in the area, transforming the fortunes of Dubai. Supported by Easa al-Gurg and other advisers, he was
in favour of an independent Dubai (on the model of Hong Kong).
However, although Dubai was a wealthy trading port in its own right,
with its own oil revenues soon to flow, it was Zayed's control over Abu
Dhabi's oil resources that gave the Al Nahyan the greater financial
clout. And Rashid's three sons and another prominent adviser, Mahdi
al-Tajir, supported a union – at that stage a union of the nine states.

It was impossible to consider the rulers' predicament in isolation
since, surrounded by larger neighbours, they were in an awkward position. The Kuwait crisis of 1961 was still fresh in the memory: the Gulf
rulers had looked on as Kuwait was threatened with annexation by Iraq
and was only rescued by the arrival of 7,000 British troops from Bahrain.
They were caught between Saudi Arabia and Iran, and exposed to their

territorial claims. Although Zayed had tried to settle the Buraimi dispute with King Faisal, the latter's insistence on having a quid quo pro for the loss of the Buraimi Oasis prevented any meaningful progress being made; the old Saudi dream of gaining access to the lower Gulf through Khor al-Udaid still burned brightly. Meanwhile the shah of Iran, Mohammad Reza Shah Pahlavi, had unresolved issues in the Gulf, not only his claim to Bahrain but over the islands of Abu Musa and the Tunbs.

It took little imagination to realize that the withdrawal of British troops would create a military vacuum in the region, and that these powers might seek to fill this in different ways: Saudi Arabia by taking Buraimi and Iran by satisfying its island claims. Divided, the sheikhdoms hardly presented an effective deterrent, but together they would at least have a louder voice. And yet there was no real sense of urgency in any of this. Nothing could bring a sense of liveliness to the debate; nothing, that is, until Harold Wilson announced Britain's withdrawal from the Gulf.

As we have seen, Goronwy Roberts had visited the rulers in November 1967 to reassure them that Britain intended to stay in the Gulf. The decision to withdraw was taken in principle by the British cabinet on 4 January 1968. Thus Roberts, barely two months after his previous visit, had to return to the Gulf and tell the rulers that Britain was leaving. For Roberts, it must have been a thankless task, meeting those to whom he had given his solemn word a short time before, particularly since a man's promise was his bond in the bedouin world. The rulers' feelings must have ranged from astonishment and disappointment to a sense of betrayal but, in the true spirit of Arab courtesy, they showed no sign of it. Wilson made the news public on 16 January 1968, telling the House of Commons that Britain would withdraw its forces from all its bases east of Suez, including those in the Arabian Gulf, by the end of 1971. For the people of the Gulf, the announcement came as a bolt out of the blue.

How had it come to this? On 18 November 1967, after another currency crisis, the chancellor of the exchequer, Jim Callaghan, had announced a devaluation of the pound from $2.80 to $2.40. There was no great planning to the decision-making process, which *The Times* likened to a sleepwalker falling out of a window. At the end of the month Callaghan resigned, thus acknowledging the failure of the government's economic policies, and was replaced by Roy Jenkins. The arrival of a man who had little faith in Britain's ability to maintain its military commitments in the world marked a shift of emphasis within Whitehall. Although it is not clear whether it was Jenkins or his officials who initiated the review of Gulf policy, he was more amenable than his predecessor to the idea of withdrawing from the region. By 14 December Jenkins had agreed to take a specific proposal forward, namely that British forces should withdraw from east of Suez by 1 April 1971. British foreign policy, once imperious and far reaching, was now grounded by the ball and chain of economic reality.

In fact, there is an academic debate around this point, whether Britain's decision to withdraw was motivated purely by economic or political reasons. The relative costs of overseas commitments were small when compared with proposed cuts to social programmes, £37 million against £606 million. It would take years for the full effect of savings to work through. Sheikh Zayed offered to share the costs of an indefinite military commitment and other rulers indicated that they too would be willing to contribute. But these offers formed no part of the final decision. Defence cuts were necessary to give credence to a wider programme of retrenchment; the National Health Service was to be cut back, expenditure on roads curtailed and house-building programmes shelved. In the end, it was a political decision, a matter of appearances, of avoiding how it might look if welfare were cut and warfare spared.

The debate moved on to the timetable for withdrawal – eventually the end of 1971 was agreed. As far as the offer of the Gulf rulers to pay the costs of military defence was concerned, this was rejected on a number of grounds. It might give the rulers a say in British policy, it was argued; it might do more harm than good, it was said. The notion of acting as mercenaries to the Gulf sheiks was also mentioned, and Denis Healey entered the arena in blustering style when he expressed his dislike for the idea of being 'a sort of white slaver for the Arab sheikhs'.[3] His remarks caused great offence in the Gulf, and he issued an apology a few days later.

Meanwhile the Americans had been watching the unfolding story with a certain dread. Already stretched by their military commitments in Vietnam, they saw no possibility of u.s. forces being able to fill the void left by Britain's departure. Since the Eisenhower Doctrine of 1957, Washington had supported a British presence in the Gulf, and it had been the exasperated secretary of state Dean Rusk who had told British foreign minister George Brown earlier in the month 'For God's sake act like Britain!', urging the UK to assert its role in the world rather than withdraw from it.[4] But now it was clear that the British government had no intention of changing its mind, and the days of gunboats in the Gulf were well and truly numbered.

It was a point well understood by the two players in the unfolding drama, Sheikhs Zayed and Rashid, once the idea of funding British troops had been rejected. On 18 February 1968, at a campsite set up in the desert near Al Semeih, near the border between Abu Dhabi and Dubai, the two rulers met and agreed in principle to merge their sheikhdoms into a union. Foreign affairs, defence, security and social services and immigration policy were all to be coordinated, while other matters were to be left in the rulers' hands. The long-standing dispute over the border between the two sheikhdoms was settled. The two rulers wrapped up the meeting in true bedouin style:

'So Rashid, what do you think?' asked Zayed. 'Shall we create a union?'

'Give me your hand, Zayed. Let us shake upon the agreement. You will be president.'[5]

Relations between the two were not quite as rosy over the next three years as this cameo might suggest. As has been noted, the idea of union went against Sheikh Rashid's competitive streak. He remained suspicious of Zayed's ambitions, fearing he would dominate the union, especially since Zayed had cultivated the northern sheikhdoms with promises of financial aid. A promise of equal rights of veto with Abu Dhabi in the new constitution went some way towards allaying Rashid's fears, but he was still raising doubts with his advisers in the later stages of the negotiations.

Nonetheless, the agreement at Al Semeih – known as the Union Accord – set the two rulers on a path towards federation. Indeed, to back up their intent, they invited the other Trucial rulers and those of Bahrain and Qatar to join them in talks for a wider federation. A week later, the nine rulers were sitting down for a three-day conference in Dubai to discuss a constitution. And, within the space of a few months, Sheikh Rashid had recognized the simple reality of his situation: with Abu Dhabi generating 80 per cent of the Trucial States' income, it was obvious that the future president of a federal state would have to be Sheikh Zayed and Abu Dhabi be the capital of the union. Sheikh Zayed's leadership was thus confirmed.

It was one thing to make declarations of intent, one ruler declaring undying friendship with another and making plans for the future, but quite another to achieve the practical steps that would lead to a union of all nine states. The pact between Zayed and Rashid was made between leaders from the same tribal confederation, the Bani Yas, members of the Hinawi alliances of old. Around the table sat the Qasimi sheikhs, the rulers of Sharjah and Ras al-Khaimah, figureheads of the Ghafiri tribes of the Trucial Coast, who were traditional enemies of the Hinawi tribes. However, now that they were among the poorer states of the proposed union, they had good reasons to support it, such as collective security and the chance to partake in the fruits of Abu Dhabi's oil bonanza.

The Dubai Agreement, as it was known, was a first step. As well as coordinating policies, it also sketched the outlines of a federal state, including a supreme council, a council of experts and a supreme court. Some suspected that the British had a grand design to unite the Trucial States with Oman, reviving the notion of a greater Oman. The ruler of Oman, Sultan Said bin Taimur, showed no design in that regard, but Abu Dhabi did develop closer links with Oman, again reflecting the old links between the Bani Yas and Al Bu Saids. Sheikh Saqr of Ras al-Khaimah, perhaps under the influence of his son, Khalid, suggested a republic but that notion was given short shrift by his fellow rulers.

In the wings, Saudi Arabia and Kuwait watched, waited and were ready to assist when they could – the Kuwaiti foreign minister, Sheikh Sabah al-Ahmad el-Jaber al-Sabah, was called in to mediate and keep the parties on track on more than one occasion. The shah also followed developments closely. Iran's historical claim to the island of Bahrain and to the islands of Abu Musa and the Tunbs were uppermost in his mind. Although these islands historically were claimed by the Qawasim, they might also be used as bargaining counters in Anglo-Iranian negotiations over the future of Bahrain. The idea of a package deal whereby the Iranians would drop their claim to Bahrain in exchange for these islands in the lower Gulf was certainly an attractive one. But the rulers of Sharjah and Ras al-Khaimah, who claimed sovereignty of the islands, had other ideas and had no intention of surrendering what they regarded as their legitimate rights.

In fact, despite his public stance, it is now clear from diplomatic records that the shah had no great interest in Bahrain. It had lost its pearl wealth, had small oil reserves and was too far from the Strait of Hormuz to be of any strategic value to Iran. But the shah was hamstrung by the strength of domestic opinion, which had long considered Bahrain

From right to left: Sheikhs Rashid and Shakhbut greeting guests in 1971.

to be the 'fourteenth province' of Iran. Such was the strength of anti-British feeling in his country that any hint of striking a deal with Britain would have been disastrous.

It was a different matter for Abu Musa and the Tunbs. These islands were considered vital to Iranian interests, a point that the shah made forcefully at his meeting when Goronwy Roberts met him in Tehran, indicating that if an agreement with the local rulers was not reached, he would use force to seize them. On 27 May 1969 the British foreign secretary, Michael Stewart, visited Tehran but refused to agree a package deal over the islands. Britain would not acquiesce in Iran's seizure of the islands, but would encourage the sheikhs to reach a settlement with the shah.

Back on the Trucial Coast, things seemed to be going well enough with the federation talks. At a meeting of rulers between 21 and 25 October 1969, Zayed was confirmed as the future president of the union and Sheikh Rashid as vice president for two years; a capital was to be established on the border between Abu Dhabi and Dubai; and the deputy ruler of Qatar was to be prime minister of a thirteen-member cabinet. But as the parties were drawing up the final communiqué, they received a request from the Political Agent for Abu Dhabi, James Treadwell, to address the meeting. They agreed, and Treadwell was admitted to the room. Reading from a prepared statement, he said: 'My government will be extremely disappointed if these difficulties are not to be overcome.' He told the assembled sheikhs: 'I strongly urge all the rulers to do their utmost to find a way of resolving their difficulties.'[6]

In another situation, his words might have raised a murmur, but in the context of the meeting, they were electrifying. The rulers of Ras al-Khaimah and Qatar – and possibly Bahrain too – walked out. There may have been a theatrical flavour to this, a spoiling tactic to avoid the decisions of the meeting being implemented. After all, Sheikh Saqr of Ras al-Khaimah had failed to gain the prized defence and interior portfolios, settling for agriculture instead, and Sheikh Khalifa of Qatar had lost the argument for cabinet meetings to be held in his home town of Doha rather than Abu Dhabi. And politically, Ras al-Khaimah and Qatar might have wanted to avoid upsetting Riyadh by endorsing Abu Dhabi as the federal capital – the Saudis still held a grudge over Buraimi. While Sheikh Saqr insisted that Treadwell's intervention had caused his walkout, the Qataris admitted that the failure to agree on portfolios had caused the breakdown. Whatever the true reason, their departure left the rulers' communiqué unsigned and put paid to their meetings for the time being.

In April 1970 a United Nations Mission reported that an overwhelming majority of Bahrainis were in favour of independence from Iran, thus giving the shah the face-saving pretext he had been seeking in order to abandon his claim to the island. A major obstacle to federation having also been removed, it seemed that a union of nine states might now go ahead, and a Saudi-Kuwaiti mission was ready to assist in this regard. Moreover, the future of the lower Gulf islands could again be considered. An opinion obtained by the Foreign Office noted that, in terms of legality, the case was tilted in favour of the Trucial sheikhs:

> We consider any international adjudication of the question of the Tunbs would have a 60–40 chance of being decided in favour of Ras al-Khaimah. Likewise, we believe that the same odds would prevail in regard to Sharjah and Abu Musa.[7]

By now the idea of Britain doing a deal over the islands, in effect giving away Arab territory, was far too dangerous to contemplate, particularly in the fragile atmosphere of its withdrawal from the Gulf.

The Bahrain settlement brought a thaw in Arab–Iran relations and allowed the British to step up their efforts to assist the Gulf rulers towards federation. Evan Luard, Minister of State for Foreign Affairs, visited the region between 24 April and 8 May 1970 and, in an attempt to free the logjam, suggested that meetings of the deputy rulers precede those of the Supreme Council. He also urged the sheikhs to disregard any promises by the British Conservative party to reverse the with-drawal, but their surprise victory in the British general election a month later changed expectations. Surely now there was hope of reprieve: had not the new prime minister, Edward Heath, made an election pledge that the decision would be reversed? In fact his arrival in office, rather than clarifying the issue, confused it all the more.

Soldiers of the Abu Dhabi Defence Force in February 1969.

The months passed. Sheikh Zayed's commitment was firm but he needed encouragement. The obstacles to union seemed to gather strength. The geographical spread of the sheikhdoms, arguments between Bahrain and Qatar – they still had their own territorial dispute over the Hawar Islands – the imbalance between their development and that of the Trucial States: all these differences might have been wrapped up in a bedouin-style confederation in another age. But too much was happening to allow any handshake deals – there was one set of advisers looking at constitutional models, another looking at communications, foreign policy and the rest.

British diplomats went to and fro in an effort to bring the rulers together, while rulers and their advisers visited London for meetings with ministers and civil servants, and so on. A last-ditch attempt was made to resolve the islands' dispute. Sir William Luce, a former Political Resident and the new foreign secretary's personal representative, shuttled between London, Tehran and the Trucial Coast, insisting that the rulers of Sharjah and Ras al-Khaimah should agree any deal with the shah. His task was made more difficult by the shah's contempt for Arabs, which he expressed by curling his lip whenever he mentioned them – a feat that Luce found physically impossible to replicate when he tried it in front of a bathroom mirror.[8] In the end, Sheikh Khalid of Sharjah made a separate peace, while Sheikh Saqr of Ras al-Khaimah resolutely refused to do any such thing.

The outcome of those decisions would become painfully apparent in due course. For the time being, it was evident that the union talks had stalled while the rulers waited to see which way the new Conservative government would jump. And now Edward Heath realized that things had gone too far to justify another policy reversal: there was a serious risk that another change of mind would significantly damage Britain's position, destabilize the withdrawal process and provoke nationalist unrest. Heath, who remains highly respected in the Gulf today, did what he could to ameliorate the decision by promising personnel and equipment for the federal forces and ordering a Defence Review that eventually resulted in a joint Anglo-American airbase being set up on Diego Garcia in the Indian Ocean – over the Gulf horizon and yet within striking distance of the oilfields. But the decision to withdraw from the Gulf would stand, and Britain would remain outwardly committed to the notion of a nine-state federation.

British diplomats delivered the unwelcome news to the Gulf rulers in January 1971, and an announcement was made in the House of Commons on 1 March; the withdrawal would proceed. If anyone had thought this would electrify the federation talks, they were sadly mistaken, for they stayed firmly in the doldrums. Soon summer was approaching and the rulers were contemplating their summer residences away from the heat of the Gulf shore. A last-gasp attempt to make progress was made on 10 July, when a meeting of the Trucial States Development Council was convened with Julian Walker, the Political Agent in Dubai, in attendance. Throughout the talks, Zayed was assisted by his son, Khalifa, and officials such as Mahdi al-Tajir of Dubai and Ahmed bin Khalifa al-Suwaidi of Abu Dhabi were helping the process along, advising their rulers about the difficult choices to be made.

A local newspaper, *Al-Ittihad*, was in no doubt about the moving force behind the talks:

> The door finally opens. The meeting is over. Camera lenses are excited. Pens are on the go. The first sight confirms that something momentously great has taken place. Out of the room walks His Greatness Sheikh Zayed bin Sultan al-Nahyan. Speak he did not. But his facial features released a fragrant breeze, watering cherished hopes and reassuring hearts that beat like puzzled birds. Zayed spoke not. He walked to a small room next to the conference hall. Then he prostrated himself on the floor, in praise of Allah Almighty. For Allah was behind the intent. And the United Arab Emirates was founded.[9]

On the first day of the talks, and into the second, there were hectic discussions about local police forces and visa regulations, where the main sticking point was over Iranian access to Dubai. Then, in the morning recess of the second day, Sheikh Zayed remarked that all the rulers were interested in was a union. He suggested that he and Sheikh Rashid – assisted by a number of their sons and advisers – should take the discussion between their sheikhdoms forward while Sheikh Khalid (the crown prince of Ras al-Khaimah) and Julian Walker would negotiate with the five northern rulers. As it happened, Sheikh Khalid withdrew after the first day, taking his air-conditioned car with him and leaving Walker to continue his 'hot and hectic' work alone.[10] After a week of hard discussion, four out of the five northern rulers were prepared to sign up, but Sheikh Saqr of Ras al-Khaimah declined to join.

Various explanations have been given for his decision. It was said that he was unhappy about Ras al-Khaimah's unequal status in the union, was expecting oil to be found in his territorial waters and, perhaps buoyed by visions of a Qasimi revival, hoped for equal treatment with Abu Dhabi and Dubai. On 18 July, Sheikh Zayed issued a communiqué announcing the formation of the United Arab Emirates (UAE) with the six rulers to take effect by the end of the year. Once he had completed his task, Walker finally reported back to the Foreign Office, only to be met by silence; after some nudging, a message was sent to the rulers congratulating them on their achievement.

The door was left open for Bahrain and Qatar. Although Saudi Arabia and Kuwait still entertained hopes for a union of the nine, most realistic observers by now believed that a federation of seven would emerge. Bahrain opted out in August, followed by Qatar three weeks later, both choosing independence over federation. There were the usual courtesies; indeed one wag suggested they were so polite that each ruler had been waiting for the other to walk through the door first.

On 29 November it was announced that Sharjah would retain sovereignty of Abu Musa and fly its flag on the island while allowing Iranian troops to be stationed in the northern part away from buildings and farms in return for a yearly payment of £1.5 million, sharing oil revenues and suspending discussions about future sovereignty. But the fate of the Tunbs remained unresolved. The following day, on the eve of the British departure, Iran occupied these islands, landing troops but meeting fierce resistance on Greater Tunb, where four Ras al-Khaimah policemen and three Iranian soldiers died in a skirmish. The islanders, many of whom were fasting for six days during *Shawwal*, the month after Ramadan, were rounded up. One resident described the scene: 'The Iranian army came inside our house, and told us to leave. We saw lights, and planes, and those things that move on the ground', meaning Iranian armoured vehicles. 'We hadn't even seen cars before.'[11] They were evacuated on fishing boats to Ras al-Khaimah, where they were left hungry, frightened and confused. The news was greeted by rioting in both emirates, and the deputy ruler of Sharjah – who had met the Iranians when they arrived on Abu Musa – was wounded by an unidentified gunman.

The action was condemned by most Arab countries – Iraq broke off diplomatic relations with Britain and Iran, and Libya used the episode as a pretext to nationalize British oil assets in the country. The British, technically in breach of their treaty obligations, declined to intervene,

Emiratis walking past a banner to Sheikh Saqr bin Mohammed al-Qasimi, ruler of Ras al-Khaimah from 1948 to 2010.

taking the view that it was too late in the day. In fact, they and the Americans were content for Iran to take on the role of policeman of the Gulf, and had no intention of starting their own dispute with the shah. In the wider context of geopolitics, the islands were expendable. None of this was any consolation to the Gulf rulers, of course. In the affected sheikhdoms, and along the coast, there was anger and a determination to regain the islands, which endures to this day.

The union of the six went ahead as planned. On 1 December 1971 the existing treaties between Great Britain and six Trucial States were revoked. The Political Resident of the Gulf, Sir Geoffrey Arthur, and Julian Walker visited each of the northern sheikhdoms in turn, hopping from one to the other in an RAF Wessex helicopter. Returning from Umm al-Qaiwain, he received a message that Sheikh Saqr bin Mohammed was prepared to see him, so he flew to Ras al-Khaimah. In what was described as 'an emotional but friendly meeting', the two exchanged notes to end treaty relations (while still staying out of the union).[12] Upon Sir Geoffrey's departure, Saqr came out of his palace and was greeted by a cheering crowd. Apparently, they had been expecting Sheikh Saqr to be arrested and were cheering more from relief than civic duty.

Abu Dhabi from the air, 1972. Almost a year after federation,
the modern city of Abu Dhabi is beginning to take shape.

The next day, the six rulers signed the provisional constitution
and duly elected Sheikh Zayed as president and Sheikh Rashid as vice
president of the newly formed United Arab Emirates. Sir Geoffrey
Arthur travelled with his staff to Sheikh Rashid's palace at Jumeirah to
sign a Treaty of Friendship. As was to be expected, the room was filled
with press reporters and photographers, many of whom were standing
on tables to get a better view. When it was all over, and after the Arab
dignitaries and press had departed, the British contingent was among
the last to leave. However, owing to the weight of bodies outside,
they were unable to open the door, and found themselves climbing
out of a window. It was, as someone remarked, a reversal of the old myth
that British imperialism leaves by the door but comes back through
the window.

Meanwhile, Sheikh Saqr had received bad news about his prospective golden egg. Oil had been found offshore but with only a light flow
rate at 4,880 metres (16,000 ft), though the operator also announced
that shows of gas had been encountered at a depth of 5,456 metres
(17,900 ft). Saqr might have lost the Tunbs and found he had no
commercial oil, yet it was not too late to change his mind about the
union. On 10 February 1972, Ras al-Khaimah joined the other six
emirates on equal terms with Sharjah, thus completing the United

Arab Emirates (UAE) in its present configuration. By then Sheikh Khalid, the unassuming and progressive ruler of Sharjah, had been assassinated by Sheikh Saqr bin Sultan. An investigation found that Saqr had been hoping to capitalize on Khalid's unpopularity after the deal had been struck between Sharjah and Iran over Abu Musa. But the rulers of the other emirates did not support Saqr's claim to rule and Khalid's brother, Sultan bin Muhammed al-Qasimi, was recognized as the new ruler, leaving Saqr to live out his days in Abu Dhabi.

——

IT IS DOUBTFUL that, amid all the flags and celebration, many people knew exactly what they were cheering for. A new state, a union of brothers and a glorious future, perhaps. At face value, the seven sheikhdoms, now officially known as emirates, were committed to working together. A new flag flew over official buildings; the nation was recognized by the Arab League and admitted to the United Nations. James Treadwell was appointed the first British ambassador to the UAE. Under the constitution, Abu Dhabi was to be the federal capital for seven years while a new capital known as Al Karama was to be constructed on the emirate's border with Dubai.

And yet, in those early days when the UAE was still finding its place in the world, there were some worrying echoes of a fragmented past. While the federal government exercised important functions over areas such as defence, immigration and foreign policy, individual emirates exercised a significant degree of autonomy. A brief war between Sharjah and the Sharqiyin (Fujairah) on the east coast in 1972 was suppressed the following spring. Iran would not quit the Tunbs, and there was an ominous silence from Saudi Arabia, which would not recognize the UAE's boundaries until the Buraimi dispute was settled. If it really had been the rulers' intention to create a viable country, then there was much more work to be done.

At the heart of the political structure was the Supreme Council – the successor to the old Trucial States Council – a Council of Ministers and the Federal National Council (FNC). The latter body was based on *shura*, meaning consultation, originally a meeting of tribal elders to advise a ruler. These were the rudimentary vehicles of a fragile union, and they would require a great degree of commitment from the rulers to ensure that they functioned as truly federal institutions. As president, Sheikh Zayed did not press the others too closely at first, since to have done so might have led to rifts and disintegration. Paradoxically, it was fortunate that the provisional constitution was flexible enough to allow a degree of autonomy in each of the emirates.

A time traveller from the 1950s would have been staggered by the changes taking place. By the mid-1970s, the tripling of the oil price had guaranteed the emirate of Abu Dhabi a yearly income of £1.5 billion. The Shakhbut era was now a distant memory as the town emerged from its bedouin past. Executives arrived at a modern airport to seek audiences in the palaces of sheikhs and air-conditioned offices of notables and advisers; foreign workers arrived from India and Pakistan to work in the many labour gangs that were building a new city while desks heaved under the weight of paperwork required to let them in. The boom was running away with itself, prices were sky high and hotel rooms in such short supply that executives had to share up to three to a room. Abu Dhabi was, it might be said, running to catch up with Dubai, now two hours' drive away on a new desert road, a town where *arrivistes* from the commercial world mixed with merchants of old.

Away from these distractions, the real question was whether the union had simply been a cosmetic exercise for the benefit of the outside world rather than a serious attempt to bring the seven sheikhdoms together. The answer was not immediately apparent; indeed some might argue that it took at least 25 years to emerge. In 1973 the problem of different currencies was resolved when a new currency board issued the UAE dirham, but such convergence was not always so evident in other matters. Across the Emirates, there were too many international airports and not enough modern roads. In the oil business, Dubai opted for total control of its industry while Abu Dhabi went for a more restrained 60-40 agreement with the oil companies.

Even achieving a cohesive foreign policy seemed elusive. Ras al-Khaimah began showing independent tendencies, first seeking recognition from the Soviet Union and then, when that came to nothing, offering military facilities to the Iraqis. In 1980 Abu Dhabi sided with Iraq in their war with Iran, but Dubai and Sharjah with their significant Iranian populations remained neutral. The currency board was replaced in 1980 by the UAE Central Bank, but this remained an ineffectual regulating authority, as witnessed by several banking collapses in the Emirates. The plan to build a new capital on the Abu Dhabi–Dubai border never materialized. Resolutions were not implemented, decrees were quietly ignored. All in all, the strength of unity appeared to be wasting away.

On the military side, individual emirates were allowed to keep their own forces, with the result that there was one large army and several smaller ones. At a strength of about 18,000, the Abu Dhabi Defence Force (ADDF) was by far the largest, followed by the UDF at about 5,000 – this was the force that had taken over from the Trucial Oman Scouts and was intended to be the military arm of the federation. The separate Dubai Defence Force had around 2,500 men in service, and Ras al-Khaimah 500. British officers on contract were being replaced by Pakistani, Jordanian and local officers, and a merger of the ADDF and UDF was achieved by presidential decree in 1978; but Zayed's decision to make his son Sultan commander of all federal armed forces caused such an uproar that the president had to hurry back from Pakistan to smooth ruffled feathers.

In 1979 matters came to a head when Zayed announced a ten-point plan to strengthen the union. Although this had the support of the smaller emirates, it was opposed by Dubai and Ras al-Khaimah. Demonstrations followed and talk of secession was widespread. In this case it took an old tribal remedy – mediation – to calm things down, with Kuwait doing the honours.

The old ways were the best ways, or so it seemed. It was clear that the politics behind these events were rooted in earlier times, characterized by a natural gravity towards tribal interests rather than the union as a whole. The rivalry between sheikhs Zayed and Rashid, which had been glossed over by the union bandwagon, ran deep. Both were re-elected to their posts in 1976, having served their first five-year terms of office. At that stage, it was Zayed that kept the union going, together with Abu Dhabi's wealth underwriting it all. The federal budget was being funded solely by his emirate and, although three of the smaller sheikhdoms promised to pay a 2 per cent contribution in 1977, the three others (including Dubai) refused to pay anything at first. Although rulers like Sheikh Saqr of Ras al-Khaimah might have suspected Zayed of personal motives in promoting the federation, their reliance on Abu Dhabi's money kept them inside the fold. Even Rashid, looking on with a measure of disdain, was prepared to use the advantages of the union while pursuing his own agenda for Dubai.

And yet the doom merchants were proved wrong. The union survived, and talk of coups being mounted by the northern Arabs – Syrians, Jordanians, Egyptians and others at the heart of the administration – proved groundless. In reality they, like the indigenous population, had

A crowd at the camel races in Abu Dhabi, November 1970. Although the oil wealth had started to flow, they had little inkling that their world was about to be turned on its head.

a stake in the UAE, a reason for ensuring its survival. With a bureaucracy of 28,000 (and growing) providing jobs for one and all, and living standards that could only be dreamt of elsewhere in the Middle East, there was no cause to overturn the established order. A few radicals might wring their hands in despair but life continued much as before; Rashid the merchant prince kept a close eye on things in Dubai while Zayed, the bedouin chief, led his colleagues along the rocky road of union.

What was required was greater cohesion, no matter how improbable that might seem. Unable to get his way on federal issues, Zayed twice tendered his resignation, once over the failure of the other emirates to contribute to the federal budget and then during the row over Sultan's appointment as head of the UDF. On both occasions, his offer was rejected. In foreign affairs, there were a few bright moments, such as the Treaty of Jeddah in 1974, when matters were settled between Zayed and King Faisal: the Saudis recognized the UAE in exchange for their receiving the Khor al-Udaid corridor to the Gulf and the entire hydrocarbons from an oilfield – known as Zarrara in the UAE and Shaybah in Saudi Arabia – that had been discovered in 1968 and was being developed on the border.[13] But the dispute with a now-revolutionary Iran over the lower Gulf islands rumbled on, the Soviets invaded Afghanistan and on 22 September 1980 Iraqi forces invaded Iran. The Gulf suddenly looked a dangerous place indeed.

10

Only One Tribe: The United Arab Emirates, 1980–Present Day

FOR THE GULF rulers, the departure of the British in 1971 raised fears of a power vacuum in the region and insecurity about the Strait of Hormuz, the main outlet for Arab oil exports to the West. But the vacuum was, in a sense, quickly filled, since the shah had occupied the Tunb islands and met no military opposition from the Arab world. Bolstered by the Nixon administration's 'Twin Pillars' policy, whereby the USA relied on Saudi Arabia and Iran to protect the region, and with the Saudis preoccupied with internal matters, the shah had something of a clear field.

And yet, however much *Pax Iranica* appeared to replace *Pax Britannica*, it could not replicate the special position the British had enjoyed with the Gulf rulers, and the occupied islands remained a running sore in relations with Iran. As it happened, Iranian primacy in the Gulf was short-lived, ending when the shah was deposed in 1979, and was never regained. The question of filling the power vacuum was then as apposite as ever. While U.S. president Jimmy Carter authorized a rapid deployment force and declared the Gulf a vital American interest, it remained to be seen whether the Gulf countries would step up and provide an effective military presence.

In May 1981, finding themselves on the precarious fringes of the Iran–Iraq war (1980–88), the Gulf rulers set out their stall. At a summit in Abu Dhabi, the UAE joined Oman, Qatar, Bahrain, Saudi Arabia and Kuwait to found the Gulf Co-operation Council (GCC). 'Thus the myth of a Gulf vacuum has been swept away forever', proclaimed an official, as if, like a clever magician, the council had conjured the problem away. It was not entirely true, of course. The idea of forming a union of states similar to the EEC by combining defence and economic systems was a commendable one, but the council was soon bemired in disagreements over an American military presence in the region. Views were mixed. 'We do not accept tutelage from anyone', a Saudi representative growled, while the sultan of Oman raised no objection to U.S. forces using bases in his country.[1]

This was all very well when there was no external threat to their states, but being spectators in the Iran–Iraq war had brought a keener edge to their deliberations. The religious ramifications of the dispute could not be ignored either. Iraq was ruled by the Sunni-backed government of Saddam Hussein while revolutionary Iran had a predominantly Shiite population. Bahrain with its majority Shiite population ruled by a Sunni sheikh was thus conflicted in its allegiances. Dubai – and to a lesser extent, Sharjah and Ras al-Khaimah – had significant Iranian and indigenous Shia contingents, and these places were keen to keep trade links with Iran open. In practice, both Abu Dhabi and Dubai were behind UAE national policy, which was to seek a peaceful resolution to the conflict, despite Saddam Hussein's offer to recapture the Tunbs if the UAE would join him, an offer that was rejected.

The First Gulf War (1990–91) turned everything on its head. When Iraqi troops invaded Kuwait, concerns about Western intervention melted away. Now the GCC countries found themselves united with the Americans and others against their former Sunni ally, who had threatened the UAE for increasing oil production to assist the Allies' war effort. According to press reports, young Emiratis jostled to sign up, their luxury cars packed into the car park at the Central Military Command in Dubai as hundreds of them queued under the blazing sun to register in a volunteer army. The recruiting officer observed that in only two hours they had accepted 130 applicants. Many boys and old men were turned away. One of the successful ones, Muhammad Abdullah, a 23-year-old civil servant from Dubai, was thrilled at the prospect of going to war, saying: 'We will fight the Iraqis with guns and bare fists. God is with us to defend our country.'[2] The country had an armed force of 43,000 men at its disposal.

In the event, UAE armed forces participated and suffered casualties in battles around Khafji, and joined in operations to drive Saddam's forces out of Kuwait. The United States used Emirati airfields and ports for military operations during the war, and the UAE increased oil production from its Abu Dhabi oilfields from 750,000 barrels to over one million barrels per day. ADCO's production operations department achieved this target in less than three weeks, helping to fuel the Allies and compensate for the disruption to oil supplies caused by the war.

Military operations in the Arabian Gulf. Today, a pipeline from Habshan (Abu Dhabi) to Fujairah provides an alternative to the Strait of Hormuz for oil exports.

By now the UAE had lost Sheikh Rashid, the ruler of Dubai, who died in 1990. He had long appreciated the value of oil to the country's development. A remark attributed to him, 'My grandfather rode a camel, my father rode a camel, I drive a Mercedes, my son drives a Land Rover, his son will drive a Land Rover, but his son will ride a camel', was not a statement of despair but a plea for the future: the country had to prepare for the day when the oil ran out.[3] His greatest legacy was a policy of diversification, which ensured that if any emirate was well placed to survive beyond the oil era, it was surely Dubai – or so it seemed. He was succeeded by his eldest son, Maktoum.

The full implications of the oil wealth were still emerging. As an economic boom created a demand for wide-ranging skills in the UAE, expatriates attracted by a zero-tax lifestyle flocked in, and Emiratis went to local schools or attended colleges across the globe in order to acquire those skills for themselves. But even today the indigenous population remains relatively small and skills shortages endure in certain industries, such as building and engineering; there are few locally educated carpenters, plumbers, nurses, car mechanics or chefs, for instance. There are targets for 'Emiratization' in various sectors, such as 75 per cent in the oil business and 50 per cent in the financial sector.

For some, the new money was invigorating, bringing ambitious schemes, impossible aspirations and mountains of debt. In Sharjah, which enjoyed revenues from oil and gas fields, ambitious construction programmes brought massive debts, estimated to be in the region of u.s.$1 billion by the late 1980s. We have seen how, in 1972, Sheikh Sultan bin Muhammed had succeeded to the emirate in difficult circumstances after the assassination of his predecessor. The sheikh was a learned man who took a close interest in literature and the arts and was determined to develop Sharjah as a cultural centre. But in June 1987, while Sultan was abroad, he was surprised to hear of his own abdication, allegedly on the grounds of financial mismanagement. There followed an intense debate between sheikhs Zayed and Rashid over whether Sultan's brother, Abdul Aziz, should be allowed to succeed. In the end, Sultan was confirmed as ruler and his brother was recognized as his heir, leaving the former to pursue a programme of reform. After a decent interval, however, Abdul Aziz was dismissed and went into exile, and Sultan ruled on.

If we imagine the Trucial Coast as a few nebulous shapes drifting without common purpose, then the new oil wealth was like the Big Bang, bringing rapid change to the emirates and utterly transforming them. But there was a darker aspect to all of this, for the new money also attracted those with different skills: the crooks and the carpetbaggers of the world. Lacking candour and despising the old ways, these intruders held the bedouin values of trust and honour in contempt. Their influence was most dramatically illustrated by the collapse of the Bank of Credit and Commerce International (BCCI) in 1991. This international bank had been set up in Abu Dhabi in 1972 with the help of a Pakistani businessman, Agha Hassan Abedi, and became the seventh-largest privately owned bank in the world. In the late 1980s, there were concerns over its links with drug-money laundering in the United States. Added to this scenario was a cast of shady characters spread across the globe, including General Manuel Noriega, the notorious 'Pineapple Face' of Panama.

If this financial chicanery sounds familiar, it is probably because it resonates with the global banking scandals of more recent times. While regulators looked on, false accounting, concealment of losses and irregular loans were added to a growing list of malpractices. In July 1991, after receiving a report of 'massive and widespread fraud', the Bank of England closed down BCCI, seizing its £13 billion in assets.[4] At this time, Abu Dhabi owned a 77 per cent share in the bank. Sheikh Zayed, who behaved honourably throughout, stepped in with a £50 million rescue bid, but the attempt failed. A seven-man task force was set up in Abu Dhabi to deal with the fallout. Appearing before a u.s. Senate subcommittee in May 1992, one of the task force members, Ahmed al-Sayegh, provided a detailed account of the affair and declared: 'Victimised is an understatement. You can't believe the sense of betrayal in Abu Dhabi.' It was reported that the emirate had lost £2 billion in the scandal. In 1994 twelve former BCCI executives were convicted in Abu Dhabi of fraud and sent to prison.

By 2004, when the GCC was planning to meet in Abu Dhabi city, the BCCI affair was long forgotten and Emiratis' admiration for Sheikh Zayed was (as always) undimmed. For the upcoming summit, highways were cleaned up and the final touches made to a new hotel on the corniche that would house the delegates. But then the venue was suddenly changed, without official explanation. It was widely known, and understood, that Sheikh Zayed was fading away. Over the next few weeks, the government carried on business as usual and, on 2 November, he died of natural causes. His eldest son, Khalifa, succeeded to both emirate and presidency without incident. As ordained several years previously, another son, Mohammed, succeeded Khalifa as crown prince of Abu Dhabi and deputy supreme commander of the UAE Armed Forces.

Foreign rumours about the succession carried no weight with the Emirati community, since Sheikh Zayed had already settled the arrangements long before his death. There were two camps in the Al Nahyan family, one around Khalifa and the other around his half brothers, the sons of Zayed's favourite wife, Fatima, who were known as the 'Bani Fatima'. Khalifa's younger half brother, Sultan, suffered from a lack of comparable status – his mother was from one of the smaller tribes and had been divorced by Zayed at a young age. This Sultan was caught between the two more powerful groupings, eventually losing out when Zayed's third son, Mohammed of the Bani Fatima, was nominated as Khalifa's heir (deputy crown prince) in January 2004. Although Sultan retains a senior position in the family, and is well respected in the emirate to this day, he is not in line for the succession.

It is in the nature of these large, diverse families that there should be sub-groups and coalitions forming around a nuclei of a ruler's wives. Sheikh Zayed had nine wives and 21 children. There was also an older family group, known as the Bani Mohammed bin Khalifa after the eldest son of the tribal patriarch, Khalifa, who died in 1945. Many from this group held prominent positions. Although members of this group made way as Zayed's sons reached maturity, a number of them still retained high office, among them Sheikh Suroor bin Mohammed, who remained chamberlain of the Presidential Court until 2004; Tahnoun bin Mohammed, the ruler's representative in the Eastern Region, Al Ain, from 1969 to the present; Hamdan bin Mohammed, deputy prime minister until 1990; and Mubarak bin Mohammed, Minister of Interior until 1979. A son of the late Sheikh Mubarak has been in the cabinet since the 1990s, another since 2004, and a son of Tahnoun has held key positions in security agencies for many years.

Fatima bint Mubarak al-Kitbi – the matriarch of the Bani Fatima – is often described as Zayed's 'favourite wife'.[5] She is in the tradition of influential *sheikhas* such as Hassa bint al-Mur of Dubai and her own mother-in-law, Salama bint Buti. She was born in a village near Al Ain and was in her mid-teens when she met Sheikh Zayed at a dance. Her eldest son, Mohammed bin Zayed (known colloquially as MBZ), was born in March 1961 when Fatima was about sixteen years old, or even younger, and she went on to have another five sons. She has seen all her sons promoted to positions of power, which includes Mohammed as crown prince and deputy supreme commander; Hamdan as former foreign minister, now ruler's representative in the Western Region; Hazza as national security adviser and deputy chairman of the Abu Dhabi Executive Council; and Abdulla as former information minister, now foreign minister.

Fatima is fondly referred to as the 'Mother of the Nation'. Besides acting as a key figure in the family, she is a strong supporter of women's rights. In 2006 the first – partial – elections for the Federal National Council took place, with both men and women included in the electoral colleges. Perhaps more significantly, the first woman cabinet minister was appointed in 2004, and there are now four women in the cabinet.

Abu Dhabi remains the largest and wealthiest of the seven emirates, and still generously redistributes its wealth among the smaller ones. As if to emphasize this point, early in his presidency Khalifa ordered a 25 per cent pay rise for all federal government employees. The Al Nahyan control three of the most important institutions in Abu Dhabi: the Supreme Petroleum Council, which supervises the oil and gas industry; the Abu Dhabi Executive Council, the emirates' cabinet; and the Abu Dhabi Investment Authority (ADIA), a sovereign wealth fund. Apart from the presence of prominent Al Nahyan figures, these bodies are populated by members of sub-sections of the Bani Yas tribal confederation:

Al Mazroui, Al Qubaisi and Al Suwaidi. There are other major tribes of great significance, the names of old, such as the Dhawahir, who include the Al Badis, from Al Ain; the Manasir, including the Al Khailis; and the Awamir. However, many of those in government, including executive council and cabinet members, come from none of these groups. Khaldoon Khalifa al-Mubarak, perhaps the most notable non-sheikhly figure among them, is a man of many business interests who also happens to be chairman of Manchester United Football Club. While tribal links are important, they are not exclusively so.

The other side of the coin is that, as tribal roles fade, so too does the risk of old rivalries sparking back to life. Relations between Abu Dhabi and Dubai were stable at the time of Khalifa's accession. This state of affairs was due in no small part to the good relations between Crown Prince Mohammed and Mohammed bin Rashid, the current UAE vice president and prime minister. Meanwhile, the 67-year-old President Khalifa has proved to be an unassuming and popular leader, although ill-health has kept him out of the limelight in more recent times.

Elsewhere in the Emirates the founding fathers have passed away and a new generation rules. In 1974 Sheikh Mohammed bin Hamad Al Sharqi of Fujairah died and was succeeded by his son, Hamad. In 1981 Sheikh Rashid bin Humaid Al Nuaimi of Ajman was succeeded by his son, Humaid. In the same year, Sheikh Ahmad II bin Rashid Al Mualla of Umm al-Qaiwain was succeeded by his son, Rashid, who in turn was succeeded by Saud in 2009. But things were not quite so peaceful in Ras al-Khaimah.

In June 2003 the sound of gunfire was heard in its streets after the ageing ruler, the long-serving Sheikh Saqr bin Mohammed al-Qasimi, replaced his eldest son Khalid as crown prince with Saud, Khalid's younger half-brother. The reason for his decision is not entirely clear, but may have arisen from a number of issues, such as Khalid's alleged involvement in burning a U.S. flag in protest at the invasion of Iraq, and his demands for greater women's rights. The ruler's decision was enforced by the intervention of Abu Dhabian troops, and Khalid went into exile. Since then, Khalid has returned to the UAE and attempted to regain his position, but to no avail. Saud became ruler upon the death of his father in 2010, and the politics of succession duly shifted to the next generation.

In Dubai, Sheikh Maktoum had been planning for the day when the oil ran out, encouraging private enterprise and promoting Dubai as

Qasr al-Hosn in 2014, surrounded by the roads and buildings of a modern city.

the financial and trading hub of the Middle East. The Al Maktoum philosophy of 'build and they will come' that had begun under Sheikh Rashid was now carried forward on an ever-growing scale, though in fact it was Maktoum's elder brother, Mohammed, who was holding the reins. The very name 'Dubai' became a symbol for entrepreneurial success as the city became famous across the world as a business and tourist centre and the home of an international airline, Emirates, founded in 1985, which now competes with the UAE national airline, Etihad, based in Abu Dhabi and founded in 2003. This trend accelerated under Maktoum's more dynamic successor, Mohammed, whose reign saw an aggressive campaign of global investment. Only a single-minded recluse could have claimed ignorance of Dubai, the poster boy for economic success.

Naturally, the critics saw things in an entirely different light. The rate of expansion was so great that the economy was in danger of spinning out of control; the construction boom was sucking in foreign workers without adequate provision for their welfare; a lack of regulation over the banking sector brought allegations of money laundering for terrorist organizations; and a surge of domestic workers from Asia gave rise to accusations of human trafficking. Above all, they saw Dubai riding for a massive fall, and the arrival of the global financial crisis in 2008 was greeted by a chorus of 'We told you so.'

Dubai was badly affected by the crisis because of its exposure in the international markets, ambitious construction projects and a real-estate market fuelled by global credit; when that credit became scarce, the market crashed. The most enduring images of Dubai's great slump are those of half-finished building sites, cars abandoned at the airport and theme parks stranded on the drawing board, all left behind by the flight of money and commerce. Residents of the Palm Jumeirah, the man-made island in the shape of a palm tree that can be seen from outer space, saw the value of their properties drop by a huge 60 per cent. The banks stopped lending and the stock market dropped by 70 per cent. The federal government's actions, as well as loans from Abu Dhabi, prevented a serious banking crisis, although firms involved in the construction sector were seriously affected. Expatriate workers made redundant immediately lost their visas and had to leave; others made a quick exit to escape debt collectors.

Something was seriously wrong but, in the opaque world of Arabian business, it was difficult to know the full extent of the problem. The Dubai authorities tried to put a brave face on matters, and Emiratis remained loyal and somewhat sensitive to criticism. When the Japanese consul general, Seiichi Otsuka, complained that Japanese firms were not being paid, the local press called for him to be expelled from the country. But on 25 November 2009 there came dramatic news that Dubai World (the Dubai government's chief investment company) had requested a debt standstill from creditors, effectively stopping payments on its U.S.$59 billion debt for six months. It was a huge reversal for the emirate, and the Dubai-based conglomerate in particular, since it was at the centre of real-estate development in the city through its subsidiary Nakheel ('date palm'), which was the most vulnerable part of the business and also announced a debt standstill. The fact that the announcement was made just as the country was closing down for a ten-day public holiday did nothing to calm nerves.

In the event, Dubai was rescued in the nick of time. By now, Abu Dhabi had one of the world's largest sovereign wealth funds and was well placed to lend the Dubai government $10 billion to pay the holders of a $4.1 billion Islamic bond, called a *sukuk*, issued by Nakheel, with the remainder to go to Dubai World's suppliers and contractors. The Central Bank as well as Abu Dhabi extended large loans, making it a concerted federal action. But reports of frantic meetings and complex negotiations rather missed the point, since this was essentially a deal struck between the two rulers, a tribal affair that 50 years before would have been settled over coffee in the desert. Its terms were not disclosed, but naming Dubai's Burj al-Khalifa, the tallest tower in the world, after the ruler of Abu Dhabi was surely a symbolic nod towards the emirate with the deeper pockets.

In foreign affairs, the UAE moved closer to the West, driven in part by concerns about Iran's power in the Gulf and its nuclear ambitions. In July 1994 a bilateral defence pact allowed U.S. warships to visit the Jebel Ali port, and airfields to be upgraded for U.S. combat support flights; the U.S. Air Force have also used Al Dhafra air base, including for the use of U2 spy planes, in the past. But the dispute between the UAE and Iran over the lower Gulf islands, Abu Musa and the Tunbs, still festered. In 1992 Teheran insisted that Emiratis visiting the islands apply for visas. In 1996 it was claimed that Iran had built an airport on Abu Musa and a power station on Greater Tunb. In August 2008 there were reports of a marine rescue centre and registration office for ships and sailors being built on Abu Musa. In April 2012 a visit to the island by Iranian president Mahmoud Ahmadinejad triggered a strong protest from the UAE government. In January 2014 much excitement was sparked by a report that Omani-brokered talks had resulted in an agreement to return the Tunbs to the UAE while the future of Abu Musa was still being negotiated. But the report proved erroneous, and the news bubble soon burst.

Relations with Saudi Arabia have been changeable. A renewed interest in the Shaybah/Zarrara oilfield brought new questions about the 1974 Treaty of Jeddah. This was the agreement signed between Sheikh Zayed and King Faisal to settle the Buraimi dispute giving the hydrocarbons from the oilfield to Saudi Arabia, which has still not been ratified by the UAE Federal National Council. In another dispute, Saudi Arabia protested about pipelines carrying gas from Qatar's Dolphin Field to Abu Dhabi that crossed its territorial waters off Khor al-Udaid. After a brief public flare-up, the argument disappeared behind closed doors.

The idea of a European-style union of Arabian states has hit the buffers over concerns about Saudi domination. In 2009 the UAE withdrew from talks between GCC states on implementing a single currency after it transpired that a proposed central bank would be located in Riyadh and not Abu Dhabi as apparently promised. But against greater threats, the two countries will presumably close ranks. In March 2011 Saudi troops and Emirati police officers were sent to Bahrain as part of a GCC deployment to protect key installations on the island during Shiite demonstrations there.

The UAE has shown an independent streak by adopting a more prominent role in foreign operations. In 2011, according to U.S. sources, the UAE sent its fighter jets against Libyan militias, the first time it had directly attacked another country. In 2012 military expenditure amounted to more than $19 billion, making the UAE the fourth-largest arms importer in the world. Another aspect of the UAE's military activities – one of the UAE's first female pilots, Major Mariam al-Mansouri, being involved with her squadron and other Arab countries in an action against ISIL fighters in Iraq – marked a startling milestone in the progress that the country has made towards women's rights.

If these events demonstrate anything, it is that there is a growing sense of national pride and self-confidence within the UAE. The new generation of leaders are less parochial and are more enthusiastic towards federal working than their fathers – with the exception of Sheikh Zayed, who had always been a staunch supporter of the cause. But even his death brought a change of tempo, and an apparent willingness to embrace democracy by introducing elections to the Federal National Council, albeit to a limited degree.

There was little succour for home-grown radicals in the Arab Spring of 2011, which passed by with relatively little incident. Western criticisms about a lack of human rights, press freedom and the treatment of foreign workers are generally regarded as misguided or exaggerated. Progress towards meeting the promise of the 1971 constitution of a 'comprehensive, representative, democratic regime' has been cautious.[6] However, one only has to look at the underlying tribal bonds of UAE society to realize that democratizing the country overnight carries certain risks. For here is a dilemma for present and future generations: how to effect meaningful change without ripping out the tribal heart of the nation.

———

VISITORS TO THE UAE might be forgiven for thinking they had entered a vast business park, the home of a shiny corporation known as 'UAE plc'. Everything seems to reinforce the impression of a homogeneous society pursuing common goals. Clichés and hyperboles abound: the Arabian 'backwater' is now in the first rank of world nations, a place of 'astonishing' growth and 'staggering' wealth, Dubai is the new

Beirut.[7] The desert spaces, once the haunt of bedouins and their flocks, are now bedecked with oil wells and pipelines, processing plants and export terminals. The first drops of crude oil that surfaced in the late 1950s were more than a simple commodity; they were the catalyst for monumental change.

The world is young again: the first picture of the UAE to spring to mind is Dubai, home of the Burj al-Khalifa, the tower that pierces the sky. Here the quiet days have long been shattered by hammering, banging and clanking from numerous building sites around the city. Abu Dhabi, the more restrained capital, has changed dramatically. Apart from a handful of relics such as the Al Maqta watchtower and the palace at Qasr al-Hosn, the old *'arish* and stone buildings have long since been bulldozed into the ground. Perhaps more impressive than the great tower of its neighbour is the Sheikh Zayed mosque, with its crisp white domes presenting a vision of ethereal beauty against a clear blue sky.

Nothing from the recent past is considered sacred. The Volcano Fountain, built in the 1980s on the corniche of Abu Dhabi city, was a meeting place where vendors mingled with locals out for an evening stroll, and National Day was celebrated with dancing to flutes and drums. At night, water cascading down its tiered sides was lit up to resemble lava flowing down a mountainside. But it is gone, demolished in 2004 as part of a redevelopment plan.

There are the museums, restored forts and archaeological sites, all evidence of a keen interest in the past. And, through the brash modernity, the voices of the older people are still heard, for every Emirati has a story to tell:

> My father was a *nakhudha*, he owned his own *baghala* and traded and carried up and down the coast, up the Gulf, to the Makran and India. In the season he went pearling in the boat, and he went fishing in it. He inherited the boat from his father, who made most of his money trading slaves from East Africa, and his father, my great-grandfather, was the last real slave trader in our family.[8]

In fact, most indigenous Emiratis can trace their tribal history and genealogy farther back, with some family trees optimistically rooted in the time of Moses. The modern descendants of these ancient patriarchs, such as the current president, Khalifa bin Zayed bin Sultan al-Nahyan, have retained their links to the past, with references to forefathers, tribal affiliation or dynasty in their names. Old tribal patterns lie at the heart of society, for the emirates of the UAE are ruled by the same families – such as the Al Nahyan, Maktoum and Qasimi – that ruled the sheikhdoms in the dim and distant past.

'We are tribe and tribe is family' is a refrain that now translates into loyalty towards the government of the day. 'Our leader is a sheikh' reflects how many people see the president of the UAE, Khalifa bin Zayed, as a bedouin chief, albeit in a vastly different world to the one of his forefathers. And the concept has been taken a stage further, as described in the recent headline of a local newspaper: 'In the UAE the Only Tribe Is the Emirati.'[9] Such assertions should be read in context, however, since 84 per cent of the UAE's 8.5 million people are expatriates, making Emiratis a minority in their own country. The real point being made here is that political power is in the hands of the seven ruling families who head the tribes to which most Emiratis belong. They are an elite, and being members of a relatively small group has heightened their perceptions of a national identity, and made them protective of it. Today, it is not enough to hold a UAE passport in order to establish full citizenship: one must also have a document known as *khulasat al-qaid*, a family book, if one is to qualify.

And yet, even though these documents confer access to generous state benefits, such as social security and free or subsidized housing, older Emiratis will still hanker after the past, remembering a time when they did things for themselves and helped each other. Apart from the patrimony of sheikhs, they had no need for welfare in the past and being relocated from their old dwellings to modern houses only uprooted and disconnected them from each other and their past. Their narrative goes something like this: 'Once we all knew each other but now we don't even know who our neighbours are.' But if this is said with a tinge of sadness for days gone by, it is only for a fleeting moment. They are immensely patriotic, though somewhat astonished by the Big Bang that has utterly transformed their world.

And while buildings fall and rise, the original institutions of the UAE have proved to be remarkably resilient, and the union has survived. The crunch came in 1996 when Sheikh Zayed, weary from the political battles of the union, at last saw the provisional constitution replaced by a permanent one. This, to all intents and purposes, was the same as the earlier document except that Abu Dhabi was made the federal capital,

The Sheikh Zayed Mosque in Abu Dhabi. It is the largest place of worship in the UAE and can accommodate 40,000 worshippers.

reflecting the fact that, over the years, it had become accepted as such. The Constitution also confirmed that the seven rulers would form the Supreme Council, the most powerful body in the land.

In this way, the constitution tied the federal structure to tribal custom, and gave the rulers a compelling reason for working together. The body politic was fitted out with a profusion of ministries, departments and councils that dressed the old tribal structures in the clothes of a modern state. And finally, a measure of democracy has since been introduced, for although the 40-member Federal National Council remains an advisory, consultative body, half of its members are now elected in an electoral college system. In 2011 there were 129,274 electors nationwide, compared to 6,689 in the 2006 contest, about 20 per cent of the potential electorate.

The notion of an advisory, consultative body brings us back to the age-old tradition of the *majlis*. The sight of a room set aside for the reception of visitors, laid with carpets and strewn with cushions, incense such as *oud* and *bakhour* smouldering in the corner, sweetmeats in a silver tray and coffee pot on a stove, is a familiar one in today's UAE. And yet this is a tradition that goes back to the days when a tent in the desert would have been used for the same purpose, as a place where the head of the household or tribe could meet and greet guests. In more formal settings, the *majlis* was any place where rulers met their tribesmen and heard their petitions. The ghost of Sheikh Saqr III of Sharjah would recognize this scene. Back in the 1950s, it will be recalled, Saqr held his *majlis* outside his palace in Sharjah, a crumbling Portuguese fort mostly used as a children's playground. This was of little consequence, for the sight of the ruler sitting with his entourage on a bench at its great gateway was enough to convey the full majesty of his office – a simple and effective way for a ruler to commune with his people.

At all events, the *majlis* reaffirmed the ties of loyalty that bound a tribe to its ruler, conveying an intimacy that would be difficult to replicate in a populous industrial society. Outside the federal structures, *majalis* live on in dialogues between citizens and members of the ruling families in each of the emirates, providing places where Emiratis can air an issue without going through official channels. Others attend the *majlis* in order to discuss government proposals, and these meetings often reach a consensus that is reflected in a final policy or scheme. However, since the *majlis* is essentially a channel of communication between tribal members and their leaders, it may provide a different experience for those who have no such connection.

The *majlis* has been adapted to meet the requirements of the modern world. During the month of Ramadan, for example, a series of lectures is held in the *majlis* of Crown Prince Mohammed at Al Bateen Palace in Abu Dhabi. Guests gather in a hall that has been designed to resemble the interior of a long tent, with a ribbed canopy draped across the ceiling. Male members of the Al Nahyan will sit in their traditional white robes and *ghutras* along one side of the room with female members dressed in black on the other side. Guest lecturers address them and invited guests on topical issues, often in the presence of the crown prince himself. Academics, scientists and business leaders using all the modern audio and visual aids deliver lectures on a broad range of subjects. In July 2014 the Canadian astronaut Chris Hadfield delivered a lecture about space exploration in which he congratulated the UAE for its decision to establish a space agency to launch a research probe to Mars. Perhaps an inquisitive Sheikh Shakhbut bin Sultan, had he been alive, would have listened with a mixture of feelings, relishing the chance to discuss the finer points of rocketry with the experts but appalled at the cost of the project, and amused that his kin should now be seeking a future in the red deserts of the solar system.

We have seen how Islam permeates every aspect of life in the region, and for the Western visitor this is most noticeable when the day is punctuated by the call of the *muezzin* and the five-times-a-day routine of prayer. In the legal field, making the transition from tribal society to industrialized nation has brought the challenge of reconciling Islamic-based Sharia law with modern commercial practice. Although Islam is confirmed in the constitution as the state religion and the main source of law, Sharia is only used in particular cases. Its influence is most evident in the field of social law – family law, divorce and succession – while commercial matters tend to be dealt with under separate codes. At first glance, usury, the charging of interest, is banned under Sharia law, but a 2011 decision of the Supreme Court ruled that it is permissible, taking the view that interest was a form of damages for late payment. In criminal law, payment of blood money after a death or injury is permitted under Sharia law. Certain crimes known as *Al Hudud* – fornication, murder, theft, adultery and homosexuality – have fixed penalties, such as flogging and amputation. Some rulers have suspended these punishments and replaced them with jail terms and fines.

Today, confronted with a wealth that was once beyond anyone's imagination, it is a miracle that anything from the past has survived in any meaningful form. At first glance, like all good miracles, this one appears to defy explanation. But in the light of the country's history and considering how the climate and environment have shaped patterns of living, how foreign invasions and tribal wars disrupted and defined the political landscape, and how human interaction brought trade and

commerce to the region, the roots of the nation can be seen. And of all the themes to emerge, continuity of tribe, language and religion are the strongest of all. Emiratis are the trustees of a great tradition, the keepers of a golden shore:

> On land and in the sea, our forefathers lived and survived in this environment. They were able to do so only because they recognised the need to conserve it, to take from it only what they needed to live, and to preserve it for succeeding generations.[10]

On 2 December, the union is celebrated by *al-Eid al-Watani*, a national holiday with flags and fireworks, just as it has been each year since 1971, all reinforcing the idea of a one-tribe nation. Today, the UAE is regarded as a beacon of stability in an unsettled Middle East, and the disagreements of the early days seem a distant memory. The seven founding fathers are all gone now, although their images will always appear on 'Spirit of the Union' posters celebrating the event. If they were looking down they would surely be amazed at how rapidly the UAE has continued to grow and prosper, and perhaps concerned by its more proactive military role and profile in the region.

Of course, the changes are largely due to oil, and the great economic challenge of the future is how to survive the eventual loss of its immense revenues. In foreign affairs the threat from powerful neighbours remains a real one. If history is anything to go by, a resilient

The modern Dubai skyline.

and pioneering spirit will see future generations through, but the stoicism and wisdom of earlier generations will be required too. For while the shore still glitters with wealth and promise, the old voices quietly fade away, washed like grains of sand into a dark, settling sea.

Maps

Regional Map of the Arabian Gulf

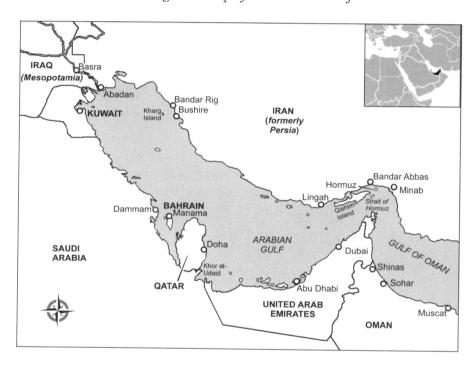

The United Arab Emirates

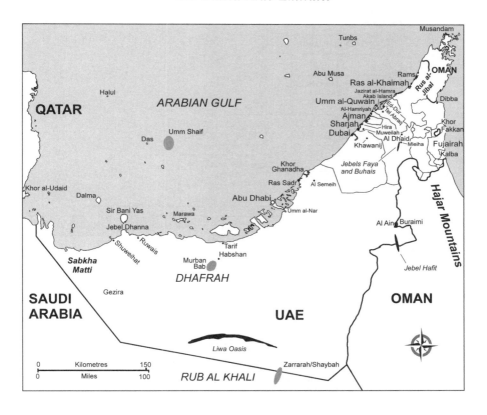

Appendices

Al Nahyan – Selected Family Tree

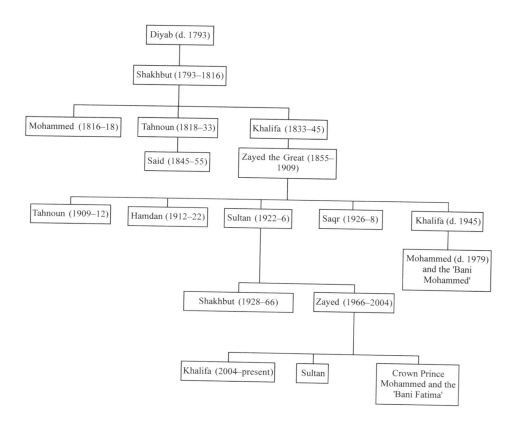

Diyab (d. 1793)

Shakhbut (1793–1816)

Mohammed (1816–18) | Tahnoun (1818–33) | Khalifa (1833–45)

Said (1845–55) | Zayed the Great (1855–1909)

Tahnoun (1909–12) | Hamdan (1912–22) | Sultan (1922–6) | Saqr (1926–8) | Khalifa (d. 1945)

Mohammed (d. 1979) and the 'Bani Mohammed'

Shakhbut (1928–66) | Zayed (1966–2004)

Khalifa (2004–present) | Sultan | Crown Prince Mohammed and the 'Bani Fatima'

Al Maktoum – Selected Family Tree

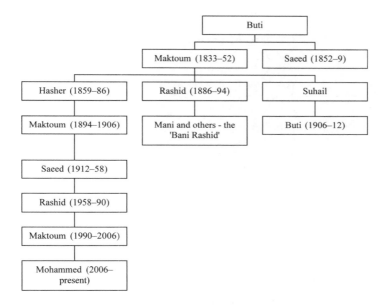

Timeline

125,000 BC — The first known inhabitants live around Jebel Faya

75,000 BC — The last Ice Age drains the Arabian Gulf, the start of the 'Gulf Oasis'

8000 BC — The end of the Ice Age brings rising sea levels, flooding the Arabian Gulf

5500 BC — Ubaid period begins

3200 BC — Hafit period begins

2600 BC — Umm al-Nar period begins

2000 BC — Wadi Suq period begins

1600 BC — Late Bronze Age begins

1300 BC — Iron Age begins

300 BC — Pre-Islamic period begins

AD 240 — Sasanian period begins

630 — The Islamic era begins with the arrival of emissaries from Mecca

1507 — The king of Hormuz agrees to pay tribute to the Portuguese

1622 — Anglo-Dutch rivalry intensifies after the Portuguese lose Hormuz

1648 — The Omanis expel the Portuguese from their last stronghold in the region, Muscat

1820 — General Treaty of Peace, the start of the British era in the Gulf

1892	– The British enter into the Exclusive Agreements with the Gulf sheikhs
1903	– Lord Curzon visits Sharjah
1922	– The Trucial sheikhs agree to exclude non-British oil companies
1939	– Sheikh Shakhbut of Abu Dhabi signs a 75-year oil concession
1952	– March: Fujairah is recognized as the seventh member of the Trucial States First meeting of the Trucial States Council – September: Saudi Arabian contingent occupies Hamasa in the Buraimi Oasis
1955	– The Trucial Oman Levies reoccupy Hamasa
1958	– Discovery of the first commercial oil offshore at Umm Shaif
1962	– Oil exports begin
1968	– Withdrawal of all UK forces from the Arabian Gulf announced
1971	– November: Iran occupies part of Abu Musa and seizes the Tunbs – December: UK forces withdraw from the Gulf – Six sheikhdoms (emirates) come together to form the United Arab Emirates (UAE)
1972	– Ras al-Khaimah joins the UAE
1974	– The Treaty of Jeddah settles the boundaries of the UAE with Saudi Arabia
1981	– The Gulf Cooperation Council is formed
1990	– The Iraqi invasion of Kuwait
1996	– A permanent constitution is agreed. Abu Dhabi is confirmed as capital of the UAE
2004	– UAE president Sheikh Zayed Bin Sultan al-Nahyan passes away and is succeeded as ruler of Abu Dhabi and president of the UAE by his son, Khalifa
2006	– First elections to the Federal National Council

Glossary

Abbasid – the ruling dynasty of the Islamic caliphate between AD 750 and 1256, having succeeded the Umayyads

aflaj (sing. *falaj*) – water channels

'arish – palm-frond house

baghala – large trading dhow

bakhour – a mixture of scents burned slowly to refresh a room

bani – the sons of (or tribe)

bin – the son of

dar – a tribal range, the extent of a tribe's grazing area

daulah – literally 'the power', a term used to describe the British government in the Gulf

Hajj – the annual pilgrimage to Mecca

haji – someone who has completed the *Haj*

hawala – an unofficial method of payment between individuals which does not involve the actual transfer of cash between vendor and purchaser. The payer delivers a sum of money to a *hawala* dealer who then notifies a dealer in the payee's district to pay over the same amount of cash (with commission added)

hijra – tribal migration

Holocene – the current geological epoch that began some 11,700 years ago

jalbut – a type of dhow, one of the most common in the Arabian Gulf

jihad – a religious war

jilla – a 25-kilogram (55-lb) basket of dates

Khaliji – people of the Arabian Gulf

Khan Bahadur – a title awarded by the Viceroy of India to Muslim employees, akin to 'Great Prince' and ranked above that of Khan Sahib, 'Master Prince'

majlis (pl. *majalis*) – a meeting room, place where a ruler holds public audiences to hear petitions

muezzin – a crier who calls the faithful to prayer

mutawwa – a local religious teacher

nahham – singer on a pearl boat

nakhudha (pl. *nawakhidah*) – captain

Nasrani – Christian

oud – small pieces of agarwood used to perfume a room or clothes

Pleistocene – a geological epoch that lasted from 2.6 million to 11,700 years ago

qadi – a judge ruling according to Sharia law

Qawasim – the principal ruling family of the northern sheikhdoms, *Qasimi* being the singular and adjective. Also describes the tribes under their control

abkha – a salt flat

shamal – wind from the north

shisha – a hookah pipe, also known as a 'hubble-bubble', used for smoking tobacco

shu'ai – a medium-sized dhow

sirdal al-ghaus – captain of a pearling fleet

tarifa – representative

terrada – native boat

Toumina – a religious celebration

Umayyad – ruling dynasty of the Islamic caliphate between AD 661 and 750

zakat – a religious tax

References

Preface

1 Donald Hawley, 'Report on a Visit to Abu Dhabi', 29 July 1960, HAW 10/3/43, Durham University Archives and Special Collections.

1 Desert, Sea and Mountain: Southeast Arabia in Prehistory

1 Story of the rock told by two Jalaji tribesmen from Sfai, Fujairah, in William and Fidelity Lancaster, *Honour Is in Contentment: Life before Oil in Ras Al-Khaimah (UAE) and Some Neighbouring Regions* (Berlin, 2011), p. 533.
2 The Mesopotamian *Epic of Gilgamesh*, dating from about 2100 BC, tells the story of a plan by the gods to destroy the world with a great flood.
3 Geoffrey Bibby, *Looking for Dilmun* (New York, 1969), pp. 225–34; Bibby to G. G. (Geoffrey) Stockwell, 8 October 1958, cited in *Fifty Years of Emirates Archaeology*, ed. D. T. Potts and P. Hellyer (Dubai, 2012), p. 14.
4 Kazmi Aftab, 'New Evidence Shows Falaj in Al Ain Is World's Oldest', *Gulf News* (16 March 2003). The department is now the Abu Dhabi Tourism and Culture Authority.
5 '"Super" camels' from D. T. Potts, *In the Land of the Emirates: The Archaeology and History of the UAE* (Abu Dhabi, 2012), p. 129; for the research, see H.-P. Uerpmann, 'Camel and Horse Skeletons from Protohistoric Graves at Mleiha in the Emirate of Sharjah (UAE)', *Arabian Archaeology and Epigraphy*, x (1999), pp. 102–18.
6 Although the name Persia is derived from a particular part of Iran, namely Fars Province, to Westerners it came to signify the whole country until its name was officially changed to Iran in 1935.
7 Cited in D. T. Potts, 'Before the Emirates: An Archaeological and Historical Account of Developments in the Region, *c.* 5000 BC to 676 AD', in *Perspectives on the United Arab Emirates*, ed. I. Al-Abed and P. Hellyer (London, 2001), p. 59.

2 Emergence: Greater Oman, the Arabian Gulf and the Bani Yas, AD 630–1909

1 Peter Hellyer, *Hidden Riches: An Archaeological Introduction to the United Arab Emirates* (Abu Dhabi, 1998), p. 17.
2 M. A. Khan, *Islamic Jihad: The Legacy of Forced Conversion, Imperialism and Slavery* (Bloomington, IN, 2009), p. 69.

3 Al Muqaddasi, cited in D. T. Potts, *In the Land of the Emirates: The Archeology and History of the UAE* (Abu Dhabi, 2001), p. 149.

4 Sirhan Ibn Said, *Keshf-ul-Ghummeh*, translated into English by E. C. Ross as *Annals of Oman* (Calcutta, 1874), cited in Hellyer, *Hidden Riches*, pp. 135–6.

5 Henry E. J. Stanley, trans., *A Description of the Coasts of East Africa and Malabar in the Beginning of the Sixteenth Century by Duarte Barosa* (London, 1866), p. 34.

6 Newsletter reported in *Nouvelles Extraordinaires de Divers Endroits*, no. 48 (17 June 1766).

7 Humaid ibn Muhammed ibn Razik, *The Imams and Seyyids of Oman* (English version published in London, 1871) and Ibn Said, *Annals*, both cited in Peter Hellyer, *Filling in the Blanks: Recent Archaeological Discoveries in Abu Dhabi* (Dubai, 1998). The presence of a fort was first reported in J. Czastka and Peter Hellyer, 'An Archaeological Survey of the Mantakha As'sirra area in Abu Dhabi's Western Region', *Tribulus*, XLI (April 1994), pp. 9–12.

8 There is evidence of an earlier occupation of Abu Dhabi Island from shards dating back to the third or fourth centuries AD.

9 Captain G. B. Brucks, 'Memoir Descriptive of the Navigation of the Gulf of Persia', India Office, *Bombay Selections*, XXIV, pp. 547–8.

10 John Barrett Kelly, *Britain and the Persian Gulf, 1795–1880* (London, 1968), p. 21.

11 India Office Records (IOR) R/15/1/173.

12 Mullah Husain to Resident, 8 October 1844, *UK Memorial*, II, Annex B, No. 9.

13 'Précis of Correspondence Regarding Trucial Chiefs', 1854–1905, IOR/L/PS/20/C248D.

14 Maria Theresa thalers (dollars) were so-named because they were first coined in Vienna during the reign of the Habsburg empress Maria Theresa. They became accepted currency throughout the Middle East and were still being used well into the twentieth century.

15 Lt-Col. E. C. Ross, *Administration Report of the Persian Gulf Residency and Muscat Political Agency for the year 18834* (Calcutta, 1884).

16 Samuel Zwemer, 'Three Journeys in Northern Oman', *Geographical Journal*, XIX/1 (1902), p. 56.

17 Kelly, *Britain and the Persian Gulf*, p. 673, n.1.

3 A Maritime Kind: The Qawasim, the British and the Trucial Coast, 1718–1906

1 Political Residency, Bushire, IOR/R/15/1/16, pp. 92–4.

2 James Wellsted, *Travels in Arabia* (London, 1838), p. 257.

3 James S. Buckingham, *Travels in Assyria, Media, and Persia*, vol. II (London, 1829), pp. 350–51; 'Emir of the True Believers', cited in Charles Davies, *The Blood-red Flag: An Investigation into Qasimi Piracy, 1797–1820* (Exeter, 1997), p. 248.

4 Bombay Archives, Secret and Political Department Diaries, No. 339 of 1809; Minto to Duncan, Fort William, 3 April 1809.

5 Sind (Sindh) is a province of today's Pakistan.

6 Buckingham, *Travels in Assyria,* p. 249.
7 Also referred to as the Trucial Sheikhdoms or Trucial Oman.
8 John Gordon Lorimer, *Gazetteer of the Persian Gulf,* I (1915), p. 719.
9 Curzon to Hamilton, 12 August 1903, cited in Briton Cooper Busch, *Britain and the Persian Gulf, 1894–1904* (London, 1967), p. 258.
10 John Gordon Lorimer, *Gazetteer of the Persian Gulf,* I/I (1915), p. 232.
11 Alan Villiers, *Sons of Sinbad* (London, 1940), p. 270.
12 'Bengal, Our Coasting Trade', *Allen's Indian Mail and Register of Intelligence for British and Foreign India,* xx (London, 1862), p. 758.

4 Jewels of the Sea: The Rise and Fall of the Pearling Industry, 1508–1949

1 Lodovico Di Barthema, *The Travels of Lodovico di Barthema, 1502 to 1508,* trans. J. W. Jones (London, 1863), p. 95.
2 W. G. Palgrave, *Personal Narrative of a Year's Journey through Central and Eastern Arabia (1862–1863)* (London, 1865), p. 28.
3 John Gordon Lorimer, *Gazetteer of the Persian Gulf,* II (1908), p. 1438.
4 'Summary of News', 20 July 1920, in *Political Diaries of the Persian Gulf, 1904–1958* (hereafter *PDPG*) (Farnham Common, 1990), vol. VI, p. 601.
5 Robert Carter, 'The History and Prehistory of Pearling in the Persian Gulf', *Journal of the Economic and Social History of the Orient,* IV/2 (2005), pp. 139–209. Discarded shells act as hard objects (substrates) for spat to colonize and grow from, creating more oysters for the next season.

5 Something in the Air: Dubai and the Northern Sheikhdoms, 1901–39

1 John Gordon Lorimer, *Gazetteer of the Persian Gulf,* I (1915), pp. 2638–9.
2 A member of the Beni Hadiya, quoted in William and Fidelity Lancaster, *Honour is in Contentment: Life Before Oil in Ras Al-Khaimah (UAE) and Some Neighbouring Regions* (Berlin, 2011), p. 314.
3 'Gun Running in the Persian Gulf', *The Times* (London) (30 December 1910), p. 3.
4 Residency (Native) Agent to the Political Resident, 20 February 1929, IOR/R/15/1/265.
5 News Report (Sharjah), no 13 of 1936, cited in Rosemarie Zahlan, *The Origins of the United Arab Emirates: A Political and Social History of the Trucial States* (London, 1978), p. 167.
6 Political Resident to senior naval officer, Persian Gulf, 17 April 1927, IOR/R/15/1/241.
7 E. Gashell for PRPG, December 1931, *PDPG,* IX, p. 635.
8 Resident to Laithwaite, 20 February 1935, IOR/R/15/1/275.
9 Martin Buckmaster, 'Trucial Coast News' (1947), 7, IOR/R/15/4/15.
10 Graeme Wilson, *Rashid's Legacy: The Genesis of the Maktoum Family and the History of Dubai* (Dubai, 2006), p. 80.
11 Weightman, *PDPG,* XIII, p. 448.
12 Ibid., p. 449.

6 The Hungry Years: The Trucial Coast in the Second World War, 1939–45

1 Political Officer, Trucial Coast (POTC), report for 11–31 October 1939, *PDPG*, XIII, p. 450.
2 Ibid., report for 1–15 November 1939, p. 474.
3 POTC, report for 1–15 December 1939, *PDPG*, XIII, p. 498.
4 POTC, report for 1–15 January 1940, *PDPG*, XIV, p. 7.
5 Raymond O'Shea, *The Sand Kings of Oman* (London, 1947), p. 61.
6 Weightman to Sheikh Sultan bin Saqr al-Qasimi, 15 July 1940, IOR/R/15/1/281.
7 Bahrain summary no. 6 for period 18–31 March 1946, *PDPG*, XXVII, p. 64, cited in Peter Hellyer and Laurence Garey, 'World War II Plane Crashes in the UAE', *Tribulus*, XIV/1 (Spring/Summer 2014), pp. 9–11.
8 Administration Report of the Persian Gulf for the Year 1941, IOR/R/15/1/719.
9 Intelligence summary of the Political Aagent, Bahrain, 16–31 May 1942, no. 10 of 1942, *PDPG*, XII, pp. 145–6.
10 Trucial Coast report, 1941, *PDPG*, XI, p. 309.

7 Sweet Crude: Abu Dhabi and the Discovery of Oil, 1909–71

1 Residency (Native) Agent to Political Resident, 1 May 1928, IOR/R/15/1/265.
2 'A.P.O.C. and Oil Concessions, Arab Coast', IOR/R/15/1/618.
3 Anglo-Persian, Royal Dutch Shell and CFP each held a 23.75 per cent share in IPC, Jersey Standard and Socony-Vacuum together held 23.75 per cent, and the British-Armenian businessman Calouste Gulbenkian 5 per cent.
4 POTC reports March 1941 and February 1942, *PDPG*, XIV, p. 31, XV, p. 55.
5 *PDPG*, XVIII, p. 641.
6 Superior Oil's withdrawal from oil operations in the Persian Gulf, see FO 371/98431; Qatar and General, Continental Shelf, BP Archive ref. 35947; Loganecker, memorandum of 6 June 1952, *Foreign Relations of the United States, 1952-1954. The Near and Middle East*, p. 597.
7 For the phrase 'Nice sweet crude', see Donald Hawley, *The Trucial States* (London, 1971), p. 209; 'general gloom', see James Bamberg, *British Petroleum and Global Oil, 1950–1975: The Challenge of Nationalism* (Cambridge, 2000), p. 207.

8 Blueprint for a Nation: The Trucial States, 1945–68

1 Rhym Gazal, 'Man Brings UAE History to Life', *The National* (24 June 2013).
2 Mohammed al-Fahim, *From Rags to Riches: A Story of Abu Dhabi* (London, 2004), p. 67.
3 Donald Hawley, interview of 7 August 2007, British Diplomatic Oral History Programme, www.chu.cam.ac.uk/archives/collections/bdohp, accessed 3 September 2014.
4 Ivor Lucas, interview of 25 January 2005, British Diplomatic Oral History Programme.

5 Letter from Balfour Paul to Luce, no. 1, 4 January 1965, FO 371/1799021.

6 Although the country's name was not changed from Persia to Iran until 1935, the name Iran is henceforth used for convenience.

7 Helene von Bismarck, *British Policy in the Persian Gulf, 1961–1968: Conceptions of Informal Empire* (Basingstoke, 2013), p. 147.

8 Easa Saleh al-Gurg, *Wells of Memory: An Autobiography* (London, 1998), pp. 119–20.

9 Anna Rubino, *Queen of the Oil Club: The Intrepid Wanda Jablonski and the Power of Information* (Boston, MA, 2008), p. 127.

10 William and Fidelity Lancaster, *Honour Is in Contentment: Life before Oil in Ras Al-Khaimah (UAE) and Some Neighbouring Regions* (Berlin, 2011), p. 2.

9 Divided We Stand: Unification and Beyond, 1964–80

1 Edward Heath, *Travels: People and Places in My Life* (London, 1977), p. 152.

2 Roberts to Brown, 17 November 1967, FCO 8/31.

3 Extract from BBC TV Panorama, 22 January 1968, PREM 13/2218, in Shohei Sato, 'Britain's Decision to Withdraw from the Persian Gulf, 1964–68', *Journal of Imperial and Commonwealth History*, XXXVII (2009), p. 111 (n. 70).

4 Memorandum of conversation between Brown and Rusk, 11 January 1969, FCO 46/43.

5 Graeme Wilson, *Rashid's Legacy: The Genesis of the Maktoum Family and the History of Dubai* (Dubai, 2006), p. 264.

6 Abdullah Omran Taryam, *The Establishment of the United Arab Emirates, 1950–85* (London, 1987), p. 135.

7 Memorandum of conversation, 11 March 1969, *Foreign Relations of the United States, 1969–76* (FRUS), XXIV, pp. 229–32.

8 Northcutt Ely, 'Recollections of the Persian Gulf', *The Fortnightly Club*, 5 December 1985, www.redlandsfortnightly.org/papers/persgulf.htm, accessed 18 August 2015.

9 *Al-Ittihad*, reported in 'The National History Project', www.thenational.ae, accessed 3 September 2014.

10 Julian Walker to the author, letter dated 10 September 2013. Sir William Luce was back in the UK at this time.

11 Kaltham al-Tamim, quoted in 'The National History Project'. Fasting for six days during *Shawwal* is considered to be the equivalent of fasting for two months, and the 28 days of fasting during Ramadan the equivalent of ten months, together making a year of fasting in total.

12 Sir Patrick Wright, 'Memories of the Political Residency', *Liwa*, II/4 (December 2010), pp. 59–65.

13 However, the treaty was not ratified by the UAE and the border remains in dispute – see Chapter Ten.

10 Only One Tribe: The United Arab Emirates, 1980–Present Day

1 'Gulf States Draft Rules for a New Grouping', *The Times* (10 March 1981).

2 Juan Carlos Gumucio, 'Rush of Emirates Men to Join Action', *The Times* (13 August 1990).

3 'The Founding Sheikhs', *The National* (1 December 2010).
4 Price Waterhouse report to the Bank of England, 1991, cited in Joseph Norton and George Walker, *Banks: Fraud and Crime* (New York, 2013), p. 124.
5 Christopher Davidson, *Abu Dhabi, Oil and Beyond* (New York, 2013), p. 98.
6 Preamble to the 1971 UAE Constitution.
7 In the 1950s and '60s, before more recent disturbances, Beirut was a glitzy, financial centre of the Arab world.
8 An elderly trader quoted in William and Fidelity Lancaster, *Honour is in Contentment: Life Before Oil in Ras Al-Khaimah (UAE) and Some Neighbouring Regions* (Berlin, 2011), p. 415.
9 Sultan Al Qassemi, 'In the UAE the Only Tribe is the Emirati', *Gulf News* (1 December 2013).
10 Sheikh Zayed bin Sultan al-Nahyan quoted in Ibrahim Al Abed, Peter Hellyer and Peter Vine, *The United Arab Emirates Yearbook 2005* (London, 2005), p. 24.

Select Bibliography

Al-Fahim, Mohammed, *From Rags to Riches: A Story of Abu Dhabi* (London, 2004)

Al Qasimi, Sultan bin Mohammed, *The Myth of Arab Piracy in the Gulf* (London, 1986)

Davies, Charles E., *The Blood-red Arab Flag: An Investigation into Qasimi Piracy, 1797–1820* (Exeter, 1997)

Hawley, Donald, *The Trucial States* (London, 1970)

Heard, David, *From Pearls to Oil: How the Oil Industry Came to the United Arab Emirates* (Dubai, 2012)

Heard-Bey, Frauke, *From Trucial States to United Arab Emirates* (London, 1996)

Hellyer, Peter, *Hidden Riches: An Archaeological Introduction to the United Arab Emirates* (Abu Dhabi, 1998)

Kechichian, Joseph A., *Power and Succession in Arab Monarchies: A Reference Guide* (Boulder, CO, 2008)

Kelly, John Barrett, *Britain and the Persian Gulf, 1795–1880* (London, 1968)

Lancaster, William and Fidelity, *Honour is in Contentment: Life Before Oil in Ras Al-Khaimah (UAE) and Some Neighbouring Regions* (Berlin, 2011)

Lorimer, John Gordon, *Gazetteer of the Persian Gulf, Oman and Central Arabia*, vol. I and II (Calcutta, 1915 and 1908 respectively)

Maitra, Jayanti, and Afra Al-Hajji, *Qasr Al Hosn: The History and Rulers of Abu Dhabi, 1793–1966* (Abu Dhabi, 2001)

Onley, James, *The Arabian Frontier of the British Raj: Merchants, Rulers, and the British in the Nineteenth-century Gulf* (Oxford, 2007)

Slot, B. J., *The Arabs of the Gulf, 1602–1784* (Leidschendam, 1993)

Walker, Julian, *Tyro on the Trucial Coast* (Crook, 1999)

Wheeler, Julia, and Paul Thuysbaert, *Telling Tales: An Oral History of Dubai* (Dubai, 2006)

Wilson, Graeme, *Rashid's Legacy: The Genesis of the Maktoum Family and the History of Dubai* (Dubai, 2006)

Zahlan, Rosemarie Said, *The Origins of the United Arab Emirates: A Political and Social History of the Trucial States* (London, 1998)

Acknowledgements

I am indebted to those who helped me, in particular Peter Hellyer, Dr Alan Heward, Sir Harold ('Hooky') Walker and Julian Walker, all of whom gave advice in their particular fields as well as making many valuable comments and suggestions. I am immensely grateful to Peter, my brother, for checking the manuscript – if any errors remain, they are entirely my own. I also owe thanks to the shareholders of the Abu Dhabi Petroleum Company (ADPC) for allowing me to use photographs from the company's archives; Peter Housego and Joanne Burman for facilitating access to the BP Archive; and Keith Todd and Nick Lee for their photographs. Finally, thank you to Gill, my wife, for her infinite patience and support.

Photo Acknowledgements

The author and publishers wish to express their thanks to the below sources of illustrative material and/or permission to reproduce it.

ADPC/BP Archive: pp. 21, 31, 41, 43, 45, 48, 51, 57, 87, 91, 97, 105, 112, 123, 127, 143, 145, 150, 155, 163, 172, 177, 182, 187, 189, 194, 198; AFP/Getty Images: p. 193; Bain Collection, Library of Congress: p. 100; BP Archive: pp. 132, 147, 167; Hathi Trust: p. 83; Nick Lee: pp. 18, 159; Matson Collection, Library of Congress: p. 109; Matthew D. Leistikow, U.S. Navy: pp. 216–17; Mike Morton Collection: pp. 25, 76, 80, 119, 138; M. Q. Morton: pp. 37, 207, 213; National Maritime Museum, Greenwich: pp. 61, 65; NASA: p. 8; P&O Archive: p. 74; Qatar Digital Library: p. 69; Keith Todd: pp. 15, 135; U.S. Navy: p. 202

Index

Abdul Aziz bin Rahman (Ibn Saud), king of Saudi Arabia 52, 131
Abdul Rahman bin Muhammed, sheikh of Hira 102
Abiel coins 23
Abu Dhabi 14, *15*, 41–2, *45*, 77, 130, *163*, 170–74, *172*, *194*, 196, 205–6, 211
Abu Musa 96, 166–7, 171, 183, 186, 187, 188, 192, 195, 209
ADMA *Enterprise 147*
al-Ahmad al-Jaber al-Sabah, Sabah 186
Ahmed bin Falaw, Humaid bin 154
Ajman 67, 71, 101, 102, 108, 117, 139, 141, 152
Akab Island 13
al-As, Amr ibn (Arab emissary) 29–30
Al Ain/Buraimi Oasis 46, 50, 158–60
Al Bu Falah 40
Al Bu Falasah 99
Al Bu Said dynasty 44, 50, 55, 186
Albuquerque, Afonso de 34
Al Utayba mosque *31*
Al Maktoum dynasty
  Buti bin Suhail 100
  Hasher bin Rashid 113
  Juma bin Maktoum 89, 112, 117
  Maktoum bin Rashid 202
  Maktoum II bin Hasher 73
  Mani bin Rashid 105–6, 114, 117–19
  Rashid bin Saeed 111, 118, 139, 161, *167*, 174–7, 181, 185–7, *187*, 197, 202

Saeed bin Maktoum 101, 102, 104, 106, 113–14, 117–18
Al Mualla dynasty
  Abdul Rahman bin Ahmed 103
  Ahmad II bin Rashid 103, 161, 206
  Hamad bin Ibrahim 103
  Rashid bin Ahmad 206
  Saud bin Rashid 206
Al Nahyan dynasty
  Dhiyab bin Isa 41–2
  Hamdan bin Zayed 130
  Khalid bin Zayed 131, 174
  Khalifa bin Shakhbut 45–7
  Khalifa bin Zayed (died 1945) 130, 132, 138
  Khalifa bin Zayed (UAE president) 191, 204, 212
  Latifa bint Hamdan 113
  Mohammed bin Khalifa 174, 204
  Mohammed bin Shakhbut 43, 44, 45
  Mohammed bin Zayed 204, 205, 214
  Said bin Tahnoun 47, 48, 68
  Saqr bin Zayed 131–2, *132*
  Shakhbut bin Dhiyab 42–3, 45
  Shakhbut bin Sultan 14, 128, 134, 137–9, 144, *145*, 148–9, 161, 170–4, 179, *187*
  Sultan bin Zayed 131
  Tahnoun bin Shakhbut 43, 44–5
  Tahnoun bin Zayed 130
  Zayed bin Khalifa ('Zayed the Great') 49–53, 98, 130

Zayed bin Sultan 16, 28, 144, *145*,
149, 159, 165, 172–4, 179, 181,
182, 184–6, 187, 197, 204, 212
Al Nuaimi dynasty
Rashid bin Humaid 161, 206
Humaid bin Rashid 206
Al Qasimi dynasty
Khalid bin Ahmed 102–3
Khalid bin Saqr 191
Khalid III bin Mohammed 169,
190
Saqr bin Mohammed 140, 161,
169, 190, 191, *193,* 194
Saqr III bin Sultan 157, 161, *167*,
168–9
Sultan bin Salim 99, 107, 135, 140
Sultan I bin Saqr 44, 47, 52, 56,
59, 62, 67
Sultan II bin Saqr 102, 108, 110,
119–21
Sultan III bin Mohammed 169,
203
Al Sharqi dynasty
Hamad bin Mohammed 206
Mohammed bin Hamad 122,
161, 206
Arab League 165, 167
Arab nationalism 162, 165, 180
Arab Spring 210
Arabian Peninsula *8*
Arabic 29
Arthur, Geoffrey 193, 194
Awamir tribe 98, 109, 107, 140, 157
Azd tribes 29

Badi, Said bin, amir of Shimal 140
Bahrain 183, 188–9
Balbi, Gaspari 40, 76
Balfour Paul, Glencairn 168
Barut (slave/acting regent of Kalba)
141
Bani Kitab 52, 98, 102, 107, 117,
140, 152
Bani Muin 57, 61
Bani Rashid 101, 105–6
Bani Yas 40–41, 42, 44, 98, 186, 205
Bank of Credit and Commerce
International (BCCI) 203–4

Bidah tribe 140
Boyat, Mohammed bin 89
Bruce, William 62, 63, 64
Buckingham, James 59
Buckmaster, Martin 109
Buraimi dispute 142, 158–60, 183
see also Al-Ain/Buraimi Oasis
Buttersworth, Thomas, *Mahratta
Pirates Attacking the Sloop
'Aurora'* (1812) *65*
Buyid dynasty 33

Callaghan, James 183
Carmathians 33
Christianity 25–6
Cousteau, Jacques 144
Cox, Percy 51, 52, 97, 101
Cox, Peter 134
Curzon, Lord George 95

al-Damuk, Muhammad bin Ahmad
89
Dalma Island 12, 75, 79, 98, 132
Dhayah 18
dhu at-Taj, Laqit bin Malik 30
Dibba 30
Dickson, Harold 83, 88, 108
Dilmun 14, 15,16, 18, 24
Dubai 45–6, 73, 77, 99–101, *105*,
110–11, 112–13, *112*, 116–17,
126–8, 152–3, *155*, 163, 174–7,
196, 206–9, 211, *216–17*
Dutch era 36–9

East India Company 36–7, 55
Ed-Dur 24
Emiratization 202

al-Fahim, Mohammed 153
falaj (pl. *aflaj*) 19–20, *21*
Fort Jahili *159*
Frifelt, Karen 17
Fujairah 67, 71, 98, 102, 139, 141,
152

Ghafiri tribes 29, 31, 50, 186
Gilgamesh, fable of 75
Gulf Oasis 10, 11

al-Gurg, Easa Saleh 169, 176, 181
Hafit period 17
Hajar Mountains 10
Halul Island 50, 147
Hamriyah 88, 101, 102
Hanno 109
al-Hariq, Salim 56
Hasan bin Ali, sheikh of Rams 59
Hasan bin Rahma, sheikh of Ras
    al-Khaimah 59, 62, 64, 65, 67
Hassouna, Abdul Khalek 167
Hawley, Donald 148, 176
Healey, Denis 178, 184
Heath, Edward 189, 190
Hengam Island 104, 166
Hili 16, *18*
Hinawi tribes 29, 31, 50, 186
Hira 101, 102
HMS *Fox 100*
Hormuz 35
Howe, John 117
Huwaidin, Mohammed bin Ali 128

Ibadis 31, 32
Ibn Majid, navigator 21, 34
Ibrahim bin Rahma 59, 65
Indian Civil Service 69
Iron Age 19
Islam 29–30, 80, 215

Jebel Buhais 11
Jebel Dhanna 100, 122, 136, 148
Jebel Faya 10
Jebel Hafit 16, 136
Jenkins, Roy 183–4
Julanda brothers 30
Julfar 32–4, 35

Kalba 110
Karim, Abdul (merchant) 49
Kennedy, Pat and Marian 164–5
Khan, Abdul Hafeez 173
Khawatir tribe 140
Khor al-Udaid 46, 47, 49–50, 183,
    198
Khor Fakkan 34–5, 152
Khor Ghanadha 139
Kier, William 64, 66

al-Kitbi, Fatima bint Mubarak 205
Kuwait 182, 186

al-Latif, Isa bin Abd 102, 103
al-Latif, Khan Bahadur Abd 98
Lermitte, Basil 136, 139
Lingah 54, 57, 61, 73, 95, 99, 104
Liwa Oasis 40, *43*, 77, 98
Luce, William 190

McCaully, Desmond 155, 164
Mahmud, Abdul Karim 123–4
Manasir tribe 26, 43, 50, 51, 98, 140,
    157, 172
Manesty, Samuel 58
Marawah Island 12
Mimimoto, Kokichi 90–91
Mir Mahanna 38–9
Mleiha 23
Murrah tribe 50, 51
Muweilah 22

Nasser, Gamel Abdel 162
Nizar tribes 29
Nofal, Sayed 168
Nur, Mohammed bin 32

O'Shea, Raymond 121
Obaid bin Juma, sheikh 117, 166
oil *see* Trucial Coast, oil operations
al-Otaishan, Turki bin Abdullah 158

Pahlavi dynasty
    Mohammad Reza Shah 183,
    186–7
    Reza Shah 104, 166
Pax Britannica 179, 200
Pilgrim, Guy 133
Pirate Coast, The 68, 69
Pirie-Gordon, Christopher 161
Political Residency 39, 70, 151
Portuguese era 34–6
Prior, Charles 128

al-Qaizi, Saif Mohammed 127
Qarn al-Harf 19
Qasr al-Hosn *37*, 42, *51*, 130, *135*,
    139, *207*, 211

Qawasim 54
Qubaisat tribe 46, 47, 49, 77, 170
al-Qubaisi, Salama bint Butti 49, 132, 172

Rams 67, 77
Ras al-Khaimah 53, 54, *57*, 60–61, *61*, 64–6, 77, 82, 139, 152, 163, 196
al-Razzaq Razuqi, Abdur 120–21, 124
Residency (Native) Agent 70
Roberts, Goronwy 181, 183
Rub al-Khali 28
Rumaithat tribe 77, 170
Rusk, Dean 184

Sabkhat Matti 28
Sasanian Empire 25, 30
Saudi Arabia 170, 186, 209–10
Sayyid Sultan (ruler of Muscat) 57
Shamailiyah 102
Sharjah 53, 70, 73, 82, 95, 102, 109, *119*, *123*, 152, 163
    airfield 108, 109–10, 116
Sharqiyin tribe 102, 195
Sheikh Zayed Grand Mosque *213*
Shihuh tribe 36, 98, 140
Shimal 18
Shuweihat *143*
Sir Bani Yas Island 25–6, 110, 122
Strait of Hormuz 10, 29, 34, 54, 166, 200
Suez Crisis 162–3
al-Suwaidi, Ahmed bin Khalifa 191

al-Tajir, Mahdi 176, 182
Tell Abraq 16–17
Temple, Richard, *Sixteen Views of Places in the Persian Gulph* 61
Thamer, Ali bin *48*
Thani, Mohammed bin 76
Treadwell, James 188, 195
Treaties and Agreements
    Exclusive Agreements (1892) 68
    General Treaty of Peace (1820) 67

Perpetual Treaty of Maritime Truce (1853) 68, *69*
Treaty of Jeddah (1974) 198, 209
Tripp, Peter 163, *167*
Trucial Coast, The 68, 123–4, 134, 139, 154
    oil operations on 133–50
    steamships and 72–3, *74*
Trucial Oman Levies, later Scouts (TOS) 158, 180, 197
Trucial States 68, 156–7, 181
Trucial States Council 160, 163–8, 181
Trucial States Development Fund 168, 170, 174, 176
Tunb Islands 104, 166–7, 183–8, 192–3, 195, 201, 200, 209
Tuwwam 29, 32

Umm al-Nar
    island 14–15
    culture 17
    period 17
Umm al-Qaiwain 67, 101, 102, 103, 107, 117, 131, 141, 152

Vasco da Gama 34

Wadi Jizzi 15
Wadi Suq
    culture 19
    period 17
Wahhabis 44, 47, 55, 56, 58, 59
Wainwright, John 60
Walker, Julian 141, 191–2
Weightman, Hugh 111, 115, 116
Wellsted, James 56
Williamson, William ('Haji') 135, 136
Williamson, T. F. ('Jock') 137–7
Wilson, Harold 178

Zaab tribe 38, 174, *182*
al-Zayani, Ali bin Ibrahim 87
Zwemer, Samuel 42, 51, 97